REA

Winston Churchill's
IMAGINATION

PAUL K. ALKON

Winston Churchill's
IMAGINATION

Lewisburg
BUCKNELL UNIVERSITY PRESS

Associated University Presses
2010 Eastpark Boulevard
Cranbury, NJ 08512

The paper used in this publication meets the requirements of the American National Standard for Permanence of Paper for Printed Library Materials Z39.48-1984.

Library of Congress Cataloging-in-Publication Data

Alkon, Paul K. (Paul Kent)
    Winston Churchill's imagination / Paul K. Alkon.
       p. cm.
    Includes bibliographical references and index.
    ISBN-10: 0-8387-5632-8 (alk. paper)
    ISBN-13: 978-0-8387-5632-4 (alk. paper)
     1. Churchill, Winston, Sir, 1874–1965—Literary art.   I. Title.
DA566.9.C5A65 2006
941.084092

                                            2006002796

PRINTED IN THE UNITED STATES OF AMERICA

for Ellen
SHIPMATE AND SOUL MATE

"Think of your unfair advantages!
You get as much out of today, and out of affairs, as any
man alive among the activists: and when you die you are
going to pass over, without a word said, into the ranks
of writers, and live again by your books."

—T. E. LAWRENCE, *in a letter to*
Winston Churchill dated September 7, 1930

CONTENTS

Preface
xi

Acknowledgments
xix

Chronology of
Winston Churchill's Major Writings and Events
xxi

One
Imagining Lawrence:
Churchill and Lawrence of Arabia
I

Two
Imagining Scenarios:
Churchill and Cinema
41

Three
Imagining Scenes:
The Story of the Malakand Field Force and *Savrola*
97

Four
Imagining Science:
Churchill and Science Fiction
155

Five
Time and Imagination in *Marlborough*
177

Six
Envoi: Churchill's Dream
213

Notes
229

Works Cited
251

Index
259

PREFACE

Although Winston Churchill is a Nobel laureate in literature whose collected works run to thirty-eight volumes, his writing has received scant attention from literary critics. His astonishing political impact has overshadowed his career as a professional writer. That so much of his writing had immediate political goals has further obscured its enduring interest. Apart from one novel and a few short stories, moreover, he concentrated on forms that many regard as offering little scope for invention: war correspondence for daily newspapers, other journalistic essays, biographies, histories, memoirs, and speeches. Few critics have deemed these genres fashionable enough to warrant much notice, or amenable to their favorite methods of commentary. Churchill's 1953 Nobel Prize was awarded "for his mastery of historical and biographical description as well as for brilliant oratory in defending exalted human values."[1] Neither oratory, no matter how brilliant, nor description, no matter how masterful, has been as easily accommodated as fiction, poetry, and drama in the curricula of English departments or as a topic in books and articles published by English department inmates. Studies of Churchill have therefore mostly come from historians and political scientists who concentrate on Churchill's involvement with important events. They analyze his works for evidence of his attitudes. They attend only briefly to the qualities of his prose, usually when they applaud his speeches or deplore the ornate flourishes that make his histories unappealing to postmodern sensibilities. Churchill's long life was so crowded with striking episodes that his biographers have perforce dealt more with the contexts than the contents of his publications. Accordingly, as the mountain of books about Churchill has approached Himalayan heights the result has mainly been accumulation of knowledge about his personal life, his methods as a rhetorician in and outside Parliament, and his political career in relation to the turbulent history of the twentieth century.

But the literary aspects of Churchill's writing have not been altogether neglected. Manfred Weidhorn's magisterial 1974 overview *Sword and Pen: A Survey of the Writings of Sir Winston Churchill* remains invaluable and ought to be reprinted.[2] I recommend it as the indispensable starting place for all who want to understand what attracted the Nobel Prize selection committee to Churchill and what ought to attract more readers today. The best single essay on how Churchill's historical imagination shaped his rhetoric and prose style is Isaiah Berlin's *Mr Churchill in 1940*.[3] David Reynolds has explained in fascinating detail how thoroughly *The Second World War*, Churchill's six-volume history and memoir of that conflict, was shaped—even to the detriment of historical accuracy—by the post-war requirements of Churchill's own political career and also by advice, amounting to commands, from the government about making final revisions to aid current foreign policy. Reynolds also brings to light the unusual extent to which for *The Second World War* Churchill relied on assistants to draft large sections of narrative which he then sometimes revised and augmented by his own memories of incidents such as meetings with Roosevelt and Stalin, but often printed largely unchanged. The result, as Reynolds rightly insists, was certainly Churchill's book in that he presided over his research team and had final say about what went in, how it was worded, and how far to agree with government recommendations (which in the event were usually accepted).[4] *The Second World War* is exceptional among Churchill's writing, however, because it is a far less unmediated and uncensored expression of his imagination than those previous works—the majority of his oeuvre—that sprang directly from his mind into words written down himself or dictated aloud to secretaries after he became a professional writer thus living, as he quipped, from mouth to hand. Reynolds has provided a definitive account of *The Second World War*. There are some other helpful commentaries, mostly of a general nature, on Churchill's writing.[5] Instead of going over the ground these pioneering studies have covered, or rehearsing yet again the tale of Churchill's life, surely familiar to anyone likely to pick up this book, I want here to advance our knowledge of his imagination.[6]

Almost everyone commenting on Churchill has remarked his active—many have said overactive—imagination. Complaints in various tones ranging from amusement to outrage have been recorded by a large roster of associates, subordinates, and allies faced with the delicate task of weeding out practical ideas from among the exuberant growth of utopian memos and conversational sallies that sprang from his fertile mind imagining how things might be done better (his way). Historians have often echoed such complaints in equally varied tones ranging from fond indulgence to solemn revisionist reproach. Among what have rightly or wrongly been considered Churchill's wilder flights of military fancy are his impulsive offer in 1914 to resign as First Lord of the Admiralty in order to lead British troops defending Antwerp, his plan for a 1915 naval attack on the Dardanelles fortifications, and his schemes during World War II for assaults on Norway and invasion via what he imagined as "the soft underbelly of Europe." Whatever their merits, all these ideas were nothing if not imaginative. So too but to better effect was Churchill's early encouragement of naval aviation and development of the tank for land warfare. His imagining before the fact of tanks as a way to end the stalemate of a trench war that condemned infantry (as he put it) to "chew barbed wire" was an idea that, as Churchill acknowledged, also had an independent imaginative genesis in H. G. Wells's 1903 short story "The Land Ironclads." As I explain in chapter 4, a characteristic feature of Churchill's mentality is his imaginative affinity with the science fiction (though not the politics) of such writers as H. G. Wells, Jules Verne, Karel Čapek, Aldous Huxley, and Olaf Stapledon.

In the run-up to World War II during Churchill's 1930s "wilderness years" he was among the very few who could vividly and accurately imagine what would happen if Hitler were not checked while there was still time. Imagining possible good and bad futures was for Churchill as statesman a no less characteristic activity than inviting readers of his biographies and histories to imagine the past. Of greatest consequence was Churchill's rare ability after the fall of France in 1940 to imagine that Britain might successfully stand alone against Nazi Germany. In his first speech as prime minister at that bleak time, Churchill even dared invite his audience to imagine that his country could adopt as an attainable goal "Victory—victory at all costs, victory in spite of all terror, victory, however long and hard the road may be."[7] That the British people turned the currents of history toward democracy and against Fascism by responding to this call to arms shows not only Churchill's powerful imagination but also his ability when it counted most to enlist the imagination of others in a noble cause.

Analysis of how Churchill's imagination operated in military and political spheres is beyond my expertise but amply provided by historians. In this book I confine myself to Churchill's literary imagination, by which I mean the ways in which his imagination is manifested in the words, scenes, and structures of his writing, and the ways in which that writing engages its readers. I avoid entanglement with abstract theories about imagination and cumbersome definitions of it. They have enlivened but seldom much edified the study of literature. I also avoid generalizations in favor of precise attention to those unique details of word deployment that for a writer are at once the hallmarks of effective imagination and its building blocks. In his autobiography Churchill reports of his English class at Harrow: "I got into my bones the essential structure of the ordinary British sentence—which is a noble thing."[8] The ways in which he used and often further ennobled "the ordinary British sentence" are an important measure of his mind. What is required now for better understanding of Churchill is the kind of close attention that works of this Nobel laureate deserve but, except for his most famous speeches, have not often enough attracted.

Of course no one book can entirely repair that neglect. Churchill's oeuvre is too vast. His mind was too capacious. Here I closely examine some key works, issues, and aspects of his imagination that have not yet had their due. Along with more familiar titles I invite consideration of little-known episodes in his literary life, and of writing by him that is now too seldom read because it is out of print (though it should not be) or only available in limited editions, is often hard to find even in large libraries, and in some cases is only available in archives. Analysis of these elusive items very much enhances understanding of Churchill's literary imagination and also of what is closely related, his moral imagination.

Chapter 1, "Imagining Lawrence: Churchill and Lawrence of Arabia," concentrates on their literary rather than political relationships. I thankfully leave to historians all discussion and debate over the Middle East settlement, such as it was, that Churchill achieved as colonial secretary in 1921 after T. E. Lawrence had worked with him as an advisor for eighteen months. My concern is how Churchill responded as a reader and book reviewer to *Seven Pillars of Wisdom*, and as elegiac essayist to Lawrence's death. Hitherto unremarked revisions of his eloquent obituary essay on Lawrence show not only how Lawrence captured Churchill's imagination but the ways in which Churchill contributed to the ever-expanding Lawrence mythology that so enthralled public imagination after the First World War. The surprising fact that these two quite different and very egotistical men became good friends as well as harmonious colleagues also reveals much about the imaginative life of each. Churchill's own ideas about imagination are best illuminated by comparing what he and Lawrence wrote about it and related matters.

Chapter 2, "Imagining Scenarios: Churchill and Cinema," takes up the revealing but largely unknown episode of Churchill's work in the 1930s for Alexander Korda's London Film Productions studio. As a paid consultant Churchill provided a critique of the script for a film that Korda hoped to make about Lawrence of Arabia. Churchill also wrote several screenplays for Korda, although the films were never produced. Analysis of these scripts, their genesis, and their revisions shows much about how actual and invented experiences were transmuted within Churchill's imagination for projection on the silver screen. This behind-the-scenes involvement with the art of filmmaking has sometimes been glanced at but never closely examined in previous accounts. These, when they mention films at all, mostly dwell on Churchill's general fondness for action movies as a way to relax after the day's work, and his unquench-able enthusiasm for *That Hamilton Woman*, Korda's film about Admiral Nelson, Lady Hamilton, and the Battle of Trafalgar. In the only essay to date on Churchill and cinema, moreover, we are told that "he consid-ered movies a diversion, not an art form. . . . he had never appreciated the aesthetic merits of silent cinema."[9] In fact Churchill's now hard to obtain 1935 essay on Charlie Chaplin, which I also closely consider, includes an extended discussion of Chaplin's artistry, a comparison of the aesthetic merits of silent and sound movies, and a forceful concluding argument on aesthetic as well as other grounds for continuing to make silent films alongside talkies. Churchill's efforts as a scriptwriter and film critic also reveal much about how he regarded the new medium of cin-ema not only as a powerful art form but as a vehicle for the transmission of ideas.

Chapter 3, "Imagining Scenes: *The Story of the Malakand Field Force* and *Savrola*," looks back to the start of Churchill's career as a writer to consider how he envisioned scenes in his first history and in his only novel. Because he took up painting as a hobby relatively late in life at the age of forty, it is generally taken for granted that during his early years he paid no attention to art and knew little or nothing about it. With con-summate comic skill Churchill partly created that impression in *Painting as a Pastime* by the way he there wryly describes his own belated discovery of what can be done with oils on canvas. But this notion of Churchill's early indifference to art is as misleading as the similar but more famous legend of his dullness as a schoolboy: a myth likewise gleefully fostered by Churchill, this one in his autobiography. In *The Story of the Malakand*

Field Force (1898) and *Savrola* (1900), however, Churchill often evoked imagination of paintings as templates for his narratives. Attention to his various methods of doing so, as well as to his ideas about book illustrations, reveals how Churchill took his first steps toward the mastery of historical and biographical description that would help earn him a Nobel Prize.

Chapter 4, "Imagining Science: Churchill and Science Fiction," explores the ways in which Churchill responded to the disturbing scientific advances that in his view made the twentieth century unlike any previous era in human history. As early as 1924 he warned that humanity faced annihilation if its warlike tendencies were not checked before its impending achievement of atomic bombs and related scientific horrors. He warned too in the 1930s about the moral and political dangers of biological engineering that might actually make it possible for a despotic government to produce android slaves of a kind for which (as Churchill notes) Karel Čapek had invented the term "robot." In an essay published a few months before Aldous Huxley's *Brave New World*, Churchill anticipates its portrait of a dystopian future by speculating that in fifty years or so "it will be possible to carry out in artificial surroundings the entire cycle which now leads to the birth of a child" and equally possible that "interference with the mental development of such beings, expert suggestion and treatment in the earlier years, would produce beings specialized to thought or toil. . . . capable of tending a machine but without other ambitions."[10] Like Huxley and, later, George Orwell, Churchill elaborates upon such speculation by way of sober warning of things to come and also as a metaphor dramatizing the dangers of totalitarian governments whose present existence is all too real and menacing. Kindred to such forays into futuristic fiction, and equally characteristic of Churchill's imagination, are his exercises in the science fiction subgenre of alternative history: speculations on what might have been the outcome and impact on the present had crucial events in the past taken a different turn. "If Lee Had Not Won the Battle of Gettysburg," Churchill's only freestanding alternative history, is a classic of its kind. Equally notable scattered throughout his major histories are the myriad miniature alternative histories that are a significant feature of Churchill's historical imagination and thus of his method as an historian.

Chapter 5, "Time and Imagination in *Marlborough*," considers Churchill's resort to alternative history in his greatest biography. In that four-volume work, which is proclaimed in its subtitle as a study of Marl-borough's life and times, Churchill uses excursions into alternative his-tory as a way of analyzing what he regarded as crucial turning points in European history as well as in the Duke of Marlborough's personal for-tunes. In this chapter I also consider Churchill's management of narrative time: the allotment of narration to each episode and interval of the nar-rated life, and hence achievement of control over the amount of reading time focused on each interval as well as, more importantly, the quality of the durations thus created for readers. Churchill's avowed purpose in *Marlborough* with respect to the Duke is "to recall this great shade from the past, and not only invest him with his panoply, but make him living and intimate to modern eyes."[11] As Churchill proceeds he often explains his methods of attempting to bring Marlborough's ghost back to life for readers while—even harder, surely—making them intimately acquainted with that aloof aristocrat from a vanished age. I discuss the ways in which and the extent to which Churchill succeeds in bringing off this difficult feat of the historical imagination.

Finally, in chapter 6, "Envoi: Churchill's Dream," I provide by way of epilogue to this book a discussion of Churchill's last work of fiction, an adroit ghost story titled "The Dream." Although first drafted in 1947 and subsequently revised over many years, at his request this short story was reserved for posthumous publication. It did not appear until 1966, almost exactly a year after his death. In this tale, Churchill imagines an encounter in which, as a seventy-two-year-old, he has a chance to explain twentieth-century history to the ghost of his father, Lord Randolph Churchill, who died in 1895. This Victorian ghost materializes one day after World War II in Churchill's studio as he is painting a copy of an old portrait of Lord Randolph. Father and son then talk about politics as they never did in real life, but with surprising omissions and reticence on Winston's part. Their dialogue provides a rare glimpse of Churchill's own view of his unsatisfactory relationship with Lord Randolph, and an equally unusual summing up of Churchill's response to the twentieth century during which he had journeyed so far from his youth in the secure world of Queen Victoria's empire. The four volumes of *Marlborough*, pub-lished over the interval 1933–38, manifest the ways in which on the brink of his finest hours in World War II Churchill was haunted by imagina-tion of the eighteenth century as embodied in the Duke of Marlborough: "this great shade from the past." Appropriately enough for a ghost story,

"The Dream" is much more fleeting and tenuous, albeit in its way equally telling as sign of how deeply the Victorian era of his origins, symbolized by the ghostly presence of Lord Randolph, haunted Churchill as he looked back in sorrow at the twentieth century's havoc. "The Dream" is Churchill's last testament in the realm of the imagination. In it I like to imagine we come as close as we ever will to an encounter with Churchill's ghost confiding to us how our world now looks to him from the other side.

ACKNOWLEDGMENTS

The University of Southern California provided research support along with enlightened administration and moral encouragement without which this book would have stalled in the slow lane. Its progress has been accelerated by opportunities to speak about Churchill at a Huntington Library conference on T. E. Lawrence, and at Churchill Centre meetings, especially its Blenheim Palace Symposium on Churchill's biography of Marlborough. The staff of the Churchill Archives at Cambridge University made research there a remarkably pleasant as well as useful experience. My subsequent queries to the Archives have been helpfully answered with saintly patience by Natalie Adams. I thought I had slipped into a utopian alternative universe while corresponding with Anthea Morton-Saner, Emma Butterfield of the National Portrait Gallery, Yvonne Oliver of the Imperial War Museum, Régis Thomas of the Musée de la Dernière Cartouche at Bazeilles, and Denise Faife of the Musée d'Orsay.

For help of various kinds, often more important to me and this book than they might have guessed, I am grateful to many friends and colleagues: to the late Bob Archibald, whom I had so much hoped would be pleased by the outcome; and to Joseph Aoun, Michael Bonnet, Leo Braudy, Terry Castle, Robert Eden, Martin Gilbert, Teresa McKenna, Jeffrey Meyers, Val Meyers, Peter Nosco, Marjorie Perloff, Joseph Perloff, John Rieley, Celia Sandys, Edward L. Saslow, Roland Schank, Elizabeth Tanner, Pascal Thomas, Ruth Wallach, Mark Weber, Howard Weinbrot, and Curt Zoller. Indispensable instruction and assistance were generously provided by Richard M. Langworth, James W. Muller, John Ramsden, and Manfred Weidhorn. Expert and amiable help over the hurdles of book production has come from Christine A. Retz, Laura M. Rogers, and Beth Anne Stuebe. I am especially indebted to Greg Clingham, good Johnsonian that he is, for allying Bucknell University Press to the proposition that what Winston Churchill wrote is no less worthy of attention than what he said and what he did.

With permission of the Churchill Centre (www.winstonchurchill.org), parts of chapter 2 are adapted from my essay "Imagining Scenarios: Churchill's Advice for Alexander Korda's Stillborn Film, 'Lawrence of Arabia'" in *Finest Hour* 119 (Summer 2003); and parts of chapter 4 are adapted from my essay "'Shall We All Commit Suicide?': Winston Churchill and the Scientific Imagination" in *Finest Hour* 94 (Spring 1997). Quotations from writings by Winston Churchill are reproduced with permission of Curtis Brown Ltd, London on behalf of the Estate of Sir Winston Churchill, Copyright Winston S. Churchill. Three paintings by Winston Churchill are reproduced with permission of Curtis Brown Ltd, London on behalf of The Churchill Heritage; Copyright © The Churchill Heritage Ltd. The Seven Pillars of Wisdom Trust has granted permission for quotations from writings by T. E. Lawrence in its purview. Quotations from *Seven Pillars of Wisdom* by T. E. Lawrence, copyright 1926, 1935 by Doubleday, a division of Random House, Inc. are used by permission of Doubleday, a division of Random House, Inc. Quotations from publications by H. G. Wells appear with the permission of A P Watt Ltd on behalf of the literary executors of the Estate of H. G. Wells. My footnotes are for F. W. Kaufmann III.

Winston Churchill

CHRONOLOGY OF MAJOR WRITINGS AND EVENTS

1874	Born November 30 at Blenheim Palace.
1895	Churchill's father Lord Randolph Churchill dies January 24.
	Graduates from Sandhurst and commissioned a 2nd Lieutenant of Cavalry.
	Military service in India.
1898	*The Story of the Malakand Field Force*
	Military service in the Sudan, including participation as a cavalryman in the Battle of Omdurman.
1899	*The River War* (2 volumes)
	Captured during the Boer War and escapes.
1900	Elected to Parliament as Conservative MP for Oldham.
	London to Ladysmith via Pretoria
	Ian Hamilton's March
	Savrola
1904	Switches to Liberal Party.
1906	*Lord Randolph Churchill* (2 volumes)
	Undersecretary for the Colonies, 1906–8
1908	Marries Clementine Hozier September 12.
	My African Journey
	President of the Board of Trade, 1908–10
1910–11	Home Secretary
1911	First Lord of the Admiralty
1915	Resigns as First Lord of the Admiralty after failure of the Gallipoli campaign.
1916	Military service as battalion commander on the western front, January–May.
1917–18	Minister of Munitions
1919–20	Secretary of State for War and Air
1921–22	Colonial Secretary
1923–31	*The World Crisis* (6 volumes)
1924	Returns to Conservative Party.
	Chancellor of the Exchequer, 1924–29

1929–39   Wilderness years: in Parliament but out of office. Warns of the increasing German menace and urges rearmament.

1930   *My Early Life: A Roving Commission*

1931   *India*: speeches

1932   *Thoughts and Adventures* (in America as *Amid These Storms*)

1933–38   *Marlborough: His Life and Times* (4 volumes)

1937   *Great Contemporaries*

1938   *Arms and the Covenant* (in America as *While England Slept*): speeches

1939   *Step by Step*: speeches
Appointed First Lord of the Admiralty in September after Britain's declaration of war against Germany.

1940   Becomes Prime Minister May 10.

1941   *Into Battle* (in America as *Blood, Sweat, and Tears*): speeches

1942   *The Unrelenting Struggle*: speeches

1943   *The End of the Beginning*: speeches

1944   *Onwards to Victory*: speeches

1945   *The Dawn of Liberation*: speeches
May 8: Germany surrenders, ending the European part of World War II.
July 26: Churchill resigns as Prime Minister and becomes leader of the opposition after Labour Party wins the general Election.

1946   *Victory*: speeches
Secret Session Speeches
"Iron Curtain" speech at Westminster College in Fulton, Missouri, warning of Soviet danger.

1948–53   *The Second World War* (6 volumes)

1949   *The Sinews of Peace*: speeches

1950   *Europe Unite*: speeches

1951   Becomes Prime Minister again.

1952   *In The Balance*: speeches

1953   Made a Knight of the Garter by Queen Elizabeth, thus becoming Sir Winston Churchill.
Awarded the Nobel Prize for Literature.

1954   *Stemming the Tide*: speeches

1955	Resigns as Prime Minister.
1956–58	*A History of the English-Speaking Peoples* (4 volumes)
1961	*The Unwritten Alliance*: speeches
1964	Retires from Parliament.
1965	Dies on January 25.
1966	"The Dream" published January 30 in the *Sunday Telegraph*.

Winston Churchill's
IMAGINATION

IMAGINING LAWRENCE:
CHURCHILL AND LAWRENCE OF ARABIA

Churchill's most revealing statement on the importance of imagination is in a speech given on October 29, 1941, to the boys at his old school, Harrow. He first reminds them that his previous visit on December 18, 1940, had occurred during the Blitz following the Battle of Britain while "we had the unmeasured menace of the enemy and their air attack still beating upon us." At that time when "we were quite alone, desperately alone, and we had been so for five or six months," Churchill remarks, there had been no way to foresee the improvement in Britain's fortunes marked by the "long lull" in aerial attacks since the German invasion of Russia in June of 1941. From this surprising turn of events Churchill draws a moral: "You cannot tell from appearances how things will go. Sometimes the imagination makes things out far worse than they are; yet without imagination not much can be done. Those people who are imaginative see many more dangers than perhaps exist, certainly many more than will happen; but then they must also pray to be given that extra courage to carry this far-reaching imagination."[1] Talking in a setting that was for him especially resonant with emotion and memories, Churchill obliquely reveals much more than he usually did in public about his mental struggle during those early months as prime minister when it was one of his hardest duties to imagine every possible scenario of invasion and related military or diplomatic disaster in order to shape countermeasures. What he had to strive for, he implies, was not courage to deal with actualities, however grim. That had never been a problem for Churchill. In action he was by all accounts fearless. What he indirectly admits having to seek and explicitly urges others in comparable situations to seek is *extra* courage to endure the terrible burden of imagining every likely danger and many unlikely hazards to boot.

This is the special ordeal of leadership, Churchill suggests while addressing boys at Harrow who may be among Britain's future leaders. But it is also the special burden of *all* "those people who are imaginative." With noble vehemence and unusually evident emotion, Churchill in his next sentence insists too on a bedrock principle closely related to that extra courage needed by the imaginative: "Surely from this period of ten months this is the lesson: never give in, never give in, *never, never, never, never*—in nothing, great or small, large or petty—never give in except to convictions of honour and good sense. Never yield to force; never yield to the apparently overwhelming might of the enemy."[2] This is Churchill's credo. Unlike T. E. Lawrence, moreover, Churchill never lacked those strong convictions that, as the juxtaposition of exhortations here suggests, serve in his view to nourish both imagination and the courage necessary to endure "far-reaching imagination."

In Churchill's terms it could be said that while Lawrence never lacked courage to deal with actualities however threatening, his postwar rejection of responsibility in favor of enlistment in the ranks was partly a failure to sustain that extra courage required to deal with his own tormenting variety of far-reaching imagination. Identification with the cause of Arab nationalism provided convictions and the courage of those convictions up through Lawrence's service in a prominent though subordinate role as advisor to Churchill during most of his tenure as colonial secretary. Establishment of Iraq and Transjordan without abandoning British commitment to the Balfour Declaration was the main political outcome of Lawrence's work under Churchill. Whether the same result would have been achieved without their collaboration is a matter for speculation, as is the much harder problem of whether more good or ill has come to the Middle East from the Cairo settlement of 1921.[3] Be that as it may, Lawrence afterward was unable to find any cause transcending his own literary concerns except belief that, as he unpersuasively insists in his memoir of postwar service in the Royal Air Force, *The Mint*, "conquest of the air is the first duty of our generation."[4]

In notes for his own obituary sent to Robert Graves, Lawrence elaborates on this bare premise but does not say what purposes should be served by mastery of flight: "Conquest of the last element, the air, seems to me the only major task of our generation; and I have convinced myself that progress to-day is made not by the single genius, but by the common effort. . . . Wherefore I stayed in the ranks and served to the best of my ability, much influencing my fellow airmen towards a pride in themselves and their inarticulate duty."[5] This seems not only another of Lawrence's many evasive half-truths but also remarkably vague as a view of the task ahead for aviation when it was written in 1935, well after Hitler's rise to power. To Lionel Curtis in 1923 Lawrence had written more candidly of his reasons for enlisting: "Seven years of this will make me impossible for anyone to suggest for a responsible position, and that self-degradation is my aim. I haven't the impulse and the conviction to fit what I know to be my power of moulding men and things: and so I always regret what I've created, when the leisure after creation lets me look back and see that the idea was secondhand."[6] Of his role in the Arab Revolt Lawrence insists that he "followed and did not institute" and "had developed ideas of other men, and helped them, but had never created a thing of my own."[7] Lawrence's ordeal in straddling two cultures erased his capacity for conviction: "The efforts for these years to live in the dress of Arabs, and to imitate their mental foundation, quitted me of my English self, and let me look at the West and its conventions with new eyes: they destroyed it all for me. At the same time I could not sincerely take on the Arab skin: it was an affectation only."[8] The resulting nihilism atrophied Lawrence's imagination even while by supreme efforts he demonstrated its flowering in *Seven Pillars of Wisdom* and recorded its odd deliquescence in *The Mint*.

In *Seven Pillars* Lawrence identifies a kind of hunger of the imagination as the force that had initially motivated him: "It was a hard task for me to straddle feeling and action. I had had one craving all my life— for the power of self-expression in some imaginative form—but had been too diffuse ever to acquire a technique. At last accident, with perverted humour, in casting me as a man of action had given me place in the Arab Revolt, a theme ready and epic to a direct eye and hand, thus offering me an outlet in literature, the technique-less art."[9] Perhaps Lawrence regards literature as a "technique-less art" only by comparison with music and painting, which often display more conspicuous though not necessarily greater technical skills. In any case, he unambiguously stresses here the importance of imagination in his life, and does so, moreover, in a book to the techniques of whose composition, typography, illustration, and binding he had lavished the attention of an apprentice consciously struggling to become a master in the same league with William Morris, Dostoevsky, Nietzsche, and Melville.[10] Lawrence makes clear that without a book to give events artful shape, even the most spectacular or apparently successful action could not have eased the cravings of his imagination. In this romantic affirmation of the primacy of self-expression, moreover, Lawrence does not leave any doubt that he saw literature not military service as the only ultimately satisfying outlet for his personality. Yet his postwar enlistments greatly impeded engagement with writing and book production after publication in 1926 of the subscriber's edition of *Seven Pillars*.

As many critics have remarked, the triumph cryptically alluded to in the subtitle of *Seven Pillars of Wisdom: A Triumph* is neither the Arab Revolt nor Lawrence's admittedly duplicitous role in helping it. The triumph is the book itself as an artifact providing at last for its author, especially in its most notoriously puzzling equivocations, "the power of self-expression in some imaginative form." Writing from his barracks in Karachi to George Bernard Shaw in 1928, Lawrence described his desire for a literary career in the past tense while explaining that when he "had writing ambitions, they were to combine" a record of fact with a work of art: "*The Seven Pillars* was an effort to make history an imaginative thing."[11] During and after creation of this masterpiece Lawrence found refuge in the ranks of enlisted men as a relief not only from the demands of imaginative expression but from the burden of having any personality at all. In *The Mint* he reports that when asked why he was in the RAF, "I explained that I'd overdone the imaginative life, as expressed in study."[12] Perhaps this sarcasm alludes only to the strain of writing *Seven Pillars*. More likely, it is another of Lawrence's evasive half-truths, revealing an imaginative exhaustion from which he certainly suffered, but also deflecting attention from the fact that during the war he had overdone not the life of study but a life of action guided by what he calls an "imaginative vision of the end" to be achieved: in *Seven Pillars* Lawrence praises "the non-commissioned of us" in the Arabian campaign as "wonderful, especially when it is taken into account that they had not the motive, the imaginative vision of the end, which sustained the officers."[13]

Exceptions were those officers hidebound by outmoded military traditions who are reproached by Lawrence with devastating sarcasm for their lack of imagination, the sine qua non of effective leadership in irregular warfare: "The staff knew so much more of war than I did that they refused to learn from me of the strange conditions in which Arab irregulars had to act; and I could not be bothered to set up a kindergarten of the imagination for their benefit."[14] Here Lawrence stresses the solitude of a man with imagination among those without it. The importance of this statement is underscored by inclusion of Kennington's amusing illustration portraying the unimaginative officers as small children compared to a gigantic adult Lawrence who disdains to begin their education in the military uses of imagination. Part of the comedy achieved by this picture arises from symbolic reversal of the actual physical relationship (stressed elsewhere in the text) of the very short Lawrence and his mostly taller compatriots.

In the lyrical chapter on solidarity that concludes *The Mint*, Lawrence affirms of the airmen's sense of belonging that "as we gain attachment, so we strip ourselves of personality."[15] As evidence of this willing erasure of selfhood Lawrence cites "the spiritual importance of such trifles as these overalls in which we shroud ourselves for work like robots: to become drab shapes without comeliness or particularity."[16] For Lawrence, however, clothing is never a trifle. This sentence elevates overalls from trivia to symbol and invites informed readers to contemplate an implied contrast between Lawrence as robotlike airman in overalls indistinguishable from the others and Lawrence elsewhere in many famous paintings, sketches, and photographs strikingly particularized—and activating every viewer's imagination—in the gorgeous white robes of a Sherif. While there is nihilism in the metaphor of airmen as dehumanized though happy robots, there is (for us if not for Lawrence) irony in *The Mint*'s last paragraph where by way of peroration celebrating a sense of solidarity with his comrades Lawrence includes among their virtues "the penurious imaginations which neither harrow nor reap their lowlands of mind."[17] A dormant or atrophied imagination is thus presented as one condition for achieving what the last words of *The Mint* proclaim: "No loneliness any more."[18] For Lawrence an active imaginative life offered the pleasures of self-expression accompanied, however, by the increasing pain of a solitude so emotionally crippling that finally it could only be escaped by severely curtailing his imagination. For Churchill imagination was a means of strengthening ties to a wider community by animating convictions in the spheres of literature and politics to serve society no less than self.

During the political epilogue to the Arab Revolt, the contrast between Churchill and Lawrence is not so stark. To the surprise of many then and later, Lawrence not only satisfied his employer but was himself satisfied with his service under Churchill from February 1921 to July 1922 as advisor on Arabian affairs to the colonial secretary. In a letter written to Robert Graves in 1927 for inclusion in *Lawrence and the Arabs*, Lawrence described Churchill as "so considerate as sometimes to seem more like a senior partner than a master," adding that "the work I did constructively for him in 1921 and 1922 seems to me, in retrospect, the best I ever did."[19] This praise was duly published by Graves along with Lawrence's modest description of his own efforts and a tribute to Churchill's imagination and courage: "I take to myself credit for some of Mr. Churchill's pacification of the Middle East, for while he was carrying it out he had the help of such knowledge and energy as I possess. His was the imagination and courage to take a fresh departure and enough skill and knowledge of political procedure to put his political revolution into operation in the Middle East, and in London, peacefully."[20] In Lawrence's original draft of this passage there is a good deal less humility though an equal appreciation of Churchill's imagination, courage, and political skill: "I take most of the credit of Mr. Churchill's pacification of the Middle East upon myself. I had the knowledge and the plan. He had the imagination and the courage to adopt it and the knowledge of the political procedure to put it into operation."[21] The revision was urged upon Graves by Lawrence as a way of reciprocating kindness while boosting Churchill's prospects: "Winston was my very friendly and kindly chief, and has still his career to make. So we must give him credit for all he can carry."[22] Only an uncharitable reader would weigh the peculiar hubris in this explanation more heavily than its engaging display of gratitude and friendship.

In *Seven Pillars of Wisdom* Lawrence wrote of his wartime career that "it was part of my failure never to have found a chief to use me. All of them, through incapacity or timidity or liking, allowed me too free a hand; as if they could not see that voluntary slavery was the deep pride of a morbid spirit, and vicarious pain its gladdest decoration."[23] With less parade of his "morbid spirit" in a letter to Churchill dated November 18, 1922, Lawrence avoided comment on any masochistic reveling in vicarious pain he may have experienced while at the Colonial Office. He reflected instead on its therapeutic benefits: "I've had lots of chiefs in my time, but never one before who really was my chief. The others have needed help at all times: you only when you want it. . . . you know it doubles the good of a subordinate to feel that his chief is better than himself."[24] In a draft preface for Edward Garnett's unpublished abridgement of the Oxford text of *Seven Pillars*, dated the same day as the letter to Churchill, Lawrence states that "when Mr. Winston Churchill took charge of the Middle East" he "set honesty before expediency in order to fulfil our promises in the letter and in the spirit."[25] The previous week in a letter to R. D. Blumenfeld Lawrence wrote of Churchill, "The man's as brave as six, as good-humoured, shrewd, self-confident, & considerate as a statesman can be: & several times I've seen him chuck the statesmanlike course & do the honest thing instead."[26] In the 1926 text of *Seven Pillars* Lawrence included a footnote making public his conviction that at the 1921 Cairo conference Churchill "made straight all the tangle, finding solutions fulfilling (I think) our promises in letter and spirit (where humanly possible) without sacrificing any interest of our Empire or any interest of the peoples concerned. So we were quit of the wartime Eastern adventure, with clean hands, but three years too late to earn the gratitude which peoples, if not states, can pay."[27] Churchill had earned Lawrence's gratitude, along with his respect, his loyal service, and not least, his friendship.

Neither in prospect nor retrospect did this outcome seem inevitable. Churchill wrote that "Lawrence's term as a Civil Servant was a unique phase in his life. Everyone was astonished by his calm and tactful demeanour. His patience and readiness to work with others amazed those who knew him best."[28] Perhaps many who knew Churchill best were no less amazed at his ability to get along harmoniously with Lawrence. Both could be difficult. Each had a considerable ego. Of Lawrence, Ronald Storrs wrote: "He was an individual force of driving intelligence, but with nothing of the administrator; having about as much of the team spirit as Alexander the Great."[29] Churchill wrote less ironically that in Lawrence "one can hardly see lacking any of the qualities of which world conquerors are made."[30] It was unnecessary to add that such qualities are not much sought after when recruiting civil servants. Churchill speculated too in one of his characteristic exercises in alternative history that "if the Great War had continued for several more years. . . . Lawrence might have realized Napoleon's young dream of conquering the East; he might have arrived at Constantinople in 1919 or 1920 with many of the tribes and races of Asia Minor and Arabia at his back."[31]

To succeed where Napoleon had failed would have been to achieve a military man's utopia. By suggesting the idea as a miniature sketch without filling in details or arguing seriously for the possibility, Churchill invites readers to exercise their imaginations in parallel with his, connecting the dots of his outline, as it were. As a posthumous tribute to Lawrence's unrealized potential this flight of fancy is magnanimous. In elegiac mood Churchill was inclined to endorse and augment the myth of Lawrence's impact on events. By daydreaming in print of Lawrence conquering Constantinople, moreover, Churchill could (yet again) covertly assuage his own regrets over the Dardanelles fiasco. Though his plan had come to grief, perhaps some one else, in some other way, even if at a much later date, could have eliminated the Turks in a coup de théâtre that, like Churchill's idea of the navy forcing the straits, would not have entailed large British casualties. Constantinople might have been won with "the tribes and races of Asia Minor" bearing the brunt instead of those British, Anzac, and French soldiers who had suffered so grievously in the real world after the landings at Gallipoli. However fantastic, Churchill finds it pretty to think so.

When setting down his considered opinion as a military historian while Lawrence was still alive, however, Churchill was more restrained. He praises Allenby for capturing Jerusalem on December 8, 1917, and thereafter "wisely fostering the Arab revolt which grew around the astonishing personality of Lawrence." This is Churchill's only mention of Lawrence in the volumes of *The World Crisis* dealing with 1916–18. On the same page Churchill praises Allenby—not Lawrence—for "brilliant and frugal operations, which will long serve as a model in theatres of war in which manoeuvre is possible." That said in justice to the tactical brilliance of Allenby's campaign, Churchill goes on to remark that from a strategic viewpoint Allenby's efforts were not used to best advantage but in fact complicated and prolonged the war:

> The very serious drain of men, munitions and transport which flowed unceasingly to the Palestine Expedition ought to have been arrested by action far swifter in character and far larger in scale. Brevity and finality, not less at this period than throughout the war, were the true tests of any diversion against Turkey. Prolonged and expanding operations in distant unrelated theatres, whether they languished as at Salonica, or crackled briskly and brightly forward under Allenby in Palestine, were not to be reconciled with a wise war policy. It would have been far safer and far cheaper in life and resources to run a greater risk for a shorter time. The advantage of

the command of the sea should not have been neglected. If, while Allenby held the Turks at Gaza, a long-prepared descent had been made at Haifa or elsewhere on the sea coast behind them, and if the railway by which alone they could exist had been severed in September by a new army of six or eight divisions, the war in Syria would have been ended at a stroke. The Eastern drain on our resources would have been stopped from February onwards; all the British troops in Palestine would have been available to meet the supreme peril in France. But in Palestine as formerly at Gallipoli, the clash of the Western and Eastern schools of thought produced incoherence and half-measures.[32]

In this more serious resort to alternative history as part of his critique of England's war strategy by giving his view of what other options actually existed and ought to have been pursued, Churchill says nothing about what Lawrence might have done. He dwells on how the navy not cavalry on camels might better have been employed. He posits amphibious operations as essential to a more decisive encounter. He speculates that the Turkish railway supply line might have been cut beyond repair not by Lawrence and his Arab irregulars but by "a new army of six or eight divisions." Whether right or wrong, here at least is Churchill's professional judgment as soldier, politician, and historian. There is in this context no romantic imagining of exploits that might have been led by some dashing young English latter-day Napoleon rallying a ragtag, lightly armed, guerrilla band to topple an empire.

Churchill never proposed *Seven Pillars* as a manual of military strategy. Its appeal as an adventure story and memoir captivated his imagination and earned his praise. Its utility to students of warfare was left for others to remark. Implicit in Churchill's dismissal of Lawrence in *The World Crisis* with a phrase highlighting his "astonishing" personality is agreement with Lawrence's own famous view (in one of his more humble moods) that his campaign had been nothing more than a sideshow of a sideshow. Lawrence, for his part, did not object to Churchill's analysis of British strategy or to his downplaying of the Arab Revolt. Commenting on the book in a letter to Edward Marsh, Churchill's private secretary and devoted friend, three months after publication in March 1927 of *The World Crisis 1916–1918,* and probably alluding as well to the previous volumes that covered 1911–15, Lawrence wrote of Churchill: "I suppose he realises that he's the only high person, since Thucydides & Clarendon, who has put his generation, imaginatively, in his debt."[33] Surely Marsh showed the letter to Churchill.

When that Napoleon manqué with the temperament of another Alexander the Great became a civil servant, a writer, a publisher, and an enlisted man serving humbly but not obscurely in the ranks, Churchill did not heap scorn on Lawrence's attempt to escape fame and renounce power. Instead Churchill, who was always ambitious and a connoisseur of achievement in others, praised the self-denial of Lawrence's postwar life as additional evidence that he "had a full measure of the versatility of genius": "He was a savant as well as a soldier. He was an archaeologist as well as a man of action. He was an accomplished scholar as well as an Arab partisan. He was a mechanic as well as a philosopher."[34] In commending Lawrence's austere refusal to pursue money, political power, and the even greater fame that he might easily have obtained, Churchill was not stooping to hypocritical praise for humility and self-restraint of a sort that he himself neither practiced nor often admired. Churchill the politician and writer had a professional interest in the methods by which Lawrence had captivated public imagination. Postmortem analysis of how Lawrence's career had achieved its imaginative appeal doubtless seemed all the more urgent to Churchill in view of the dangers posed by rearmament of Nazi Germany and the aggressive designs of Fascist Italy. Hitler's rise to power and Mussolini's ability to rally Italians behind his dreams of conquest were reasons enough for any thoughtful person to reconsider all the ways popularity could be achieved and the purposes for which it might be used or abused in the twentieth century. The accelerating tempo of Europe's plunge toward war informs not only Churchill's first summing-up of Lawrence's life but also significant revisions of that initial evaluation.

——————— ◯ ———————

"Lawrence of Arabia's Name Will Live!", Churchill's obituary article on his former colleague, appeared in *News of the World* on May 26, 1935, only seven days after Lawrence died from the injuries of his motorcycle accident. Churchill reprinted this essay with minor omissions as his contribution to the 1937 memorial volume *T. E. Lawrence by His Friends*. For convenience here I will refer to the latter of these two essentially identical texts as the early version. Churchill drew upon but also heavily revised some parts of this text for his remarks on October 3, 1936, at the unveiling of a memorial at the Oxford High School for Boys. Then for the essay on

Lawrence in his own 1937 opus *Great Contemporaries*, Churchill included much of this speech along with other substantial changes. The differences have gone unremarked, probably because with the latter version Churchill included a misleading footnote suggesting that it was just a reprinting of the previous appearances with some additions of no particular consequence: "Most of this essay has already been published in 'T. E. Lawrence, by his Friends, 1937,' and is also drawn from my address at the unveiling of his memorial at his Oxford school. It is reprinted here for the sake of completeness."[35] Churchill's bibliographer Frederick Woods propagated the confusion by remarking of the essay on Lawrence in *T. E. Lawrence by His Friends* that "it was also published in *Great Contemporaries*, having first appeared in *News of the World*, 26 May 1935."[36] It was the revised version in *Great Contemporaries* incorporating large parts of the Oxford remarks that Churchill intended to stand as his most considered and complete view of Lawrence.

When the Oxford address was reprinted in 1954 as "The Allocution" to *The Home Letters of T. E. Lawrence and His Brothers*, Churchill sent for publication with it a letter from 10 Downing Street dated March 4, 1954, affirming that "eighteen years have passed since those words were spoken, but now, pondering them again, I find not one to alter." Looking back on "the vast perils and catastrophes of the years between" the 1936 Oxford address and 1954, Churchill in this letter then switches to his ex cathedra tone as historian and concludes of Lawrence that "it is the measure of his greatness that his multiple achievement has passed beyond opinion into history."[37] Thus Churchill the historian ratifies (as usual) the opinions of his earlier self as essayist, speechmaker, and politician expressing opinions apt to the moment of their pronouncement. What most conspicuously defined that moment between 1935 and 1937 during which Churchill revised for political effect his summing-up of Lawrence was a series of steps toward another world war: Italy's invasion of Abyssinia on October 3, 1935; Germany's reoccupation of the Rhineland on March 7, 1936; and the outbreak in July 1936 of civil war in Spain. With an eye to bolstering Britain's military response to the growing threat posed by these and related events, Churchill while revising his essay undertook some mythmaking in order to reshape the legend of Lawrence of Arabia.

In the early version Churchill laments the passing of Lawrence by writing flatly: "I do not see his like elsewhere. I fear whatever our need we shall never see his like again."[38] This echoes Hamlet's lament for his father:

"He was a man, take him for all in all, / I shall not look upon his like again." In *Great Contemporaries* Churchill's hesitant allusion to "whatever our need" is replaced by a more ominous and elaborate statement expressed not in first person as merely what the writer sees and fears but in plural voice as an articulation of what everybody perceives: "All feel the poorer that he has gone from us. In these days dangers and difficulties gather upon Britain and her Empire, and we are also conscious of a lack of outstanding figures with which to overcome them."[39] By the switch in voice to express what "we" "all" understand, Churchill here quietly assumes the role, always congenial to him, of spokesman for the nation. When this version was published in 1937 while Churchill was still in the political wilderness criticizing governmental apathy and watching with dismay the pageant of mediocrity as Stanley Baldwin was succeeded as prime minister on May 28 by Neville Chamberlain, readers of *Great Contemporaries* might well take the remark as both another hit at recent occupants of 10 Downing Street and a hint that despite the shortage of outstanding figures one at least, whose book they held in their hands, was still available.

Later in the revised essay Churchill describes even more specifically the sinister historical moment that renders Lawrence's absence all the more grievous: "Those who know him best miss him most; but our country misses him most of all; and misses him most of all now. For this is a time when the great problems upon which his thought and work had so long centred, problems of aerial defence, problems of our relations with the Arab peoples, fill an ever larger space in our affairs."[40] This list of difficulties facing Britain in 1937 puts foremost one that had also become Churchill's special bailiwick. Problems of aerial defense were filling an ever larger space in his life as well as the country's affairs both on account of his well-founded concern over growth of the Luftwaffe and because since July 1935 Churchill, though still out of office, had been serving at Prime Minister Baldwin's invitation as a member of Britain's Air Defense Research Committee.[41] Far more than Lawrence had done in the RAF, Churchill was centering his thoughts and public pronouncements on large problems of aerial defense. Lawrence while in the ranks was more absorbed in the minutiae of motors, motorcycles, motorboats, aerial photography, and aircraft maintenance.

In the early version for *T.E. Lawrence by His Friends* Churchill writes of Lawrence's enlistment in the Royal Air Force that "in an honourable service, 'the simple round, the common task' furnished him with a way of living." Here Churchill echoes a familiar stanza from John Keble's "Morning," a hymn then widely known throughout England:

> The trivial round, the common task,
> Would furnish all we ought to ask;
> Room to deny ourselves; a road
> To bring us, daily, nearer God.[42]

Churchill does not stress that despite some resemblance to religious austerities Lawrence's self-denial was hardly an exercise designed to bring him nearer to God. Churchill enhances the dignity of Lawrence's RAF work by changing Keble's "trivial round" to "simple round." There is no way of telling how often this change passed unnoticed by Churchill's readers. But in any event it at least avoided any explicit statement that Lawrence's postwar service was trivial. Here too after citing Lawrence's explanation that by enlisting in the ranks "he was setting an example, and that there was nothing in life better than to be a good aircraftman" Churchill remarks in agreement: "He was certainly that, but how much more besides!"[43] In *Great Contemporaries* Churchill imputes a loftier and more specific rationale for Lawrence's enlistment than merely earning "a living" while setting a modest example as "a good aircraftman." In the revised version Churchill takes readers inside Lawrence's mind to describe what he understood, what he felt, and accordingly what motivated him politically as well as personally:

> He saw as clearly as anyone the vision of Air power and all that it would mean in traffic and war. He found in the life of an aircraftsman [*sic*] that balm of peace and equipoise which no great station or command could have bestowed upon him. He felt that in living the life of a private in the Royal Air Force he would dignify that honourable calling and help to attract all that is keenest in our youthful manhood to the sphere where it is most urgently needed. For this service and example, to which he devoted the last twelve years of his life, we owe him a separate debt. It was in itself a princely gift.[44]

Even without benefit of reading Lawrence's account in *The Mint* of his RAF comrades, who there hardly seem all that is keenest in Britain's

youthful manhood, one might well conclude that Churchill is here romanticizing. His adjective "keenest" is less apt to those enlisted men doing
humdrum maintenance alongside Lawrence on the ground than to those
pilots (mostly officers) whom Churchill was later with more plausibility
to ennoble as the Few. Although it has some basis in Lawrence's own more
grandiose post facto explanations of why he enlisted, Churchill's conversion here of Lawrence into an apostle of invigorated English air power
takes on a mythic quality that allows it to do double duty as a tribute
and as a part of Churchill's now famous rhetorical response to the Nazi
menace while acting as prophet in the wilderness calling for renewed
patriotism, for rearmament, and especially for a stronger air force.

In his early version for *T.E. Lawrence by His Friends*, Churchill includes a paragraph attributing Lawrence's imaginative appeal to attitudes
that set him apart from others as both solitary and superior: "His grip
upon the imagination of the modern world was due to his indifference
to all the delights which nature offers to her multitudes of children. He
could fee her pangs to the full. Her prizes did not stir him. Home, money,
comfort, fame, power itself—meant little or nothing to him. The modern
world had no means of exerting the slightest pull upon him. Solitary,
austere, inexorable, he moved upon a plane apart from and above our
common lot. Existence was no more than a duty, yet a duty faithfully to
be discharged."[45] Here Churchill specifies with unqualified admiration
the combination of Lawrence's human ability to suffer ("He could feel
her pangs to the full") and his exceptional if not superhuman detachment
("Her prizes did not stir him"). Churchill's focus is on Lawrence himself,
especially his imperviousness to outside influences: "The modern world
had no means of exerting the slightest pull upon him."

In the revision of this paragraph for *Great Contemporaries*, Churchill
retains and indeed strikingly enhances the tone of admiration. He also
generalizes to suggest how those like Lawrence, those in whose small class
he belongs, may influence the world. Churchill's focus shifts from why
others could not sway Lawrence to how Lawrence could sway others.
The revised paragraph is introduced by another revised passage in which
Churchill dwells on Lawrence's uncanny ability to dominate people, in
effect to rule over them as a kind of monarch, by virtue of sheer willpower
and force of personality: "Alike in his great period of adventure and command or in these later years of self-suppression and self-imposed eclipse, he
always *reigned over those with whom he came in contact*. They felt themselves

in the presence of an extraordinary being. They felt that his latent reserves of force and will-power were *beyond measurement*."[46] Churchill's image of Lawrence unofficially reigning over those around him is a distant echo of Lowell Thomas's myth of Lawrence as "The Uncrowned King of the Arabs."[47] Admiration of willpower and exercise of it are hallmarks of Churchill's own life, although tempered by awareness of corollary hazards. Hitler's career prompted Churchill to reflect most deeply on the dangers of unmeasurably strong willpower. In his chapter on Hitler in *The Gathering Storm* Churchill recounts how in 1918 while recovering amid "the shock of defeat" from a gas attack at the front that had blinded Hitler, "this convalescent regimental orderly" experienced "an agony which consumed his being, and generated those portentous and measureless forces of the spirit which may spell the rescue or the doom of mankind."[48] In Hitler's case they spelled doom. Even looking back on his career after doing so much to terminate it, however, Churchill stresses the potential for good as well as the potential for evil inherent in those "measureless forces of the spirit" paradoxically achieved via suffering ("agony") by Hitler and apparent in Lawrence, however generated, as what Churchill calls somewhat more specifically "reserves of force and will-power . . . beyond measurement."

According to Churchill in the passage revised for *Great Contemporaries*, the class of extraordinary people of immeasurable force and willpower that includes Lawrence all display similar potentialities for great good or great evil. They are the most highly gifted and therefore, Churchill implies, the most dangerous or the most helpful of all depending on how they use their talent:

> Part of the secret of this stimulating ascendancy lay of course in his disdain for most of the prizes, the pleasures and comforts of life. The world naturally looks with some awe upon a man who appears unconcernedly indifferent to home, money, comfort, rank or even power and fame. The world feels, not without a certain apprehension, that here is someone outside its jurisdiction; someone before whom its allurements may be spread in vain; someone strangely enfranchised, untamed, untrammeled by convention, moving independently of the ordinary currents of human action; a being readily capable of violent revolt or supreme sacrifice, a man, solitary, austere, to whom existence is no more than a duty, yet a duty to be faithfully

discharged. He was indeed a dweller upon the mountain tops where the air is cold, crisp and rarefied, and where the view on clear days commands all the Kingdoms of the world and the glory of them.[49]

Here nothing is said of Lawrence's ability to suffer, to feel nature's "pangs to the full." Churchill replaces "his grip upon the imagination of the modern world" with the phrase "this stimulating ascendancy," thereby placing emphasis upon Lawrence's domination rather than merely upon his imaginative appeal. "Ascendancy" denotes superiority as well as—or perhaps in most cases by virtue of—de facto control and rulership. Churchill's carefully chosen qualifying adjective, "stimulating," has in this context (and usually) a favorable connotation that might be paraphrased as "pleasantly arousing or invigorating." Thus insofar as "ascendancy" may suggest domination that is potentially unpleasant or unwelcome, "stimulating" works to defuse the negative connotation while nevertheless making clear that if Lawrence was, as the passage goes on to affirm, outside the world's jurisdiction the reverse was not true. Though Lawrence could not be commanded by the ordinary inducements ("home, money, comfort, rank or even power and fame"), by his very renunciation of "the prizes, the pleasures and comforts of life" he could dominate and command others.

Well might people be made uneasy by this one-way flow of power. Accordingly Churchill adds in the revised passage that a person so endowed is regarded "with some awe" and "not without a certain apprehension." Churchill's ironic understatement leaves readers to decide just how much apprehension Lawrence and his like generate or should generate as well as what the exact balance may be of awe and apprehension. To explain why some degree of fear is reasonable Churchill also remarks that such a person is "readily capable of violent revolt or supreme sacrifice." It could go either way: toward destructive rebellion against authority or redemptive immolation of self. The implied archetypes are Satan and Christ.

The last sentence which Churchill adds to this passage for *Great Contemporaries* hyperbolically resolves the matter in Lawrence's favor and ends whatever suspense the paragraph arouses about whether to regard that "strangely enfranchised" man as Satanic or Christlike. In describing him as a "dweller upon the mountain tops where . . . the view on clear days commands all the Kingdoms of the world and glory of them," Churchill presents Lawrence's life as an imitation of Christ by echoing and applying a familiar passage from the King James Version of Matthew 4:8 describing the satanic temptation which Christ rejected: "Again, the devil taketh him up into an exceeding high mountain, and sheweth him all the kingdoms of the world, and the glory of them." Attention in 1937 to the potential dangers of personalities "moving independently of the ordinary currents of human action" was timely in the light of Hitler's recent ascendency. Awe not apprehension, however, is the prevailing sentiment toward Lawrence evoked by Churchill, who well understood the temptations of worldly kingdoms but neither succumbed to totalitarian misuse of his own very considerable "reserves of force and will-power" nor made any secret of his fondness for "the prizes, the pleasures and comforts of life."

Churchill's heightened description of Lawrence as a kind of lost savior, Christlike rather than Satanic in his renunciation of worldly glory, intensifies the elegiac tone of the essay as revised for *Great Contemporaries*. The elegiac note is sounded more strongly too in the revised conclusion, which Churchill introduces by adding to the early version an account of his own conviction that Lawrence was both willing and able to assume again the burdens of leadership had there been a compelling occasion for his talents: "For all his reiterated renunciations I always felt that he was a man who held himself ready for a new call. While Lawrence lived one always felt—I certainly felt it strongly—that some overpowering need would draw him from the modest path he chose to tread and set him once again in full action at the centre of memorable events."[50] This wishful thinking on Churchill's part, thus presented in retrospect, intensifies a mythic sense of Lawrence as an Arthurian figure—a sort of once and future uncrowned king—merely biding his time in suspension until the right moment for a return to greatness "in full action at the centre of memorable events." The very vagueness of this phrase allows readers to indulge their own fantasies of what Lawrence might have done had he lived. Thus readers may become secret sharers in Churchill's imaginings of Lawrence redivivus. Here as often elsewhere Churchill's imagination does not preclude parallel imagining by his readers. He invites it.

But Churchill quickly damps down such fantasies by a turn at the start of the revised essay's last paragraph:

> It was not to be. The summons which reached him, and for which he was equally prepared, was of a different order. It came as he would have wished it, swift and sudden on the wings of Speed. He had reached the last leap in his gallant course through life.

All is over! Fleet career,
Dash of greyhound slipping thongs,
Flight of falcon, bound of deer,
Mad hoof-thunder in our rear,
Cold air rushing up our lungs,
Din of many tongues.[51]

Here Churchill (the ex-cavalry officer, polo champion, and future owner of racehorses) brings to bear appropriately enough—though perhaps somewhat mawkishly for readers not so steeped in equine pleasures and equine sentimentalities—the first stanza of "The Last Leap" from the collection *Sea Spray and Smoke Drift* by the Australian horseman-poet and renowned steeplechase rider Adam Lindsay Gordon (1833–70).

The poem's speaker laments the demise of a horse that has come to grief attempting a jump while racing. The second and third stanzas set the sorrowful scene:

Once again, one struggle good,
One vain effort; —he must dwell
Near the shifted post, that stood
Where the splinters of the wood,
Lying in the torn tracks, tell
How he struck and fell

Crest where cold drops beaded cling,
Small ear drooping, nostril full
Glazing to a scarlet ring,
Flanks and haunches quivering,
Sinews stiffning, void and null,
Dumb eyes sorrowful.[52]

The poem continues describing the dying horse in this melancholy vein, of which these stanzas are a sufficient sample, until the moment of death, whereupon the speaker's focus shifts to his own stoic responses to what has happened:

All is over! This is death,
And I stand to watch thee die,

Brave old horse! With 'bated breath
Hardly drawn through tight-clenched teeth,
    Lip indented deep, but eye
    Only dull and dry.[53]

Thus far Gordon's elegy in a country racecourse sketches a situation that supplies Churchill with an apt though not altogether flattering metaphor comparing Lawrence to the faithful and dashing but unfortunate and now departed horse. Motorcycle accident and fatal missed jump are comparable ends. The poem's speaker and Churchill in his essay on Lawrence stand in the same relationship of elegiac meditation to the subject of their lament.

Before rushing to judgment of this poem it is well to recollect that neither Gordon nor Churchill were alone during their times in romanticizing beyond what is now customary the human relationship with horses. Nevertheless both tempered this inclination by firsthand knowledge of the actualities of dealing with horses: Churchill as a cavalry officer and polo player, Gordon as a sportsman and member of the Australian mounted police force. Both accepted without sentimental regret the purely utilitarian aspects of using and when necessary using up these animals for purposes of no concern to the horses. When writing, both alluded to horses in ways less calculated to convey their actual attitudes toward these creatures than to establish or strengthen literary effects.

In his celebrated chapter on "the Sensations of a Cavalry Charge" in *My Early Life*, for example, Churchill only remarks of his own horse that carried him safely through during the charge of the 21st Lancers at the Battle of Omdurman that when "the ground began to fall away beneath his feet" as they reached a declivity teeming with hostile Dervishes "the clever animal dropped like a cat four or five feet down on to the sandy bed of the watercourse, and in this sandy bed I found myself surrounded by what seemed to be dozens of men."[54] The tone here is descriptive rather than effusive in noting the animal's intelligence. There is a similar absence of sentimentalizing about horses (or war) in Churchill's account of the aftermath: "But now from the direction of the enemy there came a succession of grisly apparitions; horses spouting blood, struggling on three legs, men staggering on foot, men bleeding from terrible wounds, fish-hook spears stuck right through them, arms and faces cut to pieces, bowels protruding, men gasping, crying, collapsing, expiring."[55] So too in summing up English casualties of the charge Churchill numbers horses and men in the same flat tone of objective appraisal: "In all out of 310 officers and men the regiment had lost in the space of about two or three minutes five officers and sixty-five men killed and wounded, and 120 horses—nearly a quarter of its strength."[56] Thus when attempting to describe how the charge looked and felt to him at the time, Churchill conveys the cold viewpoint of a military officer to whom horses and men alike must be regarded as neither more nor less than components of effective combat. Churchill leaves it up to his readers to distribute their sympathy between the wounded, dying, and dead men and horses. He reigns in sentimentality to further realism. Emotion could not be indulged on the battlefield. Accordingly he does not indulge it on these pages recounting the charge of the 21st Lancers.

Elsewhere, however, Churchill freely draws upon sentimental connotations evoked by a romanticized view of equine loyalty to humans. A famous comic instance of such allusions, for example, was (as a transcript and recording show) much appreciated by his audience when Churchill spoke after receiving an honorary degree at Harvard University on September 6, 1943. During a lighter moment in his call on that occasion for continued Anglo-American cultural as well as political unity in view of the fact that "the empires of the future are the empires of the mind," Churchill remarked with some regret displacement of the horse by machines that have contracted the world "in relation to our powers of locomotion at a positively alarming rate": "We have learned to fly. What prodigious changes are involved in that new accomplishment! Man has parted company with his trusty friend the horse and has sailed into the azure with the eagles, eagles being represented by the infernal (loud laughter)—I mean internal—combustion engine."[57] The drollery of Churchill's witty and carefully scripted slip of the tongue here is enhanced by his equally contrived anthropomorphism in referring to horses as our trusty friends.

Gordon too, though certainly evincing in his poetry more consistent sentimentality about horses, alludes to them mainly for symbolic purposes rather than simply to indulge in heartwarming emotional outbursts of fellow feeling toward them. This is clear even in so anthropomorphic an exercise as "The Roll of the Kettledrum; or, the Lay of the Last Charger," a poem in which it is a horse as speaker who narrates the sensations of a cavalry charge. Gordon gives this old warhorse some moments of philosophizing to inculcate humility in the human audience that he is addressing:

The wide gulf that parts us may yet be no wider
  Than that which parts you from some being more blest;
And there may be more links 'twixt the horse and his rider
  Than ever your shallow philosophy guess'd.[58]

Application of this lesson at the poem's conclusion turns out to be a chilling insistence that humans finally understand no more than horses about the riddles of existence:

We labour to-day, and we slumber to-morrow,
Strong horse and bold rider! —and *who knoweth more?*[59]

This existential note sounds throughout Gordon's poetry. His people, like his horses, most often come to sad ends devoid of religious consolation. Death, disappointment, and bereavement are prominent themes. Isolation, pain, and bewilderment at the end of life define the human condition in Gordon's verse. Love and enjoyment of life, often symbolized by the joyous cooperation of horse and rider in sport and war, are balanced by longing for the oblivion of death as an escape from the predominant pain of existence. At the age of thirty-seven, on the day after his final collection of poetry *Bush Ballads and Galloping Rhymes* was published, Gordon killed himself.

Gordon's poetry thus afforded Churchill more than equine imagery inviting a far-fetched sentimental metaphor equating Lawrence with a splendid racehorse who misjudged his jump. Gordon's bleak outlook on life resonates with Lawrence's nihilism and Churchill's usually concealed moments of depression and weariness that he called his Black Dog. Readers of his revised essay on Lawrence for *Great Contemporaries* might have recalled the concluding stanzas of "The Last Leap" in which the speaker bids farewell to the fallen horse:

Rest, old friend! Thy day, though rife
  With its toil hath ended soon;
We have had our share of strife,
Tumblers in the mask of life,
  In the pantomime of noon
  Clown and pantaloon.

With a flash that ends thy pain,
      Respite and oblivion blest
Come to greet thee. I in vain
Fall: I rise to fall again:
      Thou hast fallen to thy rest—
      And thy fall is best![60]

Implicit but not explicit in Churchill's quotation of "The Last Leap" are additional metaphors that might characterize Lawrence and his relationship to Churchill. The penultimate stanza describes life as a mere pantomime of no serious import enforcing its players—or at least the poem's two dramatis personae—to put on the disguise of stock characters, here both comic. Applied metaphorically in the context of Churchill's elegiac essay, Lawrence becomes clown and Churchill the older figure of ridicule called pantaloon. The final stanza expresses envy of the oblivion found in death, as well as longing to achieve it on the part of a speaker who must nevertheless keep rising only to experience more falls. If applied metaphorically, the conclusion hints at an undercurrent or transient mood of yearning by Churchill to experience such respite as Lawrence has been granted.

    I cannot tell whether Churchill counted on readers of his revised essay to recall the rest of "The Last Leap" and make such applications. Many might have done so, because Gordon's poetry was again in vogue. Stimulated by the 1933 centennial of his birth, two new biographies were published, along with new editions of his poetry.[61] Although on a far smaller scale than Lawrence, Gordon too was being mythologized as a national hero—of Australia but also of the empire at large. Such literary worthies as Rudyard Kipling, James Barrie, John Galsworthy, and Arthur Quiller-Couch had enthusiastically supported the project of a Westminster Abbey memorial. Its progress toward fruition was reported by many newspaper stories until at last an idealized bust of him by Lady Scott, the explorer's widow, was unveiled in Poet's Corner of Westminster Abbey by the Duke of York (later George VI) on May 11, 1934. This has been described as "the portrait of a hero, glaring defiantly at fate with his 'unconquerable soul.'"[62] The oration on that occasion, broadcast live on the BBC, was delivered by a no less astute judge of poetry than the Archbishop of Canterbury, who summed up his tribute to Gordon by pronouncing him "the voice of the national life of one of the young nations of the British race" to whom, "exiled once and now brought home, England

gives a place among her own most honoured dead." His Grace ended this widely diffused (and subsequently published) eulogy of Gordon by affirming that "the Memorial of him here will be an enduring link between Australia and the Motherland."[63] Surely this high-water mark of Gordon's reputation prompted many to revisit his poetry. Churchill must have been well aware of how the attention culminating in Gordon's apotheosis ensured a receptive audience for allusions to his poetry. Its ex cathedra ratification at Westminster Abbey was only a year before Lawrence's death on May 19, 1935, and publication seven days later of the first version of Churchill's obituary essay. I doubt that Churchill expected or would have wanted explicit extensions to himself as well as to Lawrence of allusions to Gordon. Nevertheless Churchill's recourse to Gordon's poetry bespeaks an emotional and philosophical affinity that reveals much about the hidden depths as well as the rhetorical surfaces of Churchill's imagination.

Recall how differently from Lawrence Churchill had placed and maintained himself in the public imagination. No Lowell Thomas was needed by a man whose genius was for running not backing into the limelight. To raise money for a political career Churchill lectured widely on his own Boer War exploits. By the time he was first elected to Parliament in 1900 at the age of twenty-six, he had not only been applauded in newspapers as a war hero. He had since 1895 served with increasing prominence as a war correspondent, providing dispatches from conflicts in Cuba, India, the Sudan, and South Africa. When he first took his seat as a Conservative MP for Oldham in 1900, moreover, Churchill had already put before the public his novel *Savrola* (1900) and four nonfiction narratives of warfare in which he had participated: *The Story of the Malakand Field Force* (1898), *The River War* (1899), *London to Ladysmith via Pretoria* (1900), and *Ian Hamilton's March* (1900). Churchill thereafter kept his name and personality current not only on campaign trails and in high public office, but via a steady stream of journalism and books. Churchill the professional writer supported and publicized Churchill the consummate politician. By the time of Lawrence's death in 1935 Churchill had also published a biography (*Lord Randolph Churchill*), four compilations of his speeches, two engaging memoirs (*My African Journey* and *My Early Life*), a volume of essays (*Thoughts and Adventures*), and his six-volume history of World War I (*The World Crisis*). Many more books followed. Just as his political career was crowned by service as prime minister—twice—his accomplishments as a writer were crowned by award of the 1953 Nobel Prize for Literature. Thus Churchill went more willingly and more deeply down the paths of glory than Lawrence ever could or cared to. Churchill's prolific literary career along with his extensive military and political experience equipped him to view almost every facet of Lawrence's life with a sympathetic as well as an expert eye.

Their affinities are no less striking than their differences. Churchill started life as a professional soldier educated at Sandhurst in a strictly military curriculum supplemented only after graduation by reading history and philosophy while serving in India as a cavalry subaltern. Lawrence concentrated in history at Oxford with only interludes of military education in the signals section of the Oxford University Officers Training Corps. Both, however, became authentic war heroes who displayed courage under fire. Both had much firsthand experience of combat, including command during combat. Both were quick to see the limitations of the conventional military mentality and inclined while serving to offend their superiors, as Churchill most notoriously did by criticizing Kitchener in *The River War*. Both were able to shape the political as well as military direction of events. Both were brilliant writers, especially gifted at blending historical narration with personal memoir. Both were interested in art. Both had a keen appreciation of the human comedy, which they sometimes delineated in light tones and sometimes in biting satiric strokes of a Swiftian cast. Not least, both had a vivid theatrical flair for signature costumes.

This last trait is worth dwelling on because of its extreme political importance, which both Lawrence and Churchill remarked in different contexts. In his 1931 essay "Cartoons and Cartoonists," after a wry survey of political cartoons endowing himself and many of his parliamentary colleagues on both sides of the aisle with a real or imaginary identifying attribute, Churchill remarks: "One of the most necessary features of a public man's equipment is some distinctive mark which everyone learns to look for and to recognize. Disraeli's forelock, Mr. Gladstone's collars, Lord Randolph Churchill's moustache, Mr. Chamberlain's eyeglass, Mr. Baldwin's pipe—these "properties" are of the greatest value."[64] Churchill then disingenuously insists "I have never indulged in any of them, so to fill the need cartoonists have invented the legend of my hats." He adds darkly that he may well "convert the legend into a reality by buying myself a new hat on purpose!"[65] Here Churchill's tone is comic. But the topic provided serious reflections for the man whose "V" for victory sign in sterner days became a rallying point of great political power and whose ever-present cigar must have attracted more than a few votes among the smoking classes.

During his long career Churchill indulged in more than cigars and new hats by way of identifying properties. Like Lawrence, he often appeared in exotic costume for purposes of politics or pleasure (or both). Churchill's daughter Mary mentions among her memories of growing up at Chartwell visits by Lawrence: he "would arrive on his (alas fatal) motor-bicycle as Aircraftman Shaw, and descend to dinner—to the amazed wonderment of my childish eyes—in the robes of a Prince of Arabia."[66] On such occasions in the privacy of Churchill's home he and Lawrence were enjoying life as a costume party. But Churchill's exotic outfits were no mere regalia for masquerades. He wore them all as by right and, like Lawrence, usually for serious political purposes on public occasions. A generous but far from complete sample of them on display now in the Uniform Room at Chartwell includes: the undress uniform of an Elder Brother of Trinity House; the service dress of an Air Commodore of the Royal Auxiliary Air Force; the robes of the Chancellor of Bristol University; the full dress of a Privy Councillor and cocked hat with ostrich plume; tropical service dress with regimental badges; full dress of the Lord Warden of the Cinque Ports; full dress uniform of an Elder Brother of Trinity House; the service dress of a full colonel in the 4th Queen's Own Hussars; and a siren suit, ten-gallon hat, and slippers embroidered in gold thread with the initials "WSC."[67]

While subjected to the hazards of trench warfare during his service at the front in 1915 and 1916 Churchill chose to wear the French steel helmet of the poilu rather than British issue headgear. At first he did so for practical as well as aesthetic reasons according to his account in a letter to Clementine dated December 8, 1915: "I have been given a fine steel helmet by the French wh [sic] I am gong to wear, as it looks so nice & will perhaps protect my valuable cranium."[68] After four days it was the helmet's appearance and effect on others that most endeared it to Churchill, as he reports in a letter to Clementine dated December 12, 1915: "My [French] steel helmet is the cause of much envy. I look most martial in it—like a Cromwellian—I always intend to wear it under fire—but chiefly for the appearance."[69] Equally striking in this remark are Churchill's characteristic sensitivity to the impression his outfit makes upon an audience and his active historical imagination. He connects present with past in a way that allows him to fancy himself cutting an especially martial figure because while wearing the helmet he imagines himself to look like one of Oliver Cromwell's fierce Roundheads. It is unknown whether his comrades envied the helmet (if indeed they did) on account of its stirring historical echoes or, what is more likely, simply because it afforded better protection than British gear and was to them somewhat exotic by virtue of being French. A less enthusiastic account of the helmet was provided years later by George Drew, who in 1964 recalled Churchill's costume at their first meeting: "He had a trench coat with the fur outside, a French helmet about three sizes too small, and [a] shepherd's stock."[70]

Lawrence's "Twenty-Seven Articles" of rules for getting on successfully with "Hejaz Arabs" include attention to the political advantages and psychological hazards of wearing native costume:

> 19. If you wear Arab things, wear the best. Clothes are significant among the tribes, and you must wear the appropriate, and appear at ease in them. Dress like a Sherif—if they agree to it.
> 20. If you wear Arab things at all, go the whole way. Leave your English friends and customs on the coast, and fall back on Arab habits entirely.[71]

In article 18 Lawrence explains the problematic side of putting on Arab dress, which epitomized for him the terrible strain of living mentally in two cultures at once: "You will be like an actor in a foreign theatre, playing a part day and night for months, without rest, and for an anxious stake."[72] After the war, as often during it when reporting to his superiors, Lawrence also appreciated the advantages of appearing in Arab dress among Europeans despite whatever stress was involved in playing a mixed role—part foreign, part English—to that very different audience.

Churchill was struck by the effectiveness of the resulting performance as well as by its difficulty for Lawrence as an actor in the theater of European diplomacy. In passages that remain the same in the early version and final revision of his essay on Lawrence, Churchill reports that on their first meeting in the spring of 1919 "after the War was over" and "when the Peace-makers, or at any rate the Treaty-makers were gathered in Paris" Lawrence "wore plain clothes, and looked at first sight like one of the many clean-cut young officers who had gained high rank and

Figure 1. Thomas Edward Lawrence by Augustus Edwin John, 1919. This is the drawing that Churchill refers to in *Great Contemporaries* when he writes in his essay on Lawrence: "I always saw him henceforward as he appears in Augustus John's brilliant pencil sketch." Courtesy of the National Portrait Gallery, London.

distinction in the struggle," although "usually at this time in London or Paris he wore his Arab dress, in order to identify himself with the interests of the Emir Feisal, and with the Arabian claims then under harsh debate."[73] Churchill here notes the Arab costume as a political statement while making clear too in his last clause, which might have been omitted without damaging the main point, that Lawrence chose to identify himself with the losing side in a "harsh debate." Churchill, who so often took stands that put him through the stress of being on the losing side of harsh debates, thus displays and invites sensitivity to the psychological cost of taking up an unpopular cause.

Of his first glimpse of Lawrence in Arab dress Churchill reminisces in the tone of one who has experienced a secular epiphany tinged with an almost erotic appreciation: "He wore his Arab robes, and the full magnificence of his countenance revealed itself. The gravity of his demeanour; the precision of his opinion; the range and quality of his conversation; all seemed enhanced to a remarkable degree by the splendid Arab head-dress and garb. From amid the flowing draperies his noble features, his perfectly-chiselled lips and flashing eyes loaded with fire and comprehension shone forth. He looked what he was, one of Nature's greatest princes."[74] This impression was lasting. It stamped itself so indelibly upon Churchill's imagination, he reports, that whether Lawrence "wore the prosaic clothes of English daily life or afterwards in the uniform of an Air Force mechanic, I always saw him henceforward as he appears in Augustus John's brilliant pencil sketch."[75] This statement records a complex imaginative transformation whereby Churchill's subsequent views of Lawrence, no matter how drably outfitted, were displaced by memories of him in Arab dress, and these memories in turn displaced by recollection of an artistic rendering that is "unquestionably the most widely published drawing of Lawrence."[76] Because the picture was (and is) so well known, Churchill could assume that many if not most of his readers would be able to share his ultimate mental image of Lawrence. That sketch by Augustus John, moreover, is the portrait which, more than any other picture of Lawrence, invites imaginative participation and completion by its viewers. Although the essay for *Great Contemporaries* is only illustrated by a photograph of Lawrence in Arab robes, not by the Augustus John sketch or any other sketch or painting, Churchill's text invites readers to share his mental displacement of a photographic likeness: in their case of the photo serving as frontispiece to the essay; in Churchill's case of memories of actually seeing Lawrence.

Figure 2. Lawrence in Arab dress seated on the ground. For Churchill's essay on Lawrence in *Great Contemporaries* this picture is the only illustration. Photo courtesy of the Imperial War Museum, London. Negative Q 73535.

What displaces these images is an artistic vision not based on canons of photographic realism. Churchill's remark displays his lively appreciation of Lawrence in costume while revealing too a preference for impressionistic modes of art that elicit active rather than passive response by viewers.

———————— ☙ ————————

Churchill's paintings, of which about five hundred survive, show development over the years and a range of styles. Without pausing here to survey all the variations, I want to note two conspicuous features of Churchill's oeuvre. First, landscapes not portraits were his favorite subjects, although some of his landscapes include people and occasionally he tried his hand at portraits and even self-portraits. He also painted still lifes and other interior scenes. Second, Churchill favored representational over nonrepresentational modes. He serenely ignored Picasso, cubism, and related postimpressionist movements about which, more's the pity, Churchill never deigned to comment. In his essay on painting, which concentrates on landscape, he explains successful art as an achievement of observation, intellect, memory, and willpower. Without himself claiming any but the status of an amateur, or advising readers of "Painting as a Pastime" to aim higher, Churchill writes of the masters with admiration. He applauds "the cold, profound, intense effort of memory, knowledge, and willpower, prolonged perhaps for weeks, from which a masterpiece can alone result."[77] He suggests that such paintings "must require an intellect on the grand scale" to produce "an intellectual manifestation, the equal in quality and intensity of the finest achievements of warlike action, of forensic argument, or of scientific or philosophical adjudication."[78] This is high praise indeed from a soldier turned rhetorician who is often regarded as something of a philistine, although even in so genial a mood Churchill is careful not to rank the best paintings *above* the greatest military and forensic feats.

To encourage the keen observation which he believes even amateurs must cultivate, Churchill assures readers that "if you do observe accurately and with refinement, and if you do record what you have seen with tolerable correspondence, the result follows on the canvas with startling obedience."[79] Churchill's premise that art is essentially mimetic is similar to the assumption underlying Lawrence's explanation in 1922 that "this long-drawn-out battle over my narrative of the campaigns of Feisal has put an ink fever into me. I find myself always going about trying to fit words to the sights & sounds in the world outside me."[80] Both Lawrence and Churchill were well aware, however, that neither observation nor its sequel in visual art or written narrative exactly corresponded to the photographic process of exposing film in a camera for later development. Although Lawrence once divided books into the photographic and the composed, he understood that even good photographs require on the photographer's part a strong sense of composition. His appreciation of that requirement is apparent in his choice of artfully composed photographs for inclusion in the subscriber's edition of *Seven Pillars*. There too in a passage describing a nightfall in Wadi Rumm Lawrence notes how the mind may call on imagination to shape observation: "Night came down, and the valley became a mind-landscape. The invisible cliffs boded as presences; imagination tried to piece out the plan of their battlements by tracing the dark pattern they cut in the canopy of stars."[81] While painting, Churchill sometimes jogged his memories of a scene by looking at a photograph. As a way of making up for his lack of drawing ability he even experimented with a "magic lantern" device for projecting slides onto a canvas together with a method of superimposing a grid on the resulting image so that proportions could be noted by attending to the contents of each square. He was taught this technique by Walter R. Sickert, who in turn had been schooled in resort to assistance from photographs by James McNeill Whistler and Degas.[82] But Churchill never supposed that art was achieved by simply transposing the photograph to oils on canvas dot by dot and square by square without any intermediate transformation of the image into something altogether different in kind.

Churchill explains the creative transformation of observation into art as an encoding by perception for later decipherment on canvas by the intellect:

> We look at the object with an intent regard, then at the palette, and thirdly at the canvas. The canvas receives a message dispatched usually a few seconds before from the natural object. But it has come through a post-office *en route*. It has been transmitted in code. It has been turned from light into paint. It reaches the canvas a cryptogram. Not until it has been placed in its correct relation to everything else that is on the canvas can it be deciphered, is its meaning apparent, is it translated once again from mere pigment into light. And the light this time is not of Nature but of Art.[83]

As in his amusing extended simile earlier in the essay arguing "that painting a picture is like fighting a battle," in which the painter must like a
good general dispose his forces according to a sound plan, Churchill here
puts his background to droll yet also serious use by providing an expla-
natory metaphor based on his appreciation of cryptography in military
and diplomatic intelligence.[84] Decipherment of perception's "cryptogram,"
he adds, is a "considerable process . . . carried through on the wings or the
wheels of memory."[85] For Churchill, moreover, the decoding of perception's remembered messages that transforms them into art depends on a
cultivated grasp of principles that allow one to determine whether the
elements of a painting disposed on canvas are in "correct" relationship
to one another. In his view the process of painting is thus very far from
a mechanically photographic reproduction of what the eye or camera has
registered.

"The larger Turners" are Churchill's examples of artistic greatness
despite Turner's differences from "the methods of the modern French
school" of Manet, Monet, Cézanne, Matisse, and their followers, for whose
work Churchill avows "an increasing attraction" because as "disciples of
Cézanne" they all "view nature as a mass of shimmering light, in which
forms and surfaces are comparatively unimportant, indeed hardly visible,
but which gleams and glows with beautiful harmonies and contrasts of
colour."[86] Turner's "gradations" according to Churchill "differ from those
of the modern French school by being gently and almost imperceptibly
evolved one from another instead of being bodily and even roughly separated; and the brush of Turner followed the form of the objects he depicted, while our French friends often seem to take a pride in directly
opposing it."[87] In his own paintings Churchill frequently appears to aim
at a midpoint between what he took to be the style of Turner and what
he describes as the methods of French impressionists.

Absent from Churchill's oeuvre are any ventures in the direction of
surrealism or the kind of expressionism that Lawrence, writing about some
of Eric Kennington's pictures for the subscriber's edition of *Seven Pillars*,
calls "wonderful imaginative things in colour—drawings, Blake-like, of
states of mind" such as the "lightning-coloured picture of the night over
Tafas which is almost painful, in spite of its beauty."[88] Absent too in
Churchill's paintings are any experiments in aerial perspectives like the
view from above adopted by Henry Lamb for *Irish Troops in the Judean
Hills Surprised by a Turkish Bombardment*. If Churchill was among the many

who flocked to view this picture at the December 1919 Royal Academy exhibit he was apparently unimpressed. Lawrence however liked it enough to include among illustrations of the 1926 *Seven Pillars*. Even in *Lawrence Farm* and *"Plugstreet" under Shell-fire*, analogous paintings of combat scenes done while at at the front in 1916, Churchill retained the conventional perspective of a ground-level observer although he might well have tried an aerial view given his important role in the establishment of naval aviation and his extensive experience of flight by that time. Apart from his admiring allusion to "Augustus John's brilliant pencil sketch," Churchill in his essay on Lawrence as revised for *Great Contemporaries* did not comment on any of the pictures included in the subscriber's edition of *Seven Pillars* beyond noting, more as an aspect of Lawrence's characteristic thoroughness than as a virtue of his book, that "every illustration had been profoundly considered and every incident of typography and paragraphing settled with meticulous care."[89]

In his review of *Seven Pillars* for the July 29, 1935, issue of the *Daily Mail* Churchill is equally unenthusiastic about Lawrence's efforts in the tradition of William Morris to make the book a pleasing artifact. After praising "the executors of the late Colonel Lawrence" for making available "to the public the full, un-expurgated" text in their posthumous trade edition, Churchill remarks in puzzlement rather than approval that for the subscriber's edition "the author lavished the thought and labours of many months merely upon the typography and illustrations. He reconstructed many of his sentences so that every paragraph should end about half-way through the line. . . . He chose various beautiful bindings for these copies." In this review as elsewhere, however, Churchill in his most ex cathedra tone applauds Lawrence as a writer: "*Seven Pillars*. . . . will take its place at once as an English classic. The richness and energy of the theme, the quality of the prose, the sense of the mystic, immeasurable personality lying behind it, raise the work at once and decisively above the level of contemporary productions. It ranks with *Pilgrim's Progress*, *Robinson Crusoe*, and *Gulliver's Travels* as a model of lucid, forcible, fascinating narrative. . . His book will be read as long as the English language is spoken."[90] This was Churchill's considered opinion after long acquaintance with the book. In the review he reports that "Reading it again for the third time, I found the interest as fresh and everflowing as at the first perusal. Indeed the more carefully it is read, the stronger and more inspiring is the impression received."[91] This is good advice. Though Churchill seldom gets much credit as a reader, he passes here with highest grade C. S. Lewis's "good test for every reader of every kind of book," of "asking whether he often *re-reads* the same story." Lewis was right to insist that "an unliterary man may be defined as one who reads books once only."[92] Far from incidentally, Churchill's comments on *Seven Pillars* reveal him to be very much a literary man with respect to reading as well as writing.

Equally revealing is Churchill's 1927 letter to Lawrence after first reading *Seven Pillars* in the subscriber's edition. This private communication also allows for comic touches unsuitable in public encomiums:

> I cannot tell you how thrilled I was to read it. Having gone on a three days' visit to Paris, I never left my apartment except for meals, & lay all day & most of the night cuddling yr bulky tome. The impression it produced was overpowering. I marched with you those endless journeys by camel, with never a cool drink, a hot bath, or a square meal except under revolting conditions. What a tale! The young Napoleon or Clive, if only the stupid 20th century had not made peace. No wonder you brood in haughty anticlimax! I think yr book will live with Gulliver's Travels & Robinson Crusoe. The copy wh [*sic*] you gave me, with its inscription, is in every sense one of my most valuable possessions.[93]

This is irresistible. The mock-lament for peace becomes a way of complementing Lawrence as a Napoleon or Clive manqué: a point, remember, that Churchill seriously makes elsewhere. Here it is primarily a disarming way of teasing him about his "haughty" inclination to "brood" rather than engage fully with the postwar world. After the Cairo conference Churchill had tried to persuade Lawrence to accept some prominent position in which he could best use his talents to benefit society as well as himself. His enlistment in the ranks only elicited Churchill's commendation for purposes of obituary eulogy and then, as the revisions of his Lawrence essay show, mainly to further mythologize Lawrence in a way that served Churchill's political goal of persuading people to approve expansion of the Royal Air Force as a counter to the German menace.

Even Churchill's most zealous revisionist biographers have been unable to dig up any sexual scandal to augment their dubious charges of political blundering. Here, as if to reduce to absurdity in advance any effort to catch him in flagrante delicto, we have from his own pen a confession that Churchill the gourmet bon vivant once hid away in the city of haute cuisine and amour to "lay all day and most of the night" for three days cuddling—a plump English book (and a book, moreover, singularly devoid of any but the most oblique sexual content). "Cuddling" is the droll mot juste to describe a bibliophile's fond physical as well as mental relationship to Lawrence's appealing fat book. It is a safe bet that Churchill, appetite whetted by imaginary camel rides alongside Lawrence tormented by thirst and hunger, dined well when he emerged from that apartment for meals. This may be the most bookish Parisian hideaway vacation on record.

Despite Churchill's keen interest in artists painting in the modes that he himself practiced, his indifference to other developments evidently blinded him to the generous sampling of contemporary art that Lawrence assembled in the subscriber's edition of *Seven Pillars*. Charles Grosvenor notes that "in it is preserved a partial cross section of English art of the 1920s" including "work from the older, more classical draftsmen . . . William Rothenstein and William Nicholson. . . . Eric Kennington's independent modernity. . . . The vorticist art of William Roberts and Edward Wadsworth. . . . the constructivist landscapes of Paul Nash; the rhythmic figure groupings of Cosmo Clark; the metaphysical woodcuts of Blair Hughes-Stanton; and the independent styles of Henry Lamb and the remainder of the young artists who contributed."[94] On all this in the 1927 letter to Lawrence, as in subsequent published remarks on *Seven Pillars*, Churchill is silent. What he did respond to in the realm of visual imagination during his encounters with the book was Lawrence's verbal presentation of landscapes.

Churchill's inclination as a painter to favor landscape over other subject matter made him especially receptive to this aspect of *Seven Pillars*. So did the bent of his own work as a writer. At the outset of his literary career in *The Story of the Malakand Field Force* and *The River War* he had wrestled perforce with the problem of providing vivid accounts of strange places that served as settings for adventure. Memories of writing such descriptions doubtless gave Churchill a keener professional interest in the ways Lawrence handled that aspect of his narrative. The challenge of weaving landscape descriptions into action narratives, moreover, was inescapable in much of Churchill's writing up to the time when he went to

Paris to concentrate his full attention on a first reading of *Seven Pillars*.
Perhaps the recurrence of this challenge partly accounts for the fascination that led him to read it three times by July 1935. No less than in his
first two histories, landscapes are significant determinants of human conduct, not merely picturesque background, in Churchill's Boer War books
London to Ladysmith via Pretoria and *Ian Hamilton's March*, in *My African
Journey*, in the six volumes of *The World Crisis*, in *My Early Life*, and in
Marlborough, whose first two volumes were published before Lawrence
died. Thereafter, except for the final two volumes of *Marlborough*, landscapes figure less prominently in Churchill's writing. As an artist, however,
Churchill remained attracted throughout his life by exotic landscapes with
affinities to those in *Seven Pillars*. Notable examples are his paintings of
the pyramids, of Cairo viewed from the pyramids, of Jerusalem, and his
scenes of Marrakech, the latter including the only painting Churchill did
during World War II: *A View of Marrakech with the Tower of the Katoubia
Mosque*.

In the 1927 letter to Lawrence recording his first impressions of *Seven
Pillars* Churchill's omission of any comment on its depiction of landscapes
while highlighting the absence of cool drinks, hot baths, and square meals
during the episodes narrated is an accurate though incomplete if not shallow account of the book as adventure story. But the letter was hasty, brief,
and informal. In it Churchill was not obliged to note everything that
caught his attention. In later obituary essays Churchill pays tribute to the
force of descriptive passages in *Seven Pillars* and sums up Lawrence's presentation of alien and alienating landscapes as accounts of "lava landscapes
of hell" in which fighting and travel take place over "blasted lands. . . .
forbidding solitudes . . . endless sands, the hot savage wind-whipped rocks,
the mountain gorges of a red-hot moon."[95] Whether on first or on subsequent readings—and most likely from the outset—Churchill certainly
appreciated how passages conveying such impressions of desolation serve
as emblems of Lawrence's wartime ordeal.

Churchill also responded to pictorial qualities that create larger effects
than those elicited by description of individual scenes. In his 1935 review
Churchill remarks that *Seven Pillars* presents "an inexhaustible series of
pictures arresting to the mind and stirring to the soul."[96] Churchill makes
clear that such "pictures" include entire episodes not just patches of verbal landscape painting. This response essentially coincides with that in a
1924 letter—doubtless unknown to Churchill—from E. M. Forster to

Lawrence in which Forster tells Lawrence that in *Seven Pillars* "you do present (though you don't see) life as . . . a series of pictures. . . . This deliberate succession-of-pictures method is (as Pater showed) triumphant at expressing frustration or the death of what's beautiful."[97] Churchill, however, does not make any attempt like Forster's to generalize about the special purposes for which a "succession-of-pictures method" is best employed. When commenting on his own or other people's writing Churchill usually confines himself to analyzing the effects or characteristics of a narrative technique in the passages under scrutiny without invoking any putative aesthetic universals of which it is a particular instance.

Lawrence himself points out within *Seven Pillars* that his work is "in the proper descent from books of adventure."[98] While doing full justice to the features of that lineage, Churchill also goes beyond this aspect to grapple with the far more compelling and far more difficult psychological dimension of *Seven Pillars*: "Intense as is the interest of the story . . . many will study it even more closely for the intimate access which it offers to a wonderful and still largely inscrutable man. . . . We will not say that those who read *Seven Pillars* will know Lawrence; but, reading with a sympathetic eye, they will know as much as anyone will ever know."[99] In the 1935 review Churchill invokes memories of Edgar Allan Poe's fiction as the best way of coming to grips with the Deraa episode that perhaps poses the greatest challenge to all who would understand Lawrence's mentality:

> The story is told with unrelenting candour. Nothing in Edgar Allan Poe excels in horror some of its pages. The description of Lawrence's torment when he fell unknown into the hands of the Turks is a terrifying, a shocking, and at the same time a necessary passage which enables us to realize better than anything else the war injuries which he sustained, and from which he never completely recovered. We have to think of him in the twenty years that followed as a man seared in body and spirit by the sufferings he had undergone for his country's cause.[100]

By inviting comparison of Lawrence with Poe Churchill picks the right literary analogue. He deserves higher marks than he usually gets as a student of comparative literature. There is no evidence that Lawrence consciously tried to imitate or excel Poe. But readers of *Seven Pillars* trying to locate a work that at first seems altogether sui generis would do well to think not only of its antecedents in travel writing, its epic qualities, and its Dostoevskian and Melvillian affinities, but of tales like "The Pit and the Pendulum" and "The Cask of Amontillado." Perhaps too comparing the Deraa episode to such fiction will allow better understanding of Churchill's ultimate preference for factual rather than fictional narratives. In the essay for *Great Contemporaries* after again ranking *Seven Pillars* alongside his touchstones *Pilgrim's Progress, Robinson Crusoe,* and *Gulliver's Travels* as "a tale originally their equal in interest and charm" Churchill adds as a decisive point of superiority that "it is fact not fiction."[101]

Churchill's emphasis on Lawrence's patriotism ("the sufferings he had undergone for his country's cause") not egotism as the strongest motive impelling him into Deraa and sustaining him elsewhere may at first seem another bit of reductive mythmaking. In *Seven Pillars*, however, Lawrence provides a menu of motives from which his readers may choose according to their taste. I agree with Churchill after reflecting on a tale of action that always benefitted Britain no matter what it also accomplished for the Arabs and no matter how hard Lawrence tried to persuade himself and his readers that he was mainly looking out for Arab interests or acting out of some grandiose private desire to please or memorialize "S. A." Lawrence's notoriously enigmatic dedicatory poem "To S. A." at the outset of *Seven Pillars* invites readers to take the book as a record of what its author gratuitously did as an expression of love for S. A. (not for England or for the Arabs in general) with the aim of augmenting a reciprocal affection that was (tragically) thwarted by S. A.'s untimely death:

> I loved you, so I drew these tides of men into my hands
> And wrote my will across the sky in stars
> To earn you Freedom, the seven-pillared worthy house,
> That your eyes might be shining for me
> When we came.

Churchill politely ignores this and the remaining stanzas of the florid poem which Lawrence may have intended as an elegy for his Arab friend Dahoum or which—the point has never been settled—may have been a romantic gesture to someone else or even to a figment of Lawrence's imagination. Whether the poem is regarded as touching and persuasive or as mawkish and implausible is again a matter of taste.

I put greater weight on a sentence from the suppressed introduction that Churchill probably never read but to which his mythmaking does good justice: "All our subject provinces to me were not worth one dead Englishman."[102] Here Lawrence bitterly echoes Bismarck's famous comment that the whole of the Balkans were not worth the bones of a single Pomeranian grenadier. Published only after Lawrence's death, this introduction records disillusionment that could only exist where there had first been patriotic illusions. Whatever Lawrence's motives, and whether the horrifying Deraa episode is entirely accurate, an imaginative embellishment of a real encounter, or (as some have argued) an outright fiction, Churchill is right that it is "a necessary passage" to convey what Lawrence suffered. Its best gloss within *Seven Pillars* is Lawrence's wry conclusion that "there was nothing loftier than a cross, from which to contemplate the world."[103] In *My Early Life* Churchill writes, "After all, a man's life must be nailed to a cross either of Thought or Action."[104] As many have remarked, Churchill's life belies this dichotomy. So does Lawrence's career. It would be hard to find two people of the twentieth century whose lives better illustrate the possibilities and the risks of excelling in both thought and action. Churchill surmounted the risks by summoning that extra courage needed to sustain his far-reaching imagination. Lawrence succumbed to the risks but survived although emotionally impaired, and at the price of finally curtailing his imagination by confining his actions to a limited though worthy sphere. No wonder he fascinated Churchill. No wonder either that Churchill was moved to shape, reshape, and refine his vision of Lawrence to one that could be enlisted in Churchill's wilderness crusade for rearmament and comfortably assimilated to the realms of literary imagination in the forms of elegiac character sketch and book review.

IMAGINING SCENARIOS:
CHURCHILL AND CINEMA

Accounts of Churchill's involvements with cinema have not gone much beyond anecdotes that are a favorite part of Churchillian folklore. Frequently mentioned is his fondness for movies as a means of late-night relaxation from wartime tensions during his first premiership. Often the spotlight hovers on his unquenchable appetite for *Lady Hamilton* (*That Hamilton Woman* in the U.S.), Alexander Korda's 1941 patriotic epic starring Laurence Olivier and Vivien Leigh. Churchill is said to have seen it seventeen times.[1] We are invited to admire the old bulldog beaming in approval at this tale of Nelson's defiance of Napoleon and glorious victory at Trafalgar. Equally admirable are the generous tears reportedly shed by Churchill at each reiteration on screen of Nelson's heroic death and Emma Hamilton's subsequent sad neglect by an ungrateful country. There are whispers that Churchill had some hand not only in urging Korda to make the film in Hollywood as pro-British propaganda to counter American isolationism, but even in writing its script of Nelson's speech, insisting that "you cannot make peace with Dictators. You have to destroy them."[2] Alas there is no evidence that Churchill wrote this.[3] Rumored too in various pleasing degrees of lurid speculation is Churchill's behind-the-scenes instigation of Korda's shadowy activities in the United States as a British agent ferreting out information for MI5, cooperating after Pearl Harbor with the OSS, and making dangerous wartime transatlantic trips "acting personally as a secret courier between British and American intelligence centres" while "allowing his New York office in the Empire State Building to be used as a clearing house for intelligence information."[4]

Whatever the actual extent of Korda's undercover exploits, and despite a disappointing estimate by the British Ministry of Information that his films "were of little propaganda importance," Churchill certainly expedited the award of Korda's knighthood in June 1942.[5] Churchill did not, however, explain his reasons for supporting this honor. For those fond of romantic tales with happy outcomes—and who does not love such stories?—it is better to leave shrouded in mystery Korda's dabbling in the world of James Bond, his rise from immigrant commoner to Sir Alexander, and Churchill's role in this real-life romance. There is better documentation of Churchill's less melodramatic though equally intriguing role during his 1930s wilderness years as a consultant and scriptwriter for Korda's studio, and as a commentator on the transition from silent to talking films. It is to these topics that I now turn.

In 1934 Alexander Korda secured film rights to *Revolt in the Desert*, with the stipulation by Lawrence's trustees that there would be "no departure from historical accuracy" and "no female characters."[6] Korda had the project sufficiently in motion by May to announce that Leslie Howard would play the lead. But then Lawrence suffered another of his periodic attacks of modesty, and requested that no film be made during his lifetime. After his fatal 1935 motorcycle accident, Korda received permission from Lawrence's trustees to proceed. On December 29, 1936, they approved a script by John Monk Saunders. Lawrence was now to be played by Walter Hudd, who had acted the role of the Lawrence figure, Private Meek, in George Bernard Shaw's *Too True to Be Good*. In 1937 a new script by Miles Malleson was taken as a starting point for what proved to be a long series of revisions and delays complicated by objections from the Turkish government, by requests from the British Foreign Office to tone down portrayal of Turkish cruelty so as not to alienate a potential ally, by threats from the British Board of Film Censors to withhold certification lest Turkey be offended, and by various legal maneuvers including sale of the project to New World Films, repurchase of it from them, sale of the rights to Paramount Pictures in 1938, and, finally, negotiations with Columbia that were broken off on June 2, 1939. Outbreak of the Second World War that September ended Korda's efforts to bring to the screen *Lawrence of Arabia* (as the final version of his London Film Productions script was titled). In addition to Leslie Howard, actors considered for the role of Lawrence during all these vicissitudes included John Clements, Clifford Evans, Robert Donat, Laurence Olivier, and (in a masterpiece of miscasting by Columbia) Cary Grant.[7]

Winston Churchill played two offstage roles as adviser in this melodrama of Korda's doomed movie: first as coach to one of the potential lead actors, and then as script consultant for Korda's studio. In the November 20, 1937, issue of *Film Weekly* there appears an interview with Leslie Howard. To dispel widespread doubts that the movie would actually be made, Howard announced himself "hard at work on the preliminaries of the picture. Everything is signed and sealed. We hope to start the actual shooting in ten or twelve weeks' time, and have the film edited and ready for presentation by the end of six or eight months."[8] Given the unforseen obstacles that usually spring up to bedevil film production, Howard's statement was not so delusional or disingenuous as it may appear in retrospect. Nor is there any reason to doubt Howard's veracity when he goes on to remark:

> I hope to bring in Winston Churchill to complete the scenario. He is one of the few statesmen of the period who saw beyond Lawrence's military importance into the real complexities of his nature.
>
> Already, in a number of informal conversations, Churchill has helped me considerably to round off my impression of Lawrence.[9]

Hope of bringing Churchill in to complete the script was not unrealistic because, as Leslie Howard must have known, Korda had secured Churchill's agreement to serve as a consultant on the Lawrence project during the month in which *Film Weekly* published Howard's interview. As far back as September 1934 Churchill had started what proved to be a long and, for him more than for Korda, quite profitable employment with Korda's studio. The 1934 news release announcing this relationship stated:

> Mr Winston Churchill has signed a contract with London Film Productions to edit a series of films dealing with subjects of topical interest.... Mr Winston Churchill, in collaboration with Mr Korda, has selected the topics which will be comprised in this series.... The following topics have provisionally been decided upon: "Will Monarchies Return?", "The Rise of Japan," "Marriage Laws and Customs," "Unemployment" and "Gold." ... London Films have

engaged a special staff of technical experts in order to ensure that Mr Churchill's ideas will be presented in the most vivid, novel and entertaining fashion. Mr Randolph Churchill (Mr Winston Churchill's son) has also been engaged by London Films to assist in the making of this series.[10]

Randolph soon faded out of this project, but Winston did much work sketching scenarios for elaboration by Korda's "technical experts." In September 1934 Churchill also agreed, in a separate contract, "to write and prepare for London Film Productions Limited a scenario of 'the Reign of King George V' for the forthcoming celebrations of the Twenty-Five Years' Jubilee." Churchill agreed moreover to "be ready as may be found desirable to introduce and explain the story myself by my own voice and to appear on the screen in this capacity if necessary."[11] Although Churchill put a great deal of well-compensated effort into writing and revising scenarios for the Jubilee project as well as conferring about it with Korda's people, legal complications prevented completion of the film. Never one to waste his own considerable brainpower, Churchill then converted his scenarios into a series of essays that were published in the *Evening Standard*, May 2 through May 9, 1935, under the general title "The King's Twenty-Five Years."

Upon receiving Korda's request to serve during November 1937 as a consultant for revisions of the Lawrence script, Churchill seems to have regarded London Film Productions as a money tree ripe for the plucking. In a letter dated October 22, 1937, to Korda's assistant David B. Cunynghame, Churchill explained his financial and literary situation in pressing but not altogether heartbreaking terms by noting that he faced a December 21 deadline to finish the last volume of *Marlborough*, "for which I am to receive £ 3,500." He continued:

> I am also writing another series of twelve articles for the News of the World for which I am to receive £ 4500. . . . If I am to make a strong personal contribution to this Lawrence film, I must derange all my existing plans, and let the subject play a large part in my thoughts during the month of November. I have some ideas upon the subject, but it will be necessary for me to re-read the Seven Pillars as well as the scenario. I have no doubt I shall get much interested in it and my other work will fall into the shade. In all these circumstances, of which I inform you confidentially, I think I should

be paid £ 2,000 for giving my best services in opinion, criticism and assistance on the film during the month of November. . . . If however my contribution should be found of sufficient importance to warrant my name being used with the editing or preparation of the scenario, which might perhaps be of advantage to the film, I should then ask for a percentage additional to the foregoing fee.[12]

Unmoved by this ambitious proposal, Cunynghame replied by return mail, in a letter dated that same day, October 22, 1937, that "Mr Korda hoped you would see your way to assist him by accepting a nominal fee of £ 250 for taking part at the . . . meetings."[13] With only this "nominal" fee in prospect, Churchill resisted the temptation to "derange all" his "existing plans" by setting everything else aside to reread *Seven Pillars*. Nor did he otherwise protract his labors on the Lawrence scenario. But neither did he sulk in his tent. On November 3, 1937, less than two weeks after their exchange concerning money, Churchill sent Cunynghame a memo of six double-spaced typewritten pages commenting on the script, which was returned therewith.

Moreover, as he explained at the outset of this communication, Churchill had also—evidently in the same brief interval since the correspondence about his fee—"consulted Lord Winterton about the scenario, which he has read." Churchill enclosed Winterton's comments. These had to be taken as authoritative because, as Churchill reminded Cunynghame, "You must remember that he was with Lawrence during some of the most important phases in this story."[14] In *Seven Pillars* Lawrence characterizes Winterton at first mention of him by stating that "Lord Winterton was our last-found recruit; an experienced officer from Buxton's Camel Corps."[15] Lawrence had also met and corresponded with Winterton after the war. The crux of Winterton's letter to Churchill, dated October 27, 1937, concerned the script's treatment of Lawrence at the Arab Bureau:

There is one falsification of history to which I do take real exception, not because I was personally concerned (because I did not join the Arab Bureau until later), but because of the reflection upon friends of mine.

In the early part of the script the people under whom Lawrence was working are made to look absolute fools, and he (Lawrence) to be the sole originator of the idea of the Arab Campaign. Of course this is the most complete nonsense as every document of authority, official and unofficial, shows (e.g. See Ronald Storr's book "Orientations" with its history of how the Arab Revolt started); the author has completely missed the real point. It was in the execution of the plan that Lawrence showed his genius, and where he was undoubtedly thwarted until Allenby arrived on the scene by the ordinary stupid type of "brass hat" but *never* by either his superiors or colleagues in the Arab Bureau; they recognized his genius from the first.

I think you ought to use your immense influence in the matter to get this portion of the script altered; the writer can have a "go" at the "stupid soldiers," if he wishes, by showing the way in which Lawrence was undoubtedly thwarted at first when he had actually set to work.[16]

Equally concerned with historical accuracy, Churchill urged revision of the Arab Bureau scenes to comply with Winterton's account, although to no avail if we may judge from the final version of Malleson's script, dated "October 4th 1938" and credited also to Brian Desmond Hurst and Duncan Guthrie.[17] Nor, judging from other places where that version fails to adopt Churchill's suggestions, was his influence over Korda's people so "immense" as Winterton supposed.

Churchill understood that compliance with Winterton's suggestion would not have been easy:

It seems to me that Paragraph 4 of his letter will be tiresome, and might entail considerable recasting of this part of the story. Yet I do not see why a good tale could not be told more in accordance with the truth. The picture of the Arab Bureau, all burning and toiling around Lawrence, should fill all this scene and would be good, especially when one saw them hampered and shut down by the "brasshats" outside. There is no doubt they were all as keen as mustard, and I can see this part of the tale well told,—Lawrence making his way with them and converting them. Anyhow I think you will have to try to re-draw this part more in accordance with the truth. Generally, I think Lord Winterton's comments are very valuable. (1)

On another matter, concerning verisimilitude not historical accuracy, Churchill disagreed with Winterton:

You will see that Lord Winterton likes your comic relief of the two sergeants riding in the desert. I can well see the necessity for this feature, but sergeants of the British Army do not talk in this common way. A sergeant is a fairly intelligent person who has risen to that position through a great deal of competition. The idea of a conventional British Tommy (odious expression!) being a person whose language is that of a half-boozed coster, is not in accordance with the facts. I am well aware that on the screen the idea is that a private soldier or sergeant begins every sentence with "Gor Blimey" etc., but I wonder whether in this film you could not afford to shake off this rubbish? (3–4)

Apparently Korda's answer was "no." To my ears, at any rate, there is nothing "fairly intelligent" or above the "common way" in the final script's exchanges between its two representative rankers, who are archly named Stokes and Lewis after their respective tasks of operating a Stokes mortar and Lewis machine gun during raids. Perhaps the disagreement between Winterton and Churchill over the propriety of the sergeants' portrayal stems from different attitudes toward lower ranks. More likely, it stems from different experiences. Although Churchill had commanded a battalion of Royal Scots Fusiliers for six months on the western front during World War I, his earliest and probably strongest impressions of army life had been formed during the reign of Queen Victoria. Winterton was more totally immersed in the post-Kitchener new-model army whose enormous expansion made promotions easier to obtain. It is also possible, as Michael Edwardes has suggested, that as Kipling's tales became more widely encountered in print and on screen by soldiers many of them actually began to speak the argot of his rankers.[18] If in this way life was imitating art, Churchill was certainly not one to encourage such a linguistic downturn.

Churchill's comment on the sergeants is most interesting for what it reveals about his notions of dramatic structure. He has no objection to comic relief per se, even granting "the necessity for this feature." He is bothered only by what he takes to be lack of verisimilitude. Here it is not a question, as it is in the Arab Bureau scenes, of accurately representing actual though unnamed people in a way that truthfully portrays the origin of the Arab Revolt and favorable opinions about Lawrence within the Arab Bureau. Churchill accepts introduction of the sergeants as typical characters whose presence illustrates aspects of what took place during Lawrence's raids, namely deployment by British army specialists of mortars and machine guns to supplement Arab rifle fire after a train had been derailed. He is even willing to make these characters a vehicle for comic relief, provided it is achieved via dialogue that doesn't sink to the level "of a half boozed coster" thereby rendering them unrepresentative of the types they are intended to portray. Thus Churchill only objects to dramatization of the sergeants in a way that lacks verisimilitude—or would if previous war films had not so thoroughly accustomed moviegoers to the convention that private soldiers are neither articulate nor at all intelligent but merely figures of fun. Knowing better, Churchill wants Korda to alter this image in the direction of greater fidelity to actual types as Churchill remembers them, and thus in the direction of greater verisimilitude for those whose experience of British army life extends beyond the cinema.

Churchill's other suggestions also concentrate on issues of accuracy, verisimilitude, and dramatic structure bearing on the artistic effectiveness of scenes or of the entire film. All these matters are interrelated and bear too on the script's degree of success in explaining what Lawrence did and why he ought to be regarded as a great man. But usually one or another issue predominates in particular remarks.

Some questions of accuracy that attract Churchill's attention are very minute. Of the word *crusade* that seems to have been deleted from the final script in accordance with Churchill's suggestion he comments: "You can hardly talk of arousing the Arabs to a *Crusade*, which were things instituted to do them in. *Jehad* is the real word. Anyhow, they have no use for the Cross" (2). Of an allusion locating Auda abu Tayi's residence somewhere north of Jerusalem, Churchill remarks: "I am quite sure Auda's home did not lie in this place. Was not Auda a desert Arab who had nothing whatever to do with the wretched Palestinian Arabs?" (5).

Most of Churchill's remarks about the need for greater accuracy deal with the key issue of geography. Churchill insists that the film cannot succeed unless it conveys a clear idea of the landscape that Lawrence had to master:

> It would be a good thing to check this whole story up with the map. *Page 24*, —What is the distance from Damascus to Wejd? It is 500 miles. Any ordinary film "fan" reading this would suppose that

it was a stepping-stone and quite close to Damascus. As a matter of fact it is hundreds of miles in the opposite direction. I do not think this tale can be told properly unless the geography is driven into the minds of the audience early in the day; otherwise they get a wrong impression, and keep on wondering why the hell people turn up here and there, and what it is all about. It is above all important to avoid confusion of mind in the audience. Unless you can carry them with you in thought at each stage, with pictures moving so quickly, they just get blurred, if not bored. Therefore I counsel forcing the audience to know where they are at each stage.

Another notable instance occurs on *Page 16*, where Feisal and his fellow-conspirators gallop out of the gates of Damascus, and in less than half of one second are in an Arab encampment outside the walls of Medina. Any ordinary ignorant person would suppose that Medina was a few hours' gallop from the gates of Damascus. Actually, it is about 650 miles. (2–3)

In these remarks, as in Churchill's own accounts of military campaigns from Marlborough's day through the Second World War, careful attention to geography is a hallmark. As film critic no less than as historian, Churchill's rather narrow military education yielded unanticipated benefits. In his autobiography he notes that "At Sandhurst. . . . Tactics, Fortification, Topography (mapmaking), Military Law and Military Administration formed the whole curriculum." He also notes that later, serving as a cavalry officer in India and extending his education while off duty by reading widely in "history, philosophy, economics, and things like that," he "now began for the first time to envy those young cubs at the university who had fine scholars to tell them what was what; professors who had devoted their lives to mastering and focussing ideas in every branch of learning; who were eager to distribute the treasures they had gathered before they were overtaken by the night."[19] If Churchill had gone to Oxford or Cambridge rather than Sandhurst he would have missed the intensive study of topography that left him with a lifelong habit of specifying geographical relationships with the utmost precision or, as in the case of Korda's script, encouraging others to do so. Moreover, this habit of precisely explaining the topography of historical events often contributes to those descriptive passages singled out among other striking features of Churchill's writing when his 1953 Nobel Prize was awarded "for his mastery of historical and biographical description as well as for brilliant oratory in defending exalted human values."[20]

Other echoes of his military education and army career are apparent in Churchill's response to Korda's script. Among "the practical work" at Sandhurst that Churchill found "most exciting" was a series of field exercises in which he "cut railway lines with slabs of guncotton, and learned how to blow up masonry bridges."[21] Reading *Seven Pillars* must have evoked happy memories of those student days messing about with explosives. Lawrence's story certainly stimulated Churchill's military imagination. He always enjoyed loud explosions, even when, as during the Blitz, he deplored their consequences. Korda's script afforded an opportunity to share such explosive pleasures with movie fans, as Churchill makes clear in an enthusiastic afterthought at the end of his comments:

> I forgot to say that the blowing-up of the trains should be more emphasized. It lends itself very well to your technique. Surely you should blow up half-a-dozen trains in different ways!—The approach in the distance; the scene in the railway carriage; the tense excitement of the ambush; the terrible explosion; the wreck of the locomotive, etc., and the fact of the sole communications of an army being cut off. . . .—all very pretty! And also the means by which the Turks were hunted away from Medina, and made to fight hundreds of miles to the north. It was because of these expeditions that the fame of Lawrence spread about Arabia, and it was not till after this process that anyone thought of asking for "Lurens." (5–6)

Although first relishing with boyish glee all the "very pretty" details of ambushing trains, and urging Korda to repeat such scenes (with variations) as a kind of leitmotif in the film because the medium is so well suited to these delightful episodes, Churchill gets a grip on himself and winds up this passage in the more adult tones of a sober historian concerned above all with accuracy. He stresses the strategic importance of Lawrence's raids in drawing the Turkish army away from Medina and explains what is equally relevant to an accurate depiction of history in the movie: that the raids were crucial to establishing Lawrence's reputation among Arabs, thereby effecting his metamorphosis from alien Englishman to their hero "Lurens."

In addition to making him a connoisseur of explosions, Churchill's army career enhanced his appreciation of the harsh climate as well as the vast distances against which Lawrence had to struggle. Thus after urging proper attention to conveying a sense of the many miles separating Medina, Wejd, and Damascus, Churchill continues:

> These points bring me to what I think should be a feature in the film, viz: —the great distances, and the enormous weight of the sun. This was the strongest impression left on my mind after reading "The Seven Pillars." One felt the unending toil of these immense marches by camel; with the most severe privations; barely enough food and water to keep body and soul together; —on and on each day under brazen skies, through hot, crisp sand, and over black jagged rocks. The script fails to give the impression of the rigours of the desert in which these strange Arabs live, and to which they are habituated. The words at the top of *Page 52* show that the author has this idea, but I suggest it should be emphasized more elaborately. (3)

In Churchill's memory—which is to say, in his imagination, his mental visions of the past—Lawrence's experiences as described in *Seven Pillars* merge with Churchill's recollections of his own 1898 campaign as a cavalry officer with Kitchener's army in the Sudan.

Looking back on the Battle of Omdurman thirty-two years later in his autobiography, Churchill writes of how, seen from afar amid the mirages of the desert, "batteries of artillery or long columns of cavalry emerged from a filmy world of uneven crystal on to the hard yellow-ochre sand, and took up their positions amid jagged red-black rocks with violet shadows. Over all the immense dome of the sky . . . pierced by the flaming sun, weighed hard and heavy on marching necks and shoulders."[22] In *The River War*, published in 1899 barely a year after the battle, Churchill places similar emphasis on heat, sand, rocks, and sun while setting the scene in his description of "the military Soudan":

> This is the Soudan of the soldier. . . . Its hot, black rocks have witnessed famous tragedies. It is the scene of the war. . . . Level plains of smooth sand—a little rosier than buff, a little paler than salmon— are interrupted only by occasional peaks of rock—black, stark, and

shapeless. Rainless storms dance tirelessly over the hot, crisp surface of the ground. The fine sand, driven by the wind, gathers into deep drifts, and silts among the dark rocks of the hills, exactly as snow hangs about an Alpine summit; only it is a fiery snow, such as might fall in hell. . . . scarcely a cloud obstructs the unrelenting triumph of the sun. . . . he who had not seen the desert, nor felt the sun heavy on his shoulders, would hardly admire the fertility of the riparian scrub [by the Nile].[23]

In Churchill's memo to London Film Productions three phrases describing his memories of what Lawrence says in *Seven Pillars* match almost exactly the words Churchill used previously while recollecting the landscape through which he rode with the 21st Lancers toward Omdurman. The memo's "enormous weight of the sun" corresponds to the autobiography's account of how "the flaming sun weighed hard and heavy on marching necks and shoulders" and to Churchill's allusion in *The River War* to what can only be appreciated by someone who "felt the sun heavy on his shoulders." The memo's "hot crisp sand" corresponds to the autobiography's "hard yellow-ochre sand" and even more closely to *The River War*'s "hot, crisp surface of the ground." The memo's "black jagged rocks" corresponds to the autobiography's "jagged red-black rocks" and to *The River War*'s "dark rocks" and "peaks of rock—black, stark, and shapeless." Reading or even recollecting *Seven Pillars* was for Churchill thus an almost Proustian experience triggering remembrance of his own time past serving as a mounted warrior in a harsh desert.

The rest of Churchill's comments to Korda center on aesthetic issues. He remarks "I think you should make more of Lawrence's execution of the murderer. It is a terrible story, and a high-spot in the story. It is very well done as it is" (3). Here "terrible" means terrifying, awe inspiring, not of inferior quality or poorly done. Churchill rightly regards the episode as one of the most arresting moments in *Seven Pillars* and, potentially, in the film. His final two suggestions take up the knotty problem of achieving a memorable ending that would provide appropriate closure to the story's action while also capping off the glorification its hero. Churchill (as usual) endorses and encourages the mythologizing of Lawrence.

Churchill first explains the military significance of a "tense scene" that Lawrence omitted from *Seven Pillars* when narrating his encounter with the retreating Turkish army:

The latter part of the film. When eventually Allenby's army—it was of course about fifty times as strong as Lawrence's force—drove the Turks back from their lines north of Jerusalem, Lawrence was far out in the desert, and in a position to ride across the communications of the retreating Turks. The remarkable episode which should be chronicled was that in defiance of all military advice, he took his little Arab force of perhaps twelve hundred men, and planted them in the path of this vast retreating Turkish mass, perhaps two hundred thousand strong. There are some grand pages in his book about what happened, but they do not tell the tense scene which occurred when the regular officers with him begged him not to sacrifice needlessly his small valuable force. He paid no attention whatever to them, and stood straight in the path of the avalanche. It was a miracle that he or any of them survived. No doubt they killed a lot of Turks and some Germans, but it was like throwing pebbles at a wave. I suggest that this episode requires further study and re-casting. It certainly reveals Lawrence in his most heroic and Napole-onic aspect. Again, however, the point cannot be made without the audience having the geographical lay-out in their minds. (4–5)

Of Talal's death ride, of the Turkish atrocities that occasioned it, and of Lawrence's "no prisoners" order that figure largely in *Seven Pillars* and in Korda's script (as later in David Lean's movie), Churchill says nothing. His concern is only to add the "tense scene" of Lawrence ignoring "all military advice" from more conventional and less suicidally inclined regular officers. Here, as in his published essays on Lawrence, Churchill presents material in a way that contributes to the Lawrence myth of selfless hero-ism. Arguably, a maneuver that ran the risk of needlessly and pointlessly sacrificing a "small valuable force" might better have been characterized as foolish, futile, and selfish bravado. Instead, Churchill in a conspicuous non sequitur calls it "heroic and Napoleonic" even though it accomplished no more than "throwing pebbles at a wave" while the Arab force's sur-vival (as Churchill describes it here) was a lucky chance not ascribed to Lawrence's leadership but to "a miracle." Perhaps Churchill sees Lawrence as Napoleonic in this reckless episode because Napoleon himself con-sidered luck a legitimate military virtue that some commanders were blessed with and others lacked. Elsewhere Churchill does not suggest that Napoleon was so recklessly quixotic.

Churchill's last idea, to reverse the sequence of presentation by starting at the story's end, was not acted upon until David Lean arrived at it
independently and put it to effective use in his *Lawrence of Arabia*:

> Finally, this film falls away, as they nearly all do, towards the
> end. We have vague galloperaverings of horsemen doing impossible
> charges, in the style of some of the absurdities of "Bengal Lancer."
> Nearly always the audience fails to keep up with the reel under these
> conditions. With horses galloping five time faster than animals' feet
> ever touched the ground, a sense of flurry is about all that results in
> the spectators' minds. "On ne règne sur les âmes que par le calme."
> Indeed I feel films ought to be begun from the end, because that is
> what strikes home, and what the audience take home. I cannot sug-
> gest alternatives at the present time, but this ending is the weak part
> of what is in many ways an excellent piece of work. (5)

If all Churchill's advice had been taken, Korda's Lawrence film, if it had
been made, would have been much better than the surviving script leads
us to suppose. But it was not to be. This unrealized outcome illustrates
in miniature the contingency of human affairs that, apropos more serious
matters, Churchill's military experiences had impressed upon him while
still a young man. When the twenty-five year old Churchill published *The
River War* in 1899 he observed that "We live in a world of 'ifs.' 'What happened,' is singular; 'what might have happened,' legion."[24]

Also remaining in the crowded world of cinematic "ifs" are Korda's "films
dealing with subjects of topical interest" on which Churchill had agreed
to collaborate. They were never completed. But his remarks dated "10th
June 1935" on a film scenario about the history of aviation show other
aspects of Churchill's imagination at work as both author and critic.
Although as usual he is not at all shy about making suggestions concerning content and arrangement of episodes, Churchill stresses throughout
this report that he can be most useful only at a later stage of production
when he can respond to film footage rather than merely to "the Air scenario you have sent me": "As soon as you have anything to show me, I
should like to come to the studio and see the pictures. I think it very likely
I could make you some helpful suggestions then. I will also gladly make

a speech for the screen, but I would rather do this when I see the picture in an advanced condition when I can realise more clearly than at present exactly what note I should strike. I see there is a new German film called 'The Miracle of the Air' which is just about to be released, and it would be a great advantage if we could see this, because one thing so often suggests another."[25] Here Churchill refers primarily to his role—a familiar one in other contexts—as writer of what will be the spoken word ("a speech for the screen") rather than to his role in helping to shape dramatized episodes illustrating the history of aviation. He refers to his capacity as speechwriter rather than dramatist, although the speeches he provides will not be freestanding but will function as choric comment upon dramatic actions.

At the end of his remarks on Korda's aviation scenario, Churchill in his concluding sentence reiterates that he can best fulfil this part of his task as consultant only in response to film he can actually see on a screen: "I should wish when I see the picture in an advanced condition to rewrite considerably the existing commentary, though I do not think it would be a good thing for me to speak the commentary in my own voice."[26] A psychological reason underlying Churchill's hunger for something more concrete to which he can respond—whether footage shot by the London Film studio or the new German aviation film, or ideally both—is made apparent in a revealing aside about his methods of composition generally: "Thoughts come to me easier from suggestion and counter-suggestion and the play of one mind upon the other."[27] Here we have an echo of Churchill the parliamentarian who thrives on debate. He is well aware that argument is always a spur to his creative imagination. Usually the results are effective. He was less alert to the danger of getting carried away. Sometimes the impulse to countersuggestion and thus to playing off his mind against another led to imbalance. Many critics agree that it does so most conspicuously in the excessive space devoted to countering Macaulay in *Marlborough*, where Churchill might have refuted his (and Marlborough's) chief opponent more effectively with greater concision. There Churchill seems to protract his match against Macaulay because he revels in the game itself—the play of mind against mind.

Churchill's uncharacteristically modest afterthought about keeping out of the limelight by not speaking any commentary in his own voice perhaps reflects lingering or growing ambivalence about association with a medium usually considered mere entertainment and thus lower on the totem pole of artistic respectability than history, biography, autobiography, essays, published versions of speeches delivered in the House of Commons, or even print journalism—forms which by then he had used effectively to bolster his image as a serious person and thus a good bet for high office. A compelling advantage of film to politicians in an age of universal suffrage, on the other hand, is its ability to reach and vividly impress a wide audience including those not much inclined to read. Churchill surely reflected upon Stanley Baldwin's shrewd propensity for appearing in newsreels. It is in any case clear enough why eight months earlier, in September 1934, Churchill had no hesitation in announcing to the press his involvement (which could "if necessary" include an on-screen speaking part) in Korda's forthcoming film on George V. This was a project that Churchill regarded as, potentially at least, of more enduring artistic and historical significance than topical films (like that on aviation) addressed to the passing moment. In a January 14, 1935, memo to London Film Productions accompanying his "second revised non-technical script of the Reign of King George V" Churchill expresses his firm belief "that our Jubilee film if we all work at it without being distracted by other matters may well be not only of great commercial but historic value."[28] In a letter dated September 24, 1934, concerning publicity for his part in making the film on George V, Churchill's enthusiasm for this venture led him to counsel Korda at amusing length on the niceties of handling publicity:

> I advise that the announcement should be made on Saturday by a communication to the Press Association, Central News and Associated Press, and that about an hour later a letter should be despatched containing it to all the newspapers who are on your publicity list; and that similar announcements should be cabled to your agents in the United States, Canada, Australia and other parts. It should be stipulated that no release should be made before Sunday morning's papers. (NB, I recommend that for all communications with the press on publicity you should have high-class envelopes marked "Urgent," and addressed to the editors of the various papers, and nothing could be better than that the admirable black trademark which you have adopted on your notepaper should appear in the corner. Much depends on the appearance of the envelope. There should be time for this before Saturday next.)[29]

Had there been a coals-to-Newcastle award, Korda might have been tempted to nominate Churchill on the basis of this advice, although it was received with polite silence. In that same month of September 1934 Churchill was equally agreeable though less directive concerning the press announcement of his involvement with Korda's topical series.

At the outset of his June 10, 1935, memo about Korda's aviation film Churchill reaffirms that he "shall be delighted to be associated with this splendid survey of the conquest of the air, and to father [*sic*] it in any way you like."[30] If Churchill had any ambivalence about this association it was only reflected faintly and obliquely by his modest reluctance to speak the commentary in his own voice. By June 1935 Churchill's interest in aviation was increasingly focused on the alarming growth of Hitler's Luftwaffe. It was only a month later, in July 1935, that Churchill accepted Baldwin's invitation to become a member of Britain's Air Defense Research Committee. In the House of Commons on November 28, 1934 (less than a month after announcing his arrangement with Korda's studio), Churchill in a major speech had warned—not for the first time—of "The German Air Menace." On June 7, 1935 (three days before sending his memo on the aviation scenario to Korda), Churchill spoke to the House on "Air Defense Research." In this speech Churchill noted that "it is only in the twentieth century that this hateful conception of inducing nations to surrender by terrorizing the helpless civil population and by massacring the women and children has gained acceptance and countenance amongst men. If it continues, one can clearly see that the conquest of the air may mean the subjugation of mankind and the destruction of our civilization."[31] The dire future possibilities of military aviation were thus looming larger in Churchill's mind than the history of flight or its benefits to humanity. This shift is apparent in his comments on Korda's air scenario and even more prominent three years later when, the film project having foundered, Churchill salvaged what he could from his comments to incorporate in an essay titled "The Effect of Air Transport on Civilization" published in the May 8, 1938, edition of the *News of the World*.

In his June 10, 1935, memo on Korda's "Air scenario" Churchill is sanguine about the film's prospects because "the air will be very prominent in our thoughts all through this year and next; painfully so indeed, and I should think your film will have great chances of success."[32] But Churchill does not suggest any overt exploitation of current worries about the German Air Force. Many of his comments address the issue of according "the great discoveries" their due historical importance while cutting back on less significant (and more boring) incidents such as the "Grahame-White-Paulhan contest across country from London to Liverpool." Thus Churchill recommends that "the long thrilling duel between the Wrights and Professor Langley should not be abridged in any way, nor perhaps the competition between Bleriot and Latham to fly across the Channel." After explaining why Alcock and Brown's 1919 transatlantic flight was a magnificent achievement, Churchill concludes: "Lindbergh's brilliant solo performance ten years later certainly does not deserve to rank at all with this. Indeed with great modesty he said so himself in the speech made in London at the welcome dinner at which I was present. I think therefore this [the Alcock-Brown crossing] should be featured in much larger proportion and the other later Atlantic flights or Australian and Brazilian flights damped down accordingly." Churchill also suggests a political advantage to keeping episodes in proper historical proportion according to their significance for the development of flight: "From the point of view of the international balance of this film this would also be desirable. For the United States Wright [sic] gained the prize of the great discovery. For the war prize none can exceed the German Von Richthofen. But the conquest of the Atlantic Ocean by air belongs to these two young British officers [Alcock and Brown] who were the first and for many years the only victors in that perilous struggle."[33] Perhaps here Churchill has his professional journalistic eye on gaining an international market for the film as a fringe benefit of making it historically correct. Due credit accorded "two young British officers" would certainly enhance the film's patriotic and box office appeal at home. Churchill never misses an opportunity to romanticize and applaud young RAF officers. In the Churchillian pantheon Alcock and Brown take an honorable place as forerunners of the Few.

On the inevitable issue of how much attention should be allotted to the part played by aviation in World War I, Churchill manages, though with evident effort, to keep under control his fondness for military history: "I think the war section is adequately dealt with. It has been often done though personally I am of course deeply interested in it." That said, the old warrior cannot resist adding a few words about how the scenario's combat episode might be enlivened by adding a few more whiffs of powder and shot: "I should have welcomed a few close-ups of the pilot in the machine with the tracer bullets ripping through the fusilage [sic] and fire breaking out. The attack upon the observation balloons might be included, with the observers escaping in parachutes pursued downwards by hostile aeroplanes shooting at them as they descend." Here Churchill grapples with the problem of how to maximize visual interest and excitement. This is more easily done in depicting aerial warfare than in episodes showing peacetime flights. Elaborating on his advice to cut back on the latter, Churchill articulates a basic principle: "Generally speaking there is a certain lack of variety in the air races and remarkable flights. . . . one aeroplane and one aviation ground and even one crowd is very much like another. And all aviators' faces in flying caps are much the same. . . . Certainly every effort should be made to introduce novelty and contrast." In here stressing the importance of holding audience attention by novelty and contrast Churchill has gone from questions of historical accuracy and prudent "international balance" to considerations that are purely aesthetic.[34]

It is "from this point of view," Churchill continues, that "the arrival of the autogiro or wingless aeroplane seems . . . a prodigious new fact." With an eye to what will best make the film appealing by virtue of greatest novelty and contrast, he then dilates upon the significance of wingless flight and recommends fanciful scenes that would provide visionary glimpses of a bright utopian future made possible by invention of the autogiro. Its imaginative appeal as a novelty in sharp contrast to conventional aircraft lures Churchill away from confining his remarks only to aviation's actual history and its most likely prospects in the real world: increasingly hideous warfare. He first explains the essential nature and corresponding advantages of "the wingless aeroplane":

> Here for the first time we openly part company with the bird and we cannot doubt that an entirely new sphere has been opened. Up to this point man has followed nature, or tried to do so. But nature had never thought of an autogiro, and would be incapable of it. Therefore the arrival of this monstrosity should be strongly featured and especially the spectacle which can easily be witnessed of the autogiro rising vertically from the ground and of men handing letters and parcels to the aviator while he remains virtually stationary in the air a few feet above the aerodrome. As the horizontal rotors become invisible when spinning the spectacle is one which seems a complete defiance of the law of gravity. One would hope that

by this means an immense measure of safety would be introduced into flight. The autogiro is nearly fool-proof already. Hitherto the problem has been to land a structure weighing a ton or more upon gossamer wheels at sixty miles an hour. Two fatal accidents, separated from him only by a second, stand at each side of every pilot who is landing a machine. If he is too steep or too flat death will overtake him and all the passengers, perhaps forty, who take this operation for granted. But with the autogiro the contact with the ground can be made gently and *anywhere*. Thus alone will flying be thrown open to the millions just as the cheap motor car is used to-day, and millions of flights will be made not from aerodrome to aerodrome, but from one field to another or from one broad flat roof to another.[35]

Knowing as we now do how and to what effect helicopters evolved from autogiros later in the twentieth century, we can see that Churchill was right to identify the advent of what he calls wingless flight as a noteworthy milestone in the history of aviation. As someone whose own flying lessons had taught him firsthand the difficulties of landing conventional aircraft, he is quick to appreciate the advantages of a different method of getting back to the ground. It is easier to see now that Churchill is a little over-optimistic in supposing that landing disasters would thereby be almost entirely eliminated, and wildly overoptimistic in jumping to the conclusion that via autogiros flying will be taken up by "the millions just as the cheap motor car is used to-day," thus relegating airports to a minor role in aerial transportation.

Three years later Churchill is a more somber prophet in his 1938 essay "The Effect of Air Transport on Civilization." With Europe all too obviously moving closer to war, and in view of the "air butchery of non-combatants, which we have witnessed in so horrible a form in China" during Japan's incursion there, Churchill's overall focus is on the impending menace of aerial warfare. Even in turning to "the more peaceful, and perhaps, more hopeful" sphere of civil aviation Churchill reigns in the utopian impulse stimulated by working on Korda's script. The only "wholly beneficent" uses for aircraft that he notes are Australia's aerial ambulance system, cropdusting as a boon to agriculture, and air patrols to spot fire outbreaks as "a great aid to forest preservation." These are bright spots in an otherwise dystopian vision. Churchill "cannot suppose that countries will be better governed because a man has learned to fly." He dismisses as "a delusion" the idea that "being able to move rapidly about from place to place makes people happier, or wiser." Of aerial tourism that will replace more leisurely ground travel he predicts with dismay that "the future modern traveller will see nothing at all except a kind of vague flat map spread out below." Such future travelers will discover upon arrival that "all aerodromes are more or less alike, and all new cities are very much alike." To Churchill the world that is now smaller and more rapidly experienced thanks to quick air travel is also intellectually diminished: "The modern, wealthy, gadabout tourist who hurries through a country, rarely looking even at the surface and never beneath it, gazing vacuously at the monuments and cities the guide-books proclaim and ticking them off as 'done' in the time-table, is probably a more narrow-minded person than a man or woman who is playing a real part in the village debating society." He discards any notion that "the millions" will fly as easily and frequently as they now drive cars. To the questions "Will air-travel ever be available for the millions?" and "Will ordinary people ever take an aeroplane as they now do a bus?" Churchill in 1938 answers: "This is to expect too much. The air will be used for important business of all kinds where speed is needed above all. It will be used for pleasure, and for many other purposes which contribute to human well-being. But it is difficult to imagine a development of civil flying in this generation which will make any great advance in the everyday life and locomotion of the masses." Despite this more chilly and more accurate prophecy, Churchill also speculates in the 1938 essay that "flying may, however, before very long, begin to be a popular sport, as youths now ride motor-cycles not so much for transport as for amusement and excitement." He adds that "here the important thing is *safety*."[36]

Under the rubric of safety in sport-flying, Churchill includes a revised version of his paragraph for Korda on the autogiro's advent. He suggests again its advantages over conventional aircraft in landing, but also concedes that "of course, there are many new difficulties, and some dangers, attaching to this novelty." With his usual scrupulous attention to nuances of meaning when revising, Churchill in the 1938 essay changes "arrival of this monstrosity" to "arrival of this helpful monstrosity."[37] By adding "helpful" to counter the negative connotations of "monstrosity" Churchill stresses more emphatically the paragraph's argument that despite and indeed *because of* its unnatural nature, which allows for safer landings, autogiros are a welcome development. Like so many of his striking turns of phrase, Churchill's paradoxical notion of a helpful monstrosity is arresting. It is not the usual view of monstrosity. This small but telling revision shows too that even while retrenching his forecast of the revolutionary potential of wingless flight Churchill retains his fondness for the autogiro as a purely human addition to the world and one of the few, moreover, that is in itself altogether beneficial—unlike those conventional aircraft that he mainly associates with warfare in its most brutal forms, not with sport flying for harmless "amusement and excitement." In the 1935 memo on Korda's air scenario, however, what most strongly grips Churchill's imagination is how an autogiro in flight presents an altogether novel "spectacle." Recall his reiteration of this word in urging Korda to include scenes depicting autogiros in action: Churchill advises showing "especially the spectacle. . . . of the autogiro rising vertically from the ground and of men handing letters and parcels to the aviator while he remains virtually stationary in the air a few feet above the aerodrome." Churchill again uses "spectacle" while going on to note an almost magical quality of such scenes by explaining that "as the horizontal rotors become invisible when spinning the spectacle is one which seems a complete defiance of the law of gravity." Hey presto! What a marvelous spectacle. As with a magician's levitation act, although we know better we may nevertheless (in the film or in real life) enjoy the special thrill of what *seems* defiance of nature's laws. But Churchill anchors his explanation of the effect in aeronautical science, not magic.

Accordingly Churchill's imagination takes a turn toward futuristic science fiction when he goes on to advise Korda on how the film can best build upon the appeal of an initial scene dramatizing invention of the "helpful monstrosity" by showing one autogiro in action as an apparently gravity-defying spectacle:

> I think the possibilities of this development should play a part in the closing sections of the film and that for instance a vision should be shown of a great air terminus in the heart of London with machines alighting in endless succession upon the platforms, folding up their helicopters and descending numerous lifts to the vast garages where they can be parked side by side and take up no more room than motor cars. Similarly [*sic*] being taken out and released into the air when the rush hour begins for going home. . . . I imagine some sort

of model could illustrate this and would start peoples' minds upon a more hopeful train of thought than if you end merely by the flights of war aeroplanes.[38]

This proposed "vision" of a utopian future London is very much in the vein of H. G. Wells, whose politics Churchill despised but whose science fiction he admired. In 1935, the year of Churchill's aviation memo, Korda was also working with Wells on scenarios for a film based on his 1933 book *The Shape of Things to Come*. The movie was released February 22, 1936, as *Things to Come*, starring Raymond Massey with Ann Todd and Ralph Richardson. Although a financial disaster for the studio, it attracted wide attention and is now regarded as a milestone in the development of science fiction films.[39] It memorably evokes dystopian future prospects via scenes of devastating air raids. Such visions of unstoppable death raining down from above were a widely shared nightmare during the 1930s, when bombers were imagined to be even more hideously destructive than they turned out to be (although reality was not far behind the most gruesome imaginings). The air raid scenes in *Things to Come* convey a sickly and depressing sense of utter helplessness before an irresistible aerial onslaught. They do not suggest any possibility of fighting back successfully, or even taking such attacks in stride, as London was later to do in ways that prompted Churchill's well-publicized claims during the Blitz that "London can take it." Looking back in 1948, Churchill noted that from 1935 to the outbreak of war in 1939, "We had entered a period when the weapon which had played a considerable part in the previous war had become obsessive in men's minds, and also a prime military factor. Ministers had to imagine the most frightful scenes of ruin and slaughter in London if we quarreled with the German Dictator. . . . these considerations . . . affected our policy, and by consequence all the world."[40] It was thus no trivial question how far any vision of the future ought to hammer home aviation's potential as an instrument of death on an unprecedented scale, thereby feeding those frightful imaginings that could among other consequences paralyze Britain's foreign policy.

Korda's *Things to Come* struck a balance by also dramatizing utopian possibilities for an ultimately peaceful and prosperous future. The purpose of this balance, as of most science fiction showing futures with utopian and dystopian elements, is to invite audience awareness that they have a present choice of paths toward a better or a worse future: "The film ends with Wells's eternal question, 'Which shall it be?'—the choice of a future for all, or one of chaotic destruction."[41] It is to introduce a similar question that Churchill suggests including at the aviation film's end his vision of a utopian London marked by the benign use of autogiros at rush hour instead of crowded underground trains or humdrum buses:

> Indeed it is the present ending that is the weakest part. For it neither strikes the note of hope nor imparts the moral lesson. I should like to see the moral lesson play its part. Man has wrested this great secret from nature and science. Is he worthy of it? If not it will destroy not only his Science, but his Civilization. It will deprive him of all that he has elaborated for centuries in a struggle for freedom, law and peace. Unless we are worthy to use the weapons of Science, they will destroy us. None but Ulysses can bend the bow of Ulysses. In this case not to be worthy is not merely to be incapable of using the weapon, but to perish by it. . . . Anyhow it is clear that the end of your film should be a vision of the future with its hopes and its fears contrasted, and the old choice of blessing or cursing offered to man in a more dire form than was ever presented in human history.[42]

By urging that a hopeful note be struck at the film's conclusion, Churchill proposes using it to illustrate three of his strongest convictions: that human affairs are contingent, not inexorably determined by historical tides beyond human control; that science—here in its aeronautical applications—may either destroy civilization or bless it with a better future; and that people have both an opportunity and an obligation to choose the path of blessing.

After the aviation scenario passed into the limbo of unmade films, Churchill prominently put into his 1938 "Air Transport" essay as its second paragraph the eloquent core of his 1935 passage questioning whether humanity can use to worthy purposes or even control the weapons that science has created by unlocking the "great secret" of flight. By specifying the most terrible consequence if we are not worthy to bend the bow of Ulysses—"to perish by it"—Churchill uses the metaphor to stress that while disaster is not inevitable it is the most likely outcome if people cannot take heroic measures. And such measures are neither easy nor obvious. Where, after all, will we find aviation's Ulysses? Churchill does not say.

Another of Churchill's strongest convictions is apparent in his insistence that the aviation film ought to end in a way that "imparts the moral lesson." His best writing is animated by didactic purposes. To him fiction and history alike impart—or ought to impart—moral lessons. He finds that almost every story he tells, whether true or invented, has its moral lessons. Sometimes he leaves them implicit. Most often he articulates them in varying ways. In an "Author's Preface" that he wrote in 1900 for his early (and only) novel, *Savrola*, Churchill disclaimed any instructive designs with evident scorn for works that have such lofty pretensions: "Books are frequently written with an ulterior object; to plead some cause or teach some great moral lesson. The object of these pages is only to amuse. Like the perfect dinner they should be agreeable at the time and never cause a thought afterwards."[43] Caught up here in the spirit of the 1890s, he echoes widespread fin de siècle aestheticism in this sturdy affirmation that his fiction has no "ulterior" instructive purpose but aspires only to achieve ephemeral pleasure. We may smile at catching Churchill momentarily in the mood of Oscar Wilde. But the mood quickly passed. The statement remains buried in the Churchill Archives. He decided against publishing the preface. There is no record of why he suppressed it, although in retrospect his decision seems right. While *Savrola* is far indeed from a great novel it does offer much to think about. Though it teaches no large moral lesson its episodes certainly amount to an introductory course of political instruction for the would-be leader. As he must have realized upon reconsideration, Churchill's disclaimer hardly does *Savrola* justice. Never one to overdo modesty, he may have decided against trivializing his own effort. Perhaps too he sensed that even if he was not to find his métier as a novelist, his destiny was to write works that aimed to plead important causes and teach great moral lessons. Better not to pull the rug out from under them in advance. As even his comments on Korda's aviation film scenario amply demonstrate, Churchill's was above all a moral imagination.

Of all his efforts for Korda's studio, Churchill worked hardest on the film about George V. Even though it too never got into production, it was this project that prompted him to consider most often and in greatest detail the nature of cinematic art. He had to define and grapple with the ways in which narration on the page differed from narration on the screen. For this attempt to dramatize twenty-five years of British history from the

1910 coronation of King George V to his silver jubilee in 1935, Churchill had first to single out the most important events from a very crowded field, and then decide what mixture of words and images would best convey the historical significance of these episodes as well as how they appeared at the time to those who experienced them. As he got started he confessed in a letter sent on December 14, 1934, to Arthur Wimperis at London Films: "I think this is quite the most difficult thing I have ever attempted on account of the enourmous [sic] mass of material, and the difficulty of selecting key notes. My mind is still almost blank on the after war period."[44] This is a striking admission from a man seldom at a loss for words, a man who had already published fifteen books, some in more than one volume, as well as many newspaper and magazine articles. Churchill was no amateur or inexperienced writer. Perhaps for that very reason he was acutely aware of looming difficulties in this task of compressing twenty-five years into a running time on screen of well under two hours. At a conference on January 4, 1935, the film's duration was specified as only eighty minutes.[45] What made the task even more daunting was his equally uneasy awareness that he was not only entering what for him personally as a writer was unknown territory, but was embarking on an enterprise for which he believed there were no precedents that could serve as models. Writing to Korda on October 3, 1934, Churchill pointed out that "after all this is the first history of a reign told by the cinematograph."[46]

Noel Coward's popular 1931 play *Cavalcade* and its 1933 Hollywood movie version might have provided a rough model, although Churchill does not mention it. Perhaps it did not come to mind because Coward does not focus on the king or empire at large, but rather on the fortunes of one upper-class family and its servants from the Boer War to the aftermath of World War I. Historical events are presented indirectly via their effects on various family members whom in a chronologically arranged series of vignettes we glimpse at such milestone moments as leaving for the Boer War; on an abbreviated honeymoon cruise aboard the *Titanic*; receiving news that a son has been killed in battle just before the November 11, 1918, Armistice; wandering bereaved and grieving through cheering crowds celebrating the war's end; and (in the last scene) sitting in a night club one evening in 1930 while listening to "Twentieth Century Blues," a song whose lyrics dwell on the bleak outlook ahead: "What is there to strive for, / Love or keep alive for?" This rather oddly gives way to a finale in which as the Union Jack flies overhead the cast sings "God Save the King."[47] The play was applauded as patriotic. The movie version has been described as "an immaculate cinematization of Noel Coward's nostalgic celebration of the class system."[48] I wonder how far that celebration is furthered by the scene in which Bridges, the discharged family butler who has become a drunkard after the Boer War, is killed when reeling inebriated in front of a moving car. It is certainly a death typical of the changing times, as are the other deaths in *Cavalcade*. Perhaps its emphasis on a wealthy family and its retainers struggling with so much gloom also pushed the play out of Churchill's thoughts as a template for his scenario. In any case, Williams, the imaginary butler Churchill creates for his scenario, is certainly (as we'll see) a more exemplary figure than Coward's deplorable Bridges. Churchill's butler is a war hero quite content after the armistice to return in becoming sobriety to his prewar niche in society, thus standing as a pillar of the class system far more than poor Bridges, who finally seems only a part of its perennial servant problem.

In production elsewhere while Churchill was contemplating his task for Korda's studio were three newsreel compilations about the reign of George V that were eventually screened, and also a film, *Royal Cavalcade*, that had better luck in getting to movie theaters, where it opened in April 1935. The rival film had proceeded along similar lines, although presumably unknown to Churchill. *Royal Cavalcade* "interweaves fictional personal stories, filmed in the studio with actors (such as the story of two lovers parted by the Great War), with newsreel and documentary footage of the great events of the reign, both royal and national. . . . all bound together by a strident and over-assertive commentary."[49] There are historical episodes offering glimpses of George V's predecessors from Elizabeth I forward, including a scene of Elizabeth's famous speech at Tilbury from the movie *Drake of England*. There is a prevailing upbeat tone, and a rousing climax with "the National government balancing the budget, people queuing to pay their income tax, American tourists talking of the strength of British traditions and massed choirs singing 'Land of Hope and Glory' and 'God Save the King.'"[50] If Korda's people had any inkling of how the rival script was being crafted no allusions to it surface in their correspondence with Churchill concerning his scenario. Nor is there evidence that he was concerned to emulate or deviate from the pattern of *Royal Cavalcade*. A few parallels were inevitable given the topic, current attitudes, and available film techniques. Apparently, however, Churchill thought out for himself what should be done for a jubilee film. Despite some coincidence of structure and tone with *Royal Cavalcade*, he wrote a scenario that is in a distinctively Churchillian imaginative mode.

In the October 3, 1934, letter to Korda, after professing himself "greatly hampered by not knowing what kind of pictures are difficult, expensive or impossible," Churchill outlines his initial ideas as a kind of warming-up exercise intended mainly to elicit information from the studio: "I must have ample technical guidance before I can cast my notes into more advanced form than what is set out here. . . . I must have more knowledge before I can see how to tell the tale I have in my mind."[51] In this first attempt to consider from a scriptwriter's perspective all the ingredients of an effective movie, Churchill makes tentative suggestions about music, sound effects ("the incidental noises"), dialogue and other spoken words ("the talkie aspect"), animation, and the use of old newsreels for documentary purposes.

The main problem with available footage is poor quality: "The existing news reels which illustrate the period are, of course, primitive. They flicker and they do not always bring out the parts or characters we wish to illustrate in our story." For episodes that were not filmed or were filmed without focus on what now seem the most noteworthy "parts or characters," the jubilee film can either resort to outright fictional dramatizations or, more dubiously, to imitation newsreels. Churchill wonders if newsreels that do show important moments can be brought up to present standards by technical means: "Surely if you throw these reels upon the screen and rephotograph them by cinema process, you would get first a greater smoothness, though possibly a little more dimness; and secondly you could throw a spotlight impression upon the parts of each old picture that you wish to illustrate. For instance if in a crowd you wish to pick out two or three figures for a few moments, can they not be rephotographed on a larger scale while the original news reel is being run through?"[52] Churchill prefers to salvage and use existing newsreels as much as possible, thereby enhancing the authenticity of Korda's film as a pathfinding effort in cinematic historiography.

Of sound effects Churchill says nothing beyond his reminder that in addition to music there will also have to be some "incidental noises." He urges Korda to provide "the orchestration . . . upon a considerable scale" because this is a "vitally important aspect": "There should be an underlying accompaniment of music throughout the film. Sometimes it rises to dominate, as in the surge and chorus of a patriotic tune—sometimes it is barely perceptible. Sometimes it should express a rising storm and stress of events, and then can fall into a lull. And ever and anon there should be a lilt, almost like an echo, of the well-known popular airs of those days which illustrate the theme."[53] Whether preexisting or composed for the occasion, musical accompaniment to a film becomes program music without, however, necessarily sacrificing all claims to attention in its own right during the film itself or when performed independently. The genre allows for variation in the degree of attention invited to a film's music per se. Churchill, whose musical tastes ran more to the music hall than to the concert hall, is here an advocate of subordinating music to the programmatic demands of the story.

Although he revels in opportunities for introducing "the surge and chorus of a patriotic tune," in his "Scenario of the Reign of King George V" dated mid-January 1935, Churchill names and specifies the placement of only a few of what were to be the film's many songs. There is to be a rendition of "Put me upon a [sic] island where the girls are few" in a 1910 music hall scene where the song elicits from a suffragette in the balcony an angry outburst: "Shame! What right have you to mock the women?" There is to be "Land of Hope and Glory" sung by survivors of an air raid. There are to be "munitions girls . . . crooning 'Keep the home fires burning'—or something like that." There is to be a grand finale at the end with a rendition of "Rule Britannia" celebrating both the jubilee and the empire over which King George V presides.[54] Churchill also specifies trumpet calls at the outset in scenes depicting ceremonial announcement of the new reign and promulgation of the news. First a "Fanfare of trumpets" is to introduce the Accession scene:

> The leads of St James's Palace with crowd and troops in the courtyard. A trumpeter comes into the picture against the sky. The drum roll ceases and the heralds proclaim:
> His Majesty King George the Fifth.
> (Note: the details of this ceremony must be obtained from the College of Heralds; also the uniforms of the heralds and the actual trumpet calls. It is most important that all this should be accurate.)[55]

This scene's trumpet calls are not accompaniment of action but part of the film's recreation of a particular historical occasion that included music.

The trumpet calls *are* the action. However, Churchill's next scene is to be a "rapid series of shots of all parts of the Empire: the trumpet blast being used instead of words to announce the Accession."[56] This too is not accompaniment, but rather substitution of music as a kind of shorthand for words after the previous scene has established that the trumpet blast means a new reign has begun.

In a "Preliminary Outline of Jubilee Film" Churchill envisions the grand finale as a musical climax that will involve theatergoers in a sing-along to accompany what is in this version apparently an offscreen orchestra and chorus as well as an offscreen voice that is not Churchill but what may for him be an alter ego, the muse of history itself:

> The finale is equally obvious and appropriate:—Clio the Muse of History (whom we shall probably require several times) pronounces the famous lines of Dibden [*sic*] in Rule Britannia:
>
> > "The nations not so blessed as thee
> > Shall in their turn to tyrants fall,
> > While thou shalt flourish great and free,
> > The dread (hope) and envy of them all."
>
> Then a rapid roll of the drums crashes into "Rule Britannia" chorus. Then "God Save the King."
> As the actual audience rise, so does an immense audience on the screen, and then successively in panels are seen simultaneously all over the empire great subsidiary audiences rising as if the whole Empire were singing together.[57]

More noteworthy than the confusion here of Dibdin (as it should have been spelled) with James Thompson, the actual author of "Rule Britannia," is Churchill's decision to quote its less often cited verse 2. Uncertainty over whether the second word in the last line is or should be "dread" or "hope" (it is "dread" in the poem) suggests that Churchill is quoting the poem from memory, as he most often seems to do—occasionally with his own improvements—when citing poetry. With or without a substitution of "hope" for "dread," the second verse is very apposite to the appeasement period during which the script was drafted, as indeed is the rest of the poem which that verse will recall to mind. In the political context of 1935 it becomes an allusion to the rising menace of Hitler's newly established tyranny and an oblique expression of Churchill's wilderness exhortations for England to stand firm against that threat. Whether audiences would have noticed the contemporary application is of course a moot point because the film was not made. But the choice of verse 2 as a spur to the theatergoer's memory of "Rule Britannia" is another small measure of how Churchill was giving imaginative expression to his political stance.

For a celebration of the jubilee, Churchill's final musical turn to the national anthem would have been expected, especially in the light of such predecessors as Noel Coward's *Cavalcade*. Only the magnitude of its rendition might have raised eyebrows. In the 1930s, as until long after World War II, English theatergoers took for granted, mostly without embarrassment or self-consciousness, that they would rise and perhaps even sing along while "God Save the King" was played (in however abbreviated a rendition) before a performance. Evidently, however, the jubilee called for more decibels than could be achieved in a single theater. Churchill's grandiose patriotic vision of the whole empire singing together is his musical ne plus ultra, a Churchillian 1812 overture.

It is altered but not retrenched for his mid-January 1935 scenario, in which by some happy strokes of the blue pencil Clio has disappeared and is replaced by one of Churchill's representative human characters, Mr. E—short for Mr. England, the man in the street. After Mr. E ("soliloquising") finishes his recitation of the lines from "Rule Britannia" there is to be a "roll and uplift of drums into Rule Britannia, during which scene changes to an enormous stadium with tremendous concourse of people, into the centre of which massed bands playing Rule Britannia, slowly advance, breaking into God save the King. At the same time in the four corners of the picture other multitudes as great become visible all rising successively with a sense of crescendo, our audience rising too. (Curtain)."[58] Churchill's concluding vision of massed bands like those in a giant military tattoo is probably modeled on the musical extravaganzas of the Royal Tournaments, a regular fixture on the London calendar from 1880 until their abolition in 1999. Churchill attended many of these tournaments with their wonderful and surely to him irresistibly appealing combination of military sporting events, military displays, and military music.[59] No doubt by 1935 this once and future First Lord of the Admiralty had often applauded the Royal Navy Field Gun Competition, a tournament event from 1907 forward that commemorated a famous Boer War exploit of the navy. At every Royal Tournament there were also spectacular displays of horsemanship bound to catch the attention of a former cavalry officer and polo enthusiast.

Wherever he got the idea for massed bands, Churchill in proposing it goes about as far away as possible from the quieter intimacies and informality of music-hall fare. But that is also to have its place in his composition as "ever and anon there should be a lilt, almost like an echo, of the well-known popular airs of those days." Though he only specifies a few of the popular tunes to be included in the sound-track score, Churchill's description of them collectively as providing a lilt implies that for the most part they will be graceful, jolly, and light tunes. However, this does not necessarily exclude some at least of the more melancholy wartime songs of love, endurance, and loss. To suggest that whatever songs are included should function "almost like an echo" implies aiming for a subtle effect of reprise even *on first appearance* of each tune within the sound-track score. By contrast with the "surge and chorus" of patriotic tunes intermittently throughout and then overwhelmingly at the film's finale, the delicacy of such recurring lilts would be all the more effective. It is just as well that Churchill's hobby was painting not composing music. Nevertheless his suggestions for the jubilee film's accompanying score, taken together, show a musical sensibility that was far from tone-deaf.

In his October 3, 1934, letter to Korda, Churchill suggests as a general principle "about the talkie aspect" that anything goes: "We should have no rule except to use everything unhesitatingly which best conveys the meaning." In successive scenario drafts Churchill included short scenes of dialogue involving a cast of representative characters. Among them are a suffragette ("a beautiful girl of nineteen, and the heroine of this part of the story"); the suffragette's disapproving father Mr. E, and his friend Mr. C; A Belfast Protestant, Mr. Orange, his daughter Lucy, and Lucy's Catholic boyfriend; a father, mother, and son in British Columbia, from whence the son departs to fight for Britain in the First World War; British and German officers talking together at the July 1914 Kiel Harbor regatta just as news arrives of Archduke Ferdinand's assassination at Sarajevo; British officers on a warship at sea receiving news that war with Germany has been declared; other naval officers at headquarters ashore; British soldiers in the trenches returning after a raid with a German prisoner; a London constable; "an intelligent foreigner" (specified in later drafts as a "Finn"); and others including Williams, "a big hulking flunkey from Buckingham Palace who becomes a War hero according to Mr. Churchill's story of the real character."[60] Churchill was alert to the danger that episodes involving dialogue among such characters might deflect attention from the historical issues they were designed to dramatize: "No doubt the dialogue can be cut and sharpened, and we must avoid exciting undue *personal* interest in the characters."[61] As docudramas in our day have made all too clear, fiction may easily displace attention away from fact even when the fiction remains a plausible representation of reality.

Churchill's primary remedy for this problem was to aim for a balance between exciting too little and too much interest in his fictional people by cutting back on dialogue after having first given reign to creative impulses he had not much indulged since publishing *Savrola* thirty-five years before turning scriptwriter. Further checks on deflecting attention from actual history were to be Churchill's own voice-overs, as he also explained in his October 3, 1934, letter to Korda: "I contemplate that I should speak some passages myself, like a Greek chorus, and thus put points that can be put in no other way."[62] Churchill reserves for himself an august role, even though it is a shade less awesome than speaking in the persona of Clio, who perhaps disappeared from the scenarios only because playing this goddess required a female voice.

Animation appealed to Churchill as means of presenting statistics and maps via what he calls a cartoon method that would by virtue of movement be more interesting and thus more likely to hold attention than a static map or graph. Animated cartoons would allow viewers to follow the rise and fall of such matters a shipping losses, as well as the ebb and flow of battle across various regions. More innovative though beyond technical capacities at that time is Churchill's suggestion in his October 3, 1934, letter to Korda about taking actual still photographs as a basis for animation that would transform them into moving pictures of the depicted scenes:

A good deal of the . . . action that I require is cramped by the difficulty of presenting the real characters moving, and still more conversing. Pray advise me whether the following is possible:—Suppose we took one of the innumerable excellent photographs of three or four pre-war Cabinet ministers, or of some pre-war scene with a group of people in it. Starting from the original photographs could not these figures be made to move on the Micky Mouse plan? Even if they only moved for a few seconds it would just enable the necessary points to be made. . . . My task would be enormously simplified if any device of photography or of rephotgraphing, or Micky Mouse methods, could make some of the excellent old snapshots move momentarily.[63]

Such a combination of photography with "the Micky Mouse plan" of animating cartoon drawings would blur the borderline between fact and fiction. Episodes involving conversations among obviously invented though representative characters like Mr. E are clearly fiction, easily identified and acceptable as such. Old newsreels incorporated into the jubilee film would be as easily identified and accepted as factual even when slightly doctored to eliminate flickering or to concentrate on a particular figure among many. Still photos transformed to moving pictures are more problematic. They would be a kind of counterfeit newsreel that could be accused of falsification.

Anticipating such criticism, Churchill suggests with conspicuous illogic the grounds on which it might be warded off: "Indeed it must be remembered that in this film we are trying to make a cinema memorial of the reign and to recall, as far as possible, such portions of the past as were indeed chronicled by the then new invention of the cinema. Therefore every device is legitimate and no question arises about 'faked' photographs and so forth. On the contrary we should proclaim our purpose and that we have used every device possible to achieve it."[64] The non sequitur here is his leap from the fact that because the jubilee film attempts to bring again to the screen and thus again to mind ("to recall") what has actually been recorded by motion picture cameras ("the then new invention of the cinema"), it *therefore* follows that it is legitimate to include imitation moving pictures made by animating snapshots. Churchill's uncharacteristically muddy logic is perhaps a sign of uneasiness at proposing a "Micky Mouse" method that would neither be totally "faked photographs" in the sense of invented scenes with no basis in a real snapshot, nor authentic newsreels showing historic figures in actual movement. Quite typical, however, is the way he cuts this Gordian knot by refusing either to pretend that differences do not exist or to dwell on any questionable aspect of differences between authentic and imitation moving pictures. Instead he simply urges Korda to "proclaim" as part of the film's publicity campaign that it can boast of having resorted to "every possible device." Churchill briskly converts a necessity into a virtue and moves on.

For the film scenario as in his other writing Churchill often takes a picture—whether painting, drawing, or snapshot—as an imaginative starting point when creating an episode. His proposal for "Micky Mouse" animation of photographs is an attempt to do this more literally than is possible on the printed page. Notes recalling "points of the discussion" during a script conference at Chartwell on December 28, 1934, record a less mechanical moment of such transformation: "Mr. Churchill suggested that a scene be introduced showing the arch of Victoria Station swallowing up soldiers going to the front. (Mr. Churchill has a slide and a painting showing an effective scene of farewells in front of this arch.) Mr. Wimperis suggested the arch should be made actually symbolical as 'Jaws of Moloch' swallowing up the men."[65] In his mid-January 1935 "Scenario of the Reign of King George V" Churchill stresses the scene's symbolism by directing that instead of being depicted only once it be repeated as a leitmotif to convey the horror of World War I's insatiable appetite for men:

> *Scene*
> 1916
> Now the War has lasted so long that leave for the fighting troops is a regular institution and we see for the first time the mouth of Victoria Station with the leave train about to go.
> (Note: steel helmets on the men's backs.)
> This picture recurs several times as a kind of motif the object being to indicate the ever-increasing strain and endless devouring of men through these dark gateways.[66]

Churchill's stage direction conveys the symbolism more subtly by avoiding any explicit allusion to Moloch while keeping the underlying idea by describing the arch of Victoria Station as its "mouth" and referring to soldiers as eaten by "devouring" gateways that are emblematically "dark" as a sign of their sinister function during wartime.

For another symbolic war scene in the jubilee film Churchill's imagination worked in the opposite direction by going from a general literary

model toward scenes rather than proceeding from a picture to an episode.
In this case Churchill was prompted by a combination of his own memories of the western front and his recollection of Edgar Allan Poe's tales.
At a "Story Conference" on January 15, 1935, Churchill suggested that part
of a "Model scene (Alps to the sea). . . . might provide our one horrifying
effect of war-skeleton hand emphasising [*sic*] size duration and horror of
Europe torn to pieces (Try an imaginative Poe-esk effect of horror.)."[67]
As the scene evolved it was to start with a soldier's-eye view through a
periscope of no-man's-land seen from an English trench, followed by an
aerial view in which "we see this scene of desolation, finally merging in
a map, stretching from the Alps to the sea," and then a dissolve into a
"Long Shot" at the sea coast: "Barbed wire with the trenches in the background. The barbed wire runs from the sand dunes into the water. On
the wires several shapeless figures. *CAMERA TRUCKING* up shows that
the shapeless figures are dead men in uniform." Opposite this typed outline of the shot Churchill's annotation written with a pen reads: "This is
our one really '*macabre*' scene. I would show the dead face like Death
itself—close up. The waves wash the seaweed and the rags of clothing
to & fro. It is a terrifying symbolism—Death growing larger & larger."
Churchill replaces his first idea of a "war-skeleton hand" with a shot
zooming in on a dead man's skeletal face as a more universally understood—and even more macabre—icon of death. In a typed "Note A"
amplifying his penned annotation, Churchill specifies exactly how the
zoom shot is to proceed and what its effects ought to be as the camera
closes in on one of the bodies pinned to the barbed wire: "A skeleton hand
clutches the wire and a skull face becomes visible. . . . Then closer up still
until the skeleton face with its helmet still on, fills the picture of a veri-
table Death's Head growing to monstrous symbolic proportions. This terrifying spectacle is our only 'macabre' shot."[68] To this typed note the word
"symbolic" has been added in ink by Churchill to make sure Korda's tech-
nicians do not neglect the transformaton here of realism into symbolism.

The final draft of directions for this shot again replaces Churchill's
initial simile of a "dead face *like* Death itself" with an outright identification of the skull as an emblematic death's head: "On the wires are several shapeless figures and sea-weed which has caught about them moves
with the waves. Death's head appears."[69] The emblem is traditional but
Churchill intends it to frighten viewers without drawing any comforting
moral, religious or otherwise, to allay the scene's horror. Less eerie but

not by much is the initial draft's typed outline of what should be depicted in the view of no-man's-land through a periscope: "Ruined country, wrecked houses, dead horses, shell holes. Three hundred yards away the German lines—the first shots of day." To the items in this scene Churchill while annotating it pens in the addition of "unburied corpses." He crosses out "the first shots of day" and replaces that phrase with more specific sounds and sights: "a few rifle shots, meanwhile and one shell burst in the ground a hundred yards away."[70] Addition of rifle shots and a shell burst doubtless brought the scene more into line with Churchill's memories of daybreak in the front lines during his time as colonel with the Royal Scots Fusiliers facing the German trenches at Ploegsteert in Belgium. Adding the shell burst also brings the scene as a composition more in line with Churchill's wartime paintings, most notably his early 1916 canvas *"Plugstreet" under Shell-fire.*[71]

For the western front panoramas Churchill as scriptwriter combines his memories of war in the trenches, his painterly instincts, and his literary sense that some effects ought to be modeled on those achieved by Edgar Allan Poe's tales of terror. Churchill is far from sugarcoating much less glorifying war in these scenes because he does not entirely domesticate them by assimilation to conventions of art and literature. The touches that bring them into a comfortable framework of familiar symbolism (the Death's head), of nicely arranged paintings (the shell burst), and of agreeable literary terror ("imaginative Poe-esk effect of horror") are in context counterbalanced by Churchill's insistence on adding "unburied corpses" and skeletal bodies in uniform pinned to barbed wire. He creates scenes that for all their affinities with Poe's stories unmistakably come not from the harmless daydreams of fantastic fiction but from actual events that have happened and could happen again in the real world. Had the film been made these panoramas would have taken it beyond Poe toward Goya's Disasters of War. As an historian venturing into a new medium Churchill wants its resources employed to make his audience apprehend emotionally as well as understand intellectually the terrors of war.

This impulse is of a piece with Churchill's usual disinclination to imagine or invite his audience to imagine that war is easy or should lightly be undertaken. Despite his reputation as a man unduly fond of war, Churchill did not gloss over its horrors. Quite the contrary. As in his jubilee scenario, he seized occasions to warn against romanticizing warfare. He praised literature that showed it for what it is. A few years before embarking on his collaboration with Korda's studio, for example, in an introduction to A. P. Herbert's *The Secret Battle*, Churchill wrote of this harrowing novel of combat and miscarriage of military justice during World War I: "It was one of those cries of pain wrung from the fighting troops by the prolonged and measureless torment through which they passed; and like the poems of Siegfried Sassoon should be read in each generation, so that men and women may rest under no illusion about what war means."[72] Doubtless for similar reasons, Churchill also admired R. C. Sherriff's acclaimed 1929 play *Journey's End*. Set in a dugout on the western front as British officers under terrible strain prepare to face a German offensive likely to overwhelm their position, *Journey's End* portrays the psychic as well as physical toll on soldiers struggling—not always successfully—to act honorably while events beyond their control sweep them toward death.

In a letter to Sherriff after seeing his play, Churchill (then chancellor of the exchequer) called it "brilliant" and expressed his "admiration for this remarkable production."[73] In the letter he also raised three questions and answered them to provide (unsolicited) advice about aspects of the action and dialogue in the light of his own firsthand knowledge of trench warfare. Churchill soon invited Sherriff to 11 Downing Street where "a servant brought . . . coffee, and Winston passed a decanter of port." In response to a question from his host about military service, Sherriff mentioned being wounded at Passchendaele while serving with the 9th East Surreys, whose regimental history during the Great War Churchill "knew at once all about." But he mainly wanted to discuss the stagecraft of *Journey's End*: "He asked me a lot of searching questions. It was as if he had watched the play through a microscope. He enquired about intricate details that had never occurred to me before, why certain actors did this or said that, and I was hard put to it to make sensible answers."[74] Churchill's admiration for works like Sassoon's poetry, *The Secret Battle*, and *Journey's End* did not waver even though such "antiwar" literature could be enlisted in the service of that strain of British pacifism that he regarded as more likely than rearmament to encourage another and even worse conflict. In Churchill's political rhetoric, imagining vividly the true face of war is the first step toward persuading people that only military strength will deter it. In his military histories Churchill had devised many ways of using the printed page to invite imagination of war.[75] His fascination with the stagecraft of *Journey's End* shows that well before trying his hand at film scripts Churchill was thinking hard about how war might most effectively be imagined by a dramatist.

Churchill's "macabre" effects in his screenplay are not intended to dominate the wartime episodes or undermine the film's overall positive assessment of George V's reign as a story of adversity overcome and progress for Britain and its empire. Churchill's fictional characters are involved in episodes that dramatize difficulties but wind up offering reassurance. The Belfast Protestant father is at last reconciled to his daughter Lucy's marriage to her Catholic boyfriend as the latter is about to leave for the front to fight with the British against the Germans. In a truly Churchillian happy ending, the father, his son (home on leave recuperating from a wound), Lucy, and her new husband celebrate their reconciliation by sharing "some Irish whisky."[76]

There is also a happy outcome for suffragettes as women earn respect and advance their cause by rallying around to help the war effort. Though no friend of the suffragette movement in its early days, Churchill treats its success magnanimously and presents its history sympathetically. Despite some acerbic strokes Churchill's characterization of the film's representative suffragette, Miss E, is a friendly if not entirely flattering portrait: "The young woman is an important figure in our story. She must be a tallish, *slender*, almost gawky but a handsome and slightly hysterical spinster of 23. Her countenance is obviously harassed by inner stresses—lines under the eyes—yet, chained to the railings among the crowd, in her rage she *must* (for us) excite the sympathy of the audience."[77] When deciding how best to dramatize women's contribution to Britain's war effort, Churchill could have opted for hospital scenes illustrating their care of the wounded but chose instead to show women bravely carrying on in a munitions factory despite air raids. A note on the December 28, 1934, script conference at Chartwell records that "Mr. Churchill was anxious that the Suffragette girl's activities in the War [*sic*] should take place in a munitions factory rather than a hospital, as shells more impressive than bed-pans."[78]

Accordingly there is an episode showing the aftermath of an attack in which, following a bomb explosion at "fuze shed No 13" viewed from about two hundred yards away, the camera is to zoom in on "havoc, dust, debris, wrecked machinery, impression of bodies." As stretcher bearers take away casualties Miss E. refuses the doctor's orders to go home, and urges the surviving women to get back to their work:

DOCTOR (holding up his hand): That will do today, Miss E. No more work. We'll get it tidied up for you.

MISS E: Why no more work, three quarters of the machines are running?

DOCTOR: No, no, you can't do that. At the other end of the hall it is a shambles . . . there are sights no woman should see.

MISS E: What do you mean? This is my shop, I am in charge here. How dare you talk this sex disqualification stuff to me! You're out of date, that's what you are, doctor! Come on, chaps, what about it?[79]

Here the temperamental inclination to disobedient insistence on equality and independence that so many men (including Churchill) found wearisome in peacetime suffragettes becomes a virtue that allows male waffling to be overruled and the good work of making ammunition to proceed apace. Churchill even includes a bit of liberated nonsexist vocabulary as Miss E addresses her female subordinates not as "girls" or "women" but as "chaps."

The scene's conclusion and sequel afford more scope for Churchill's sentimental and patriotic musical impulses:

The women all come forward, hesitatingly at first, and take their places at the machines. The doctor goes off shaking his head, while at the same time stretcher-bearers come in at one end and shapeless forms are carried towards them from the other. Through all this scene the clack of the machinery is continuous, but through it rises at the end the sound of the women crooning "Land of Hope and Glory" which lasts and gets louder in the black out and then dies away. (Black out)

Scene

After this episode with its noise and clatter as the black out comes the munition girls are heard crooning "Keep the home fires burning"—or something like that.[80]

There is no record of whether Churchill hoped that moviegoers would hum along with his crooning women as a kind of warm-up for the film's musical grand finale. He certainly intended the music to reinforce this episode's implied argument that by their contribution to victory the bothersome suffragettes have redeemed themselves and deserve what concessions they have won.

Another wartime episode is based on Churchill's recollection of an incident he witnessed while serving at the front. In a letter to his wife Clementine dated December 15, 1915, Churchill explains the circumstances of what he calls a "scene . . . to stay in the memory":

> 10 grenadiers under a kid went across by night to the German Trench wh they found largely deserted or waterlogged. They fell upon a picket of Germans, beat the brains out of two of them with clubs & dragged a third home triumphantly as a prisoner. The young officer by accident let off his pistol & shot one of his own Grenadiers dead: but the others kept this secret and pretended it was done by the enemy—do likewise. Such men you never saw. The scene in the little dugout when the prisoner was brought in surrounded by these terrific warriors, in jerkins & steel helmets with their bloody clubs in hand—looking pictures of ruthless war—was one to stay in the memory. C'est très bon. They petted the prisoner and gave him cigarettes & tried to cheer him up. He was not vy unhappy to be taken & to know he wd be safe & well fed till the end of the war.[81]

For Churchill the imaginative nucleus of this report is not an encounter in the German trenches but "the scene in the little dugout" which takes on in his description the air of a symbolic painting in which British soldiers with oddly primitive weapons ("bloody clubs") become emblems: "pictures of ruthless war."

Churchill describes the participants in relation to one another as though he were composing a painting or providing stage directions for a dramatic "scene" (or both). First there is the arrival of the raiding party, an action that in Churchill's narration quickly dissolves into the impression of a static picture showing the prisoner "surrounded by these terrific warriors, in jerkins & steel helmets with their bloody clubs in hand." Specification of the dugout as "little" and the warriors as "terrific" makes the now symbolic soldiers loom large in relation to the "little" but otherwise undescribed space which the reader must suppose them pretty much filling up even if, as was likely, all ten raiders did not accompany their prisoner into the dugout. Churchill focuses attention on the imposing warriors not their unremarkable physical setting, which he only specifies sufficiently to call the reader's imagination into play.

Then it is as if this tableau, which Churchill commends to Clementine as an altogether memorable image, is again animated to provide a less striking because less ferocious sequel that is a bizarre tapering-off to a happy ending of sorts as the German prisoner is "petted," given a gift of cigarettes, and otherwise cheered up by his now kindly captors until he recovers sufficiently from his ordeal to be content with the prospect of remaining "safe and well fed till the end of the war." Unlike the British grenadiers who captured him, the German is evidently no "terrific" warrior. He has allowed himself to be ignominiously "dragged" back from their hunt to a captivity which does not much displease him. His stature is further diminished as, transformed at least momentarily into a harmless mascot, he is "petted."

The intellectual nucleus of this episode is its casual glossing over of the inept accidental shooting of one of his own men by the inexperienced young officer. To his band of ruthless-looking "terrific warriors" this senseless death matters no more than do the German casualties they have inflicted during their raid. Nor was there any reprimand by his superiors of the "kid" in charge. Instead, as we know from other sources, that young officer, 2nd Lieutenant William Parnell, received the Military Cross for his success in bringing back a prisoner for interrogation.[82] Churchill had no difficulty finding out the truth although he was only an observer without command authority over those involved. To all present the accidental shooting was apparently an open secret. Churchill in his letter goes along by instructing Clementine to keep quiet about the young officer's blunder. Getting information from the prisoner—which was the raid's object, although Churchill does not spell this out—takes precedence over everything else and makes up for any mistakes along the way. Thus by its very lack of repercussions the careless fatal accident becomes an even more shocking example of the harsh nature of war than allusion to enemy soldiers having their brains beaten out with bloody clubs as though in a combat between cavemen.

When Churchill turned the incident into an episode for the jubilee film he provided a more complete description of the dugout setting, fictitious names for the young officer and two of his subordinates, dialogue to make clear what happened during and after the raid, other touches that stress the brutality of modern warfare, and a fictitious postwar scene to round off the incident with a storybook happy ending that had no basis in fact but contributes to the film's generally positive portrayal of World War I as (despite its horrors) an instance of adversity overcome by the British Empire under the benign rule of George V. Churchill's dugout setting, along with the incident's tense atmosphere, may owe something to his memories of Sherriff's *Journey's End*. All its action takes place in a similar dugout. A central episode is an offstage raid on German trenches to capture a prisoner for interrogation, which is accomplished albeit at the cost of an English officer and six men killed by enemy fire. A frightened young prisoner, described as a German boy, is brought into the dugout escorted by a sergeant-major and two soldiers with fixed bayonets for brief questioning before being sent away for further interrogation (offstage) at headquarters. Churchill's stage direction describes the dugout for his scenario as "small, perhaps 15´ by 12´ with bunks on one side, and a small table with candles in bottles. At the dugout entrance is a staircase to the ground level. In the corner a telephone ringing, and an adjutant speaking." A colonel is also present. The prisoner is escorted in by three soldiers, "begrimed and in steel helmets." Among them is "Williams the bomber," a "big fellow who was a Buckingham Palace flunky" who has fought heroically with the grenadiers. He is "the one who broke the German counter attack in the brick-field, with his bag full of bombs." Williams has just agreed with the others to testify that "8207 private Mowlen" was killed by a German not by their officer, "Mr Bullock." Further stage directions specify that Williams while reporting to the colonel "holds an iron-headed mace in his right hand, with its head resting on the ground" and that "these big men dwarf the dugout, and their helmets almost touch the roof" whereas "the prisoner is much smaller."[83] Instead of a club as in the letter to Clementine, Churchill specifies the weapon of choice for nighttime trench raids as an "iron-headed mace."

This brings the implied level of civilization forward from the stone age when cavemen wielded clubs to the medieval period (usually dismissed by Churchill as the Dark Ages), when refined battlefield versions of the primitive club were termed maces. Presumably Churchill's specification of iron-headed mace is also a more accurate and complete description than "club" of the weapon actually employed, and thus a more helpful directive to the London Film studio's costume department. Whether thought of as cave dweller's club or medieval man's mace, the weapon as Churchill describes it symbolizes a horrifying regression of modern civilization toward the savagery of earlier eras.

The mace is also a reminder that whatever its weaponry all war is regressive toward a lower stage of civilization, thus inherently savage, and must be understood as such and practiced accordingly to achieve success, as the British raiders have and as the British Empire eventually did. Looking back at the period of administrative paralysis before he took over as prime minister, Churchill in his memoir of the Second World War remarks with devastating sarcasm the futility of trying to manage a war as though it were a matter for amiable discussion among committee members anxious above all not to offend each other by any disagreements. At meetings of the Military Co-ordination Committee during April 1940, Churchill records, "There was a copious flow of polite conversation, at the end of which a tactful report was drawn up by the secretary in attendance and checked by the three Service departments to make sure there were no discrepancies. Thus we had arrived at those broad, happy uplands where everything is settled for the greatest good of the greatest number by the common sense of most after the consultation of all." Such happy consensus, however, cannot cope with the realities of war: "Alas, I must write it: the actual conflict had to be more like one ruffian bashing the other on the snout with a club, a hammer, or something better. All this is deplorable, and it is one of the many good reasons for avoiding war, and having everything settled by agreement in a friendly manner, with full consideration for the rights of minorities and the faithful recording of dissentient opinions."[84] The real-life prototypes of Williams with his iron-headed mace evidently lingered in Churchill's imagination as emblems of the fact that war, however regrettable (as for Churchill both world wars were), had to be understood once embarked upon as essentially "like one ruffian bashing the other on the snout with a club." The incident he described for Clementine and dramatized for Korda eventually provided in the trench raiders' "bloody clubs" a powerful image "of ruthless war" illustrating Churchill's explanation of why after becoming prime minister he minimized the constraints of warfare directed by committee consensus. Although never heedless of his many advisory groups, by also appointing himself minister of defense Churchill achieved greater control of military decisions in hopes of making Britain more efficient at "bashing the other on the snout with a club."

As the screenplay continues, Bullock arrives and admits that he accidentally killed private Mowlen. Questioned by the colonel, Williams and the other two soldiers stick to their story that it was a German who shot

Mowlen. Not deceived, the colonel joins their benevolent conspiracy to save Bullock from pointless disgrace:

> COLONEL (to young Officer): I think it manly of you, Mr Bullock, to say what you have done, and only, if I may say so, what would be expected from the character you bear in the regiment. But no one's judgment can really be trusted about what happens in a scrimmage. There are always contradictory accounts, and the weight of independent testimony is three to one against you. You are evidently mistaken. Dismiss the matter from your mind . . .
> YOUNG OFFICER: But, sir . . .
> COLONEL (interrupting): There is nothing more to be said, and besides I have given an order, a definite order.
> COLONEL (to adjutant): Get a party to take the prisoner to the brigade and let these men turn in. That'll do Mr Bullock.
> WILLIAMS: Party, left turn, quick march.
> (Black out as they begin to shuffle through the narrow doorway and up the steps.)[85]

It is impossible to know how much of what Churchill heard during the actual incident is echoed in this dialogue.

Nor is it clear whether Churchill had a real-life model for Williams, the former "Buckingham Palace flunky" turned war hero via his exploits with hand grenades, who is now the protector of his inept young lieutenant as well as master of the mace. This character may owe something to memories of Crichton, the butler in J. M. Barrie's 1902 play *The Admirable Crichton*. In this popular comedy satirizing the class system, Crichton at his post in London is a model of deference to his wealthy employers and a staunch advocate of the social order who knows his place and that of everybody else. When the family is shipwrecked on a desert island, however, he turns out to be the most capable of them all and takes charge, becoming their ruler. After eventual rescue he returns once more to his role of arch humility as the lowly and loyal butler while the blundering upper-class idiots again resume their antics. If Williams was to any extent modeled on Crichton, little trace remains of Barrie's satire except insofar as Churchill's once and future Buckingham Palace flunky proves a more capable man than his social superior, Bullock. In any case, Williams is certainly Churchill's beau ideal of a servant. He displays equal sangfroid whether coping with palace protocol or with the demands of trench warfare. He is an embryonic version of Dorothy Sayers's Bunter: a capable person who is cool in a crisis, able to exercise intelligent initiative in a complex situation, and loyal to his superior in a way that manifests some genuine friendship cutting across class lines while nevertheless accepting and even affirming the validity of social differences.

Whatever its mix of fact and fiction, Churchill's script effectively conveys essential elements of the real "scene" that made such a strong impression on him. But Churchill's sequel set "after the war" turns away from the episode's horrors in favor of stressing England's return to a normalcy where virtue is rewarded, where people know their place, where different social classes get along harmoniously in peace just as they did in wartime although less scrambled together, and where our favorite characters are thriving:

> *Scene*: anteroom in Buckingham Palace. A long string of officers moving slowly forward to receive decorations for gallantry. In the string Lieutenant (now Captain) Bullock gives his ticket on which is written 'Captain Bullock . . . Regiment to receive the Military Cross with bar.' (As he hands this to the Equerry he catches the eye of the crimson-liveried powdered footman who stands just behind and receives another ferocious wink.)[86]

Alas poor Mowlen, forgotten here along with other casualties as Churchill focuses attention on a utopian world as it should be: where the virtuous are rewarded for what they have done well, are not held to account for their mistakes, and are living happily ever after. It is a romanticized and anodyne closure to a painful episode whose real-life sequel offered less comfort. Lieutenant Parnell was later among those who died in the Battle of the Somme.[87] As fictionalized by Churchill, this tragic story of a promising life cut off in its prime becomes a grim comedy of military manners with a reassuring happy ending.

Working as a scriptwriter and consultant for London Film Productions was nothing if not educational. At considerable cost to Korda but no tuition expense for Churchill, this work taught him much that students learn in those pricey film schools that now adorn so many institutions of higher learning. At the School of Cinema-Television in my university, for example, one beginning course is Screenwriting Fundamentals. Another is described in our catalogue as "an experiential course dealing with the technical and aesthetic principles of directing, cinematography, editing, sound, and the development of ideas through a cinematic vocabulary." Although Churchill never tried his hand at directing actors on a set, which he might have enjoyed, he certainly had in effect an "experiential course" with assignments and expert instruction from Korda's people about a wide range of technical and aesthetic issues involving screenwriting, editing, sound, and cinematic development of ideas. Had he been given a final exam he would surely have done well, though not well enough even to think about dropping all else to follow the yellow brick road to Hollywood. Nobody can regret Churchill's decision to keep his efforts centered on politics and literature, with painting and bricklaying not home movies as his hobbies. Nor can there be much regret that the films on which Churchill worked for Korda were never produced. They are not lost masterpieces. Neither, however, to judge from what clues remain, would they have been contemptible by the standards of their day. Surviving script drafts, memos, and conference minutes actually provide better glimpses of Churchill's imagination in action than completed films that would have been shaped by many other people involved in their production, especially during filming and in the final progression from cutting room to projection booths.

In his publications Churchill occasionally put to use what he learned about films thanks to his spell of on-the-job training, although not in ways that alter the overall bent of his writing. The most noteworthy single application of his cinematic education is "Everybody's Language," Churchill's essay about Charlie Chaplin published in the October 26, 1935 issue of *Collier's*. Reprinted only twice subsequently, it deserves to be more widely known. Churchill wrote this essay just after his most intensive involvement with Korda's studio working on the jubilee film and short subject series. If regarded as a kind of seminar paper on film theory, and taken as a measure of what he learned during his adult "school days" with Korda's people, "Everybody's Language" further belies the myth that Churchill was an indifferent student. But it is no mere final-exam recital of filmmaking fundamentals. Nor is it a memoir of his scriptwriting days, entertaining as that might have been. Drawing on his own studio experience without alluding to it, Churchill in "Everybody's Language" moves to fresh and more difficult ground by analyzing Chaplin's artistry as the basis for a provocative reconsideration of silent movies.

The essay starts like the outset of a novel or short story, then in its second paragraph describes a scene as though for a stage play or film:

> In a room in St. Thomas's Hospital, London, a man lay dying. He had had a good life—a full life. He had been a favourite in the music halls. He had tasted the triumphs of the stage. He had won a measure of fame as a singer. His home life had been happy. And now death had come for him. While he was yet in the prime of manhood, with success still sweet in his mouth, the curtain was falling—and forever.
>
> The other windows of the hospital were dark. In this one alone a light burned. And below it, outside in the darkness, shivering with cold and numbed with fear, a child stood sobbing. He had been told that there was no hope, but his wild heart prayed for the miracle that could not happen, even while he waited for the light to go out and the compassionate hesitations that would tell him his father was no more. The dying man and the child outside the window both bore the same name—Charles Chaplin.[88]

The single light that will soon be extinguished leaving a child sobbing alone in the cold darkness of bereavement—and implausibly leaving a large London hospital showing no illumination at all from within—is an unlikely detail whose symbolism would be more effective on screen than it is on the printed page. A film would move on from this scene, taking the audience's attention with it. Readers may pause to wonder why there aren't a few other lighted windows.

Nevertheless the melodramatic beginning does arouse curiosity about how the boy's story—and the essay—will develop. Churchill's next paragraph switches away from his storytelling and scenario-writing mode toward analytical reflections on the social, psychological, and artistic consequences of hardship. The transition is a platitudinous but undeniable generalization about the inscrutability of individual fate: "Destiny shifts us here and there upon the chequerboard of life, and we know not the purpose behind the moves." Churchill then considers the formative influence of Chaplin's childhood poverty as an illustration of the more interesting propositions that "poverty is not a life sentence. It is a challenge. To some it is more—it is an opportunity." Churchill explains that thanks

to young Chaplin's genius for observation his predicament was turned
to good advantage: "In the kaleidoscopic life of London's mean streets
he found tragedy and comedy—and learned that their springs lie side by
side. He knew the problems of the poor, not from the aloof angle of the
social investigator, but at first hand." Churchill then compares Chaplin's
start in life with the early days of Charles Dickens and Mark Twain: "Both
[Dickens and Chaplin] knew hardness in childhood. Both made their
misfortunes stepping-stones to success. They developed along different
lines, chose different mediums of expression, but both quarried in the
same rich mine of common life and found there treasure of laughter and
drama for the delight of all mankind. Mark Twain, left fatherless at twelve,
had substantially the same experience, though in a different setting. He
would never have written *Huckleberry Finn* had life been kinder in his
youth."[89] We can only speculate on whether Twain talked about his youth
with Churchill when they met in 1900 while he was on an American
speaking tour and at his first lecture was introduced by Twain. Of their
meeting Churchill in *My Early Life* reports merely that despite a disagreement about the Boer War, he "did not displease" Twain, who autographed each volume of a set of his works that Churchill brought along
for the famous writer to sign. Churchill ruefully adds that "to convey a
gentle admonition" Twain inscribed in the first volume the maxim "To
do good is noble; to teach others to do good is nobler, and no trouble."[90]
However Churchill learned about Twain's start in life, his being "left
fatherless" is what struck the deepest chord, impelling in "Everybody's
Language" an imaginative leap of empathy that brings Twain into the
company of Dickens, Chaplin, and by implication Churchill himself.
Those familiar with Churchill's own youth (as by 1935 many were thanks
to his 1930 autobiography) might recall that his father Lord Randolph
Churchill died when Winston was twenty-one years old.

Without any allusion to Lord Randolph's death, however, Churchill
in "Everybody's Language" switches his theme from the death of fathers
back to the wider topic of how talented people can make "their misfortunes stepping-stones to success." From poverty as experienced by
Dickens, Chaplin, and Twain, Churchill leaps to a rather distantly related
order of adversity:

> Genius is essentially a hardy plant. It thrives in the east wind. It
> withers in a hothouse. That is, I believe, true in every walk of life.

> The reason the historic English families have produced so many
> men of distinction is that, on the whole, they have borne great re-
> sponsibilities rather than enjoyed great wealth. Their younger sons,
> especially, have usually had to make their own way in the world, to
> stand on their own feet, to rely on their own merits and their own
> efforts. I am glad that I had to earn my living from the time that I
> was a young man. Had I been born heir to millions I should cer-
> tainly have had a less interesting life.[91]

This reflection tails off anticlimactically to Churchill's modest conclusion that with more money his life would have been "less interesting."
Nevertheless he has managed to include himself among the "men of distinction" and "Genius" whose accomplishments have been spurred by
lack of money (or at least lack of millions). That point made, he gets back
to Chaplin.

Churchill identifies the attributes of Chaplin's famous tramp as a
consequence of the actor's experiences in America where society is less
rigidly stratified ("more fluid") than in England, and where especially
"the American hobo of twenty-five years ago" when Chaplin first arrived
was "not so much an outcast from society as a rebel against it." It is this
American ethos that Churchill finds reflected in Chaplin's screen persona:
"His portrayal of the underdog is definitely American rather than British.
The English working man has courage in plenty, but those whom prolonged unemployment has forced on the road are nowadays usually broke
and despairing. The Chaplin tramp has a quality of defiance and disdain." After surveying Chaplin's film career from its outset and dwelling
with approval on his "dream to play tragic roles as well as comic ones,"
Churchill identifies the unique predicament created for Chaplin the master of pantomime by the advent of sound: "Had it not been for the coming of the talkies, we would already have seen this great star in a serious
role. He is the one figure of the old silent screen to whom the triumph
of the spoken word has meant neither speech nor extinction. He relies,
as of old, upon the pantomime that is more expressive than talk . . . . It
is the supreme achievement of Mr Chaplin that he has revived in modern times one of the great arts of the ancient world." Churchill notes that
"the golden age of pantomime was under the early Caesars." He adds that
"Augustus himself . . . is sometimes credited with its invention" and then
by way of comic relief remarks that "Nero practiced it, as he wrote poetry,

as a relaxation from the more serious pursuits of lust, incendiarism and gluttony." The greatness of pantomime as an art in the ancient world stemmed in Churchill's view not from the eminence of its amateurs, however, but from the fact that its many less conspicuous devotees "gave their whole lives to acting in dumb show, till they had mastered the last potentialities of expression in movement and gesture." It is in this worthy tradition of serious artists that he locates Chaplin to reinforce insistence that "no mere clown, however brilliant, could ever have captured so completely the affections of the great public. He owes his unrivalled position as a star to the fact that he is a great actor, who can tug at our heartstrings as surely as he compels our laughter."[92]

Where "Everybody's Language" becomes decidedly more original is in Churchill's argument that film history might have taken a different turn instead of so completely discarding silent movies, and that studios should still produce them as well as talkies, although for separate audiences. At the moment of transition to sound, Churchill suggests, Americans who dominated the film industry overlooked a viable possibility: "Had their producers and stars learned from Chaplin and the Europeans, the silent screen might have defied the talkies. The sound picture would have come just the same, but it would not have scooped the pool."[93] Churchill is always aware of the contingency of events, and hence willing to invite speculation about what might have been. But even in 1935 (let alone now) what actually happened to movies after the advent of sound could only render implausible an alternative history in which sound and silent films coexist in anything like equal numbers and with anything like equal significance.

The interest of Churchill's essay rises in proportion to the resistance its readers are likely to feel on this point. His mode switches from analysis to argument defending a thesis that he knows to be going against the grain and perhaps relishes the more on that account: "If we are ever to realize to the full the art of the cinema, I believe that it may be necessary deliberately to limit the mechanical aids we now employ so freely. I should like to see films without voices being made once more, but this time by producers who are alive to the potentialities of pantomime. Such pictures would be worth making, if only for this reason, that the audience for a talkie is necessarily limited by the factor of language, while the silent film can tell its story to the whole of the human race. Pantomime is the true universal tongue."[94] This is Churchill's version of the Enlightenment dream of a universal language. No doubt he would have preferred English. He recognizes, however, that there is simply too much linguistic diversity, especially "throughout Asia and Africa," for any spoken language to prevail: "There are millions of people whose mother tongue will never be heard in any cinema and who understand thoroughly no other speech."[95] Eight years later in his 1943 Harvard address on Anglo-American unity, after noting the very real war-making advantages derived by England and America from the "gift of a common tongue," Churchill toyed in a more utopian vein with the idea of Basic English becoming the world's new lingua franca: "It would certainly be a grand convenience for us all to be able to move freely about the world . . . and be able to find everywhere a medium, albeit primitive, of intercourse and understanding. Might it not also be an advantage to many races, and an aid to the building-up of our new structure for preserving peace?"[96] The hesitant tone of this second sentence that is a question rather than a statement suggests at once the noble possibility that even a primitive universal language might contribute to maintaining peace, and a doubt that any such thing will really happen.

In the 1935 essay "Everybody's Language" an unblushing imperialism—although on behalf of America as well as the British Empire—underlies Churchill's utopian vision of pantomime revived to become "the true universal tongue" thanks to modern film technology along with Chaplin's guiding genius as master teacher whose works can instruct the ancient art's new practitioners: "The English-speaking nations have here a great opportunity—and a great responsibility. The primitive mind thinks more easily in pictures than in words. The thing seen means more than the thing heard. The films which are shown amid the stillness of the African tropical night or under the skies of Asia may determine, in the long run, the fate of empires and civilizations. They will promote, or destroy, the prestige by which the white man maintains his precarious supremacy amid the teeming multitudes of black and brown and yellow."[97] Churchill's belief in the importance of maintaining white supremacy over "the primitive mind" of Asians and Africans is a Victorian attitude that he assumes (no doubt correctly) will be shared by most of his 1935 readers. I hope there is no need to dwell on the differences between his Kiplingesque ideas of economic and cultural supremacy maintained (in theory) for civilizing purposes and that virulent Nazi racism which Churchill even then was eloquently denouncing. Of more significance than the obsolescent Victorian outlook that Churchill manifests here is his forward-looking and far less widely shared understanding that "the white man" has only a "precarious supremacy" and that films may do more than wars to "determine, in the long run, the fate of empires and civilizations."

In affirming the political importance of both ideas and methods for impressing them upon the world's "teeming multitudes" via images ("in pictures"), Churchill anticipates the most striking statement of his 1943 Harvard address: "The empires of the future are the empires of the mind."[98] This prediction rings true and is easier to understand in the twenty-first century. Churchill is ahead of his time in appreciating how "empires of the mind" will prevail over older forms of imperialism. Before the twentieth century's midpoint the man who in 1895 had received from Queen Victoria his commission as a cavalry officer understood better than most then or even now that new modes of communication were undermining and would eventually topple empires of the kind he had served in Victoria's heyday. His recognition of the forces shaping cultural and political change in the twentieth century did not stop Churchill from struggling vainly throughout his life to preserve intact what remained of the old-style British Empire. Famously, however, this "child of the Victorian era" (as Churchill described himself in 1930) was to fight his most important battles not on horseback, in the trenches, or even at the Admiralty in command of the world's greatest navy, but at a BBC microphone.[99] While those battles were certainly for his country and its empire, his speeches were to a far greater extent (as his Nobel Prize citation describes them) oratory "defending exalted human values." It was to be via words not pictures that Churchill sought to preserve and extend those democratic ideals that he knew could sustain an empire of the most viable kind: an empire of the mind.

After further discussion of Chaplin's films and his yearning to get away from comedy, which because of "the world's need for laughter" Churchill hopes Chaplin will not forsake altogether, "Everybody's Language" winds up with Churchill's hopeful but hesitant prediction that "the future of Charlie Chaplin may lie mainly in the portrayal of serious roles in silent, or rather, non-talking films, and in the development of a universal cinema." Churchill's conditional phrase concedes that in fact this may not be what lies ahead for Chaplin. But in any case such a "universal cinema," though devoid of dialogue, could include as "accessories" music and "natural sounds." Such films could be shown "without any serious weakening of their appeal, in cinemas which were not wired for sound." Thus by the completion of his apprenticeship with Korda Churchill believed that sound effects and music, though not indispensable, do add to a film's "appeal." This is primarily an aesthetic dimension that would attract audiences and in that way indirectly but only indirectly help convey whatever messages are embodied in the universal language of the actors' pantomime. As Churchill concludes "Everybody's Language" its focus shifts back to artistic issues and away from the awesome possibility that movies "may determine . . . the fate of empires and of civilizations." Without dwelling further on that "great responsibility," and without prescribing any particular political messages to be promulgated, Churchill assures readers that "if Mr Chaplin makes pictures of this kind . . . he will not only increase his already great reputation, but he will blaze a trail which other will follow, and add enormously to the range of cinematic art."[100] By "films of this kind" Churchill means the "silent or rather non-talking" movies that he has defined as a new genre falling between the old entirely silent movies and the new talkies.

His definition is precise. It is a workable generic formula that has occasionally occurred independently to others but rarely been put to use. A brilliant example approximating Churchill's "non-talking" kind of movie, though of course not indebted to his suggestion, is Cornel Wilde's 1966 *The Naked Prey*. Such a tour de force is not easy to bring off, if only because it flies in the face of audience expectations for dialogue. Churchill is well aware that his suggestion defies what by 1935 was already conventional wisdom about movies:

> It is a favourite cliché of film critics, in discussing talking pictures, to say that we cannot go back. In effect, they suggest that, because technical progress has given us sound, all films must be talkies and will continue to be so for ever. Such statements reveal a radical misconception of the nature of progress and the nature of art. As well say that, because there is painting in oils, there must be no etchings; or that because speech is an integral part of a stage play, dialogue must be added to ballet. To explore the possibilities of the non-talking film, to make of it a new and individual art form, would not be a retrograde step, but an advance.[101]

Churchill's disdain for "film critics" locked into their clichés reflects his involvement with Korda's studio as an insider helping to make movies and no longer just a passive spectator of the finished products. As usual in so many other spheres, Churchill has thought for himself, arrived at an unpopular position, and is willing to stand by his own conclusions while vigorously defending them via cogent argument that compels serious consideration of the issues if not agreement. There is no way to tell whether he would have written "Everybody's Language" as it now stands had he not worked for Korda. By the end of Churchill's involvement with London Film Productions and surely not coincidentally, however, he had achieved far more than an average moviegoer's understanding of cinematic art. Though in this field he does not deserve the accolade of highly gifted amateur earned by his efforts as a painter, Churchill nevertheless was by 1935 certainly a remarkably well-informed film critic and a far from inexperienced scriptwriter. He could look at movies with what he would have called comprehending eyes.

IMAGINING SCENES:
THE STORY OF THE MALAKAND FIELD FORCE AND *SAVROLA*

Although Churchill did not take up painting as a hobby until he was forty years old, a catalogue of this energetic amateur's output lists over five hundred works.[1] Many of them are on display in Churchill's studio at Chartwell. There have been exhibitions of his paintings in England, North America, Australia, and New Zealand.[2] Over fifty color reproductions illustrate Lady Soames's account of his life as a painter.[3] In 1948 he was elected Honorary Academician Extraordinary by the Royal Academy. Churchill's 1948 *Painting as a Pastime* "was an instant success and had the widest circulation of any of his post-war single volume works."[4] Illustrated with some of his paintings, this perennial favorite has been reprinted several times, most recently in a beautiful Levenger Press edition in 2002, and translated into Finnish, French, German, and Japanese. Its text combines "Painting as a Pastime," first published in the December 1921-January 1922 issue of *Strand Magazine*, and "Hobbies," first published in the December 1925 issue of *Nash's Pall Mall*. These essays were given further currency by inclusion in *Thoughts and Adventures* in 1932, in its many subsequent printings in Britain and the United States, and in translations of *Thoughts and Adventures* into Danish, French, German, Korean, Spanish, and Swedish.[5] In "Painting as a Pastime" Churchill recounts his first steps "upon the pathway of painting" partly to encourage readers to follow his example: "Try it, then, before it is too late and before you mock at me."[6]

In the resounding first sentence of "Painting as a Pastime" Churchill stresses the dramatic and sudden nature of his belated engagement "with paints, palettes and canvases": "To have reached the age of forty without ever handling a brush or fiddling with a pencil, to have regarded with mature eye the painting of pictures of any kind as a mystery, to have stood agape before the chalk of the pavement artist, and then suddenly to find oneself plunged in the middle of a new and intense form of interest and action with paints and palettes and canvases, and not to be discouraged by results, is an astonishing and enriching experience."[7] As Churchill piles up his parallel clauses ("to have reached. . . . to have regarded. . . . to have stood. . . . Then suddenly to find"), he achieves a lighthearted echo of those accounts of religious conversion that have been a staple of autobiography since Augustine's *Confessions*. Like any convert telling how his life "suddenly" changed for the better, Churchill's stance is that of an erstwhile benighted outsider to whom in an "astonishing . . . experience" what was once "a mystery" is now understood, thus creating a better (an "enriching") way of life. By including an implausible image of himself standing in wonderment "agape before the chalk of the pavement artist" Churchill comically enhances the sense of an absolute dividing line between a passive preconversion existence without any understanding of even the lowest manifestation of art and his postconversion transformation into a person zealously engaged in "a new and intense form of . . . action" who now writes to win over more converts.

This impression of almost miraculous instant transformation from ignorant "before" to enlightened "after" is further enhanced by Churchill's amusing account of his first feeble attempt at painting in 1915. After his initial efforts had succeeded only in making on the canvas nothing more than "a mark about as big as a bean," he was cured of his "so halting, indeed so cataleptic" state by the unanticipated intervention of a deus ex machina in the form of Sir John Lavery's wife:

> At that moment the loud approaching sound of a motor-car was heard in the drive. From this chariot there stepped swiftly and lightly none other than the gifted wife of Sir John Lavery. "Painting! But what are you hesitating about? Let me have a brush—the big one." Splash into the turpentine, wallop into the blue and the white, frantic flourish on the palette—clean no longer—and then several large, fierce strokes and slashes of blue on the absolutely cowering canvas. Anyone could see that it could not hit back. No evil fate avenged the jaunty violence. The canvas grinned in helplessness before me. The spell was broken. The sickly inhibitions rolled away.

I seized the largest brush and fell upon my victim with Berserk fury. I have never felt any awe of a canvas since.[8]

By identifying her vehicle as "a motor-car" and then calling it by the archaic term "chariot," Churchill creates an implied image of Mrs. Lavery as a goddess descending in this machine to initiate him into the mysteries of painting. She frees him from "sickly inhibitions" that amounted to a comically malign enchantment holding him in thrall: "The spell was broken." Henceforward he is an adept, although (as he insists with charmingly uncharacteristic modesty) only a humble one by comparison with the real masters. Throughout the essay he is also at pains to show that at last he can intelligently appreciate them because, thanks to Mrs. Lavery's spell-breaking manifestation as muse at the crucial moment, he has set out to follow the great painters, however distantly, "upon the pathway of painting." By thus dwelling on his tardy conversion from gaping spectator to active artist, "Painting as a Pastime" suggests that Churchill had little interest in art or understanding of it before he himself took up painting as a hobby.

This impression may be strengthened for any reader who notices how the older postconversion Churchill quietly corrects a mistaken reference to art made years before. In his 1899 book *The River War* Churchill recalls that while on advanced patrol at the outset of the Battle of Omdurman he had witnessed from horseback the entire Dervish army advancing to attack, and found "most striking of all" the sight of its "centre, commanded by Yakub," over which "the sacred Black banner of the Khalifa floated high and remarkable": "They could not have mustered less than 6000. Their array was perfect. They displayed a great number of flags— perhaps 500—which looked at the distance white, though they were really covered with texts from the Koran, and which by their admirable alignment made this division of the Khalifa's army look like the old representations of the Crusaders in the Bayeux tapestry."[9] Of course the Bayeux tapestry shows not crusaders but William the Conqueror's army campaigning against England. For his later account of the Battle of Omdurman in *My Early Life*—published in 1930, fifteen years after he had taken up painting—Churchill rectifies his allusion to the Bayeux tapestry in *The River War* but retains a comparison of the Dervish army to medieval warriors via a different reference to the crusaders. In *My Early Life* Churchill remarks of the "6000 men" at the center of the advancing enemy army: "I called these Dervishes 'The White Flags.' They reminded me of the armies in the Bayeux tapestries, because of their rows of white and yellow standards held upright." In the first part of his chapter on the battle Churchill switches to present tense for immediacy, compresses his description of its opening phase as the Dervish army advances, and identifies his *own* side with crusaders not in appearance but because the British were seeing (and about to fight) Islamic foes identical in appearance and outlook to those the crusaders had confronted: "The masses have defined themselves into swarms of men, in ordered ranks bright with glittering weapons, and above them dance a multitude of gorgeous flags. We see for ourselves what the Crusaders saw."[10] Here Churchill invites readers to perform a twofold imaginative leap of envisioning how the Dervish army looked to him and his comrades in arms that morning in 1898 while also understanding that what they saw—"the successors of the Saracens"— would have looked exactly the same hundreds of years earlier.

He thereby stresses that "ancient and modern confronted one another" at the Battle of Omdurman: "The weapons, the methods and the fanaticism of the Middle Ages were brought by an extraordinary anachronism into dire collision with the organisation and inventions of the nineteenth century."[11] This underscores Churchill's observation that "nothing like the Battle of Omdurman will ever be seen again. It was the last link in the long chain of those spectacular conflicts whose vivid and majestic splendour has done so much to invest war with glamour."[12] As a historian Churchill had to devise ways of describing "spectacular" scenes like the Battle of Omdurman and also later varieties of warfare that were hideously divested of glamour and impossible to take in at a glance as spectacle, but not therefore without interest or importance. Nor were challenges to his descriptive powers limited to such topics. Like all writers he had to find imaginatively effective ways of portraying places, people, and events. Despite his late debut as a painter, despite his professions of earlier ignorance about artistic techniques, and despite occasional mistakes when referring to particular works of art, at the outset of his career as an author Churchill was inclined to invite imagination of scenes as they might be depicted in a painting. He often arranged episodes and parts of episodes as though they were pictures. He described many of his narrative procedures—and even suggested ways of reading his narratives—by metaphors involving painting. In the medium of words he thus aimed at many effects of painting.

⌒

Churchill's early awareness of art derived partly from instruction and viewing opportunities but mainly from the fact that he grew up and turned seriously to writing during the golden age of book illustration. At Blenheim Palace as at other upper-crust residences where Lord Randolph Churchill's son had entrée, paintings formed a backdrop to his social life and must sometimes have attracted at least his casual notice. There were probably a few visits, however unwilling, to museums and art exhibitions. If so, they did not rate special comment in his letters and memoirs. He received instruction in drawing while at Kate and Charlotte Thomson's school in Brighton from 1884 to 1888, age ten to fourteen. A report dated April 1885 shows that in drawing during spring term that year he ranked eighth out of a class of eighteen.[13] At Harrow he enjoyed drawing. But as he explained in a January 1890 letter to his mother, he was motivated to sign up for lessons because he might thereby pile up in the "further" exam Army Class points that could help him toward admission to Sandhurst, and because he had been sternly rebuked by Lord Randolph for wasting time in singing class: "I am very anxious to learn drawing. Papa said he thought singing was a waste of time, so I left the singing class & commenced drawing. But Mr Davidson said that it was one thing to 'take drawing lessons' & another to 'Learn Drawing' I get now an hour & a half a week & if I had another hour with the army class boys who learn Drawing in the Evening I am sure I should get on, as you know I like it. Drawing count [sic] 1200 marks in the further & every mark is useful."[14] This pragmatic surrender to Lord Randolph's disdain for singing is ironic because in later life it was the Harrow songs about which Churchill waxed most sentimental at appearances there, and which he regarded as the school's finest feature: "I enjoyed the Harrow songs. They have an incomparable book of school songs. At intervals we used to gather in the Speech Room or even in our own Houses, and sing these splendid and famous choruses. I believe these songs are the greatest treasure that Harrow possesses."[15] Writing again to his mother on March 12, 1890, Churchill describes his drawing exercises at Harrow: "I am getting on in drawing and I like it very much. I am going to begin shading in Sepia tomorrow. I have been drawing little Landscapes and Bridges and those sorts of things."[16] After he took up painting Churchill's canvases mostly depicted landscape scenes. I cannot tell how far that bent was facilitated by his early lessons. There was probably little carryover from his Harrovian drawings to his adult quasi-impressionist oil paintings. Churchill by his own admission never excelled as a draftsman. The small ink sketches on many of his surviving letters are charming but hardly suggest that he was a star pupil in drawing class. His lessons, however, including as they did experiments with sepia shading, must have heightened his awareness of forms and shadings of color in the world around him.

In his Army Class, drawing was divided into geometrical drawing and freehand drawing, graded separately, with the former more useful because it was preparation for required courses in mapmaking at Sandhurst. In this he did well. Writing to his mother from Bangalore on February 2, 1898, Lieutenant Churchill of the 4th Queen's Own Hussars, as he then was, apologized boastfully for sending only "a short letter" because "as I am a better sketcher than most of the subalterns all the reconnaisance [sic] sketching falls on me. I have ridden nearly forty miles this day map making."[17] This kind of sketching results in topographical features delineated on what was termed a sketch map, not perspective drawings designed to suggest a three-dimensional view from some vantage point. In correspondence with his parents from Harrow, drawing fades away with tight-lipped reports on Churchill's hard but eventually victorious struggle to master geometrical drawing. The nadir of this battle is a gloomy remark to Lord Randolph probably written on June 8, 1890: "I am not going in for my Preliminary this term as I am not strong enough in Geometrical drawing."[18] Perhaps the difficulty was somehow related to the fact that geometrical drawing curbs the imagination in favor of a premium on accuracy. Writing to his mother in November 1890 Churchill reports himself "very hard at work" for the exam, "sure of English," "nearly sure" of geography, Euclid, and French, and confident he "can work up Geometrical drawing."[19] After taking his preliminary exam for Sandhurst but before hearing the good news that he had passed in all subjects, Churchill in a letter postmarked December 10, 1890, reported to his mother "a very successful day" in which he can say he passed English and Geography "& I should [not] be at all surprised if I passed in Geometrical Drawing."[20]

Inevitably looming more frequently in Churchill's early experiences than drawing lessons were illustrated books, magazines, and newspapers as he held them in his hands, perused their texts, and looked at their pictures. There is no record of all the books he read before commencing as author, but he must have encountered a great many illustrated editions. In his essay "Cartoons and Cartoonists" he relates the lasting impact on himself and on other schoolboys of the political art in Punch:

I always loved cartoons. At my private school at Brighton there were three or four volumes of cartoons from *Punch*, and on Sundays we were allowed to study them. This was a very good way of learning history, or at any rate of learning something. Here, week after week, all the salient events of the world were portrayed in caricature, sometimes grave and sometimes gay. The responsibility of Sir John Tenniel and other famous cartoonists must be very great. Many are the youthful eyes that have rested upon their designs, and many the lifelong impressions formed thereby.[21]

Perhaps included in the "something" that Churchill absorbed in addition to or instead of history from the illustrations of famous artists like Tenniel was an intuitive appreciation of what made for an effective picture. In cartoons the disposition of elements in a composition is easier to appreciate than in most other modes of art.

In "Cartoons and Cartoonists" Churchill includes and discusses a Tenniel cartoon for *Punch* on the American Civil War showing North and South as "two savage, haggard men in shirts and breeches, grappling and stabbing each other with knives as they reeled into an abyss called Bankruptcy." Churchill mentions that "in later volumes and later years" he "saw the most famous of all cartoons—Tenniel's 'Dropping the Pilot,'" occasioned by Kaiser Wilhelm's dismissal of Bismarck in 1890.[22] At the conclusion of his essay on cartoons Churchill praises the "fierce and terrible" cartoons of Louis Raemakers, who was "able to put into his drawings a passion of protest and scorn which no words, spoken or written, could ever convey." This is a generous tribute from a man whose career depended upon mastery of spoken and written words. This praise even hints that Churchill longs for some verbal method of conveying political emotions as effectively and economically as an artist like Raemakers could do visually. More surprisingly, Churchill singles out Max Beerbohm as another artist who "has also great dramatic power." Of Beerbohm's series depicting "the last hundred years" of Franco-German relationships Churchill remarks that "in twelve pages of drawings the history of a terrible century is laid bare so plainly that everyone can feel it, and so profoundly that even the most deeply-instructed person finds his imagination and memories stirred."[23] Thus for Churchill one measure of success in political art—and by implication also in political writing including history is stimulation of appropriate emotions and reawakening of accurate memories together with a less well-defined but equally important stirring of those ideas and images that comprise imagination as it brings home to vivid awareness current or past events.

As photography, movies, and television rose to prominence in the twentieth century, books illustrated with specially drawn or painted pictures dwindled in numbers and became increasingly associated with children's literature. It was otherwise in the nineteenth century. A large proportion of book illustrations were the handiwork of artists rather than photographers. By 1865 when *Alice in Wonderland* was published—with illustrations by one of Churchill's favorites, John Tenniel—its opening sentence recounting Alice's exasperation with her sister's unillustrated book would have seemed at once amusing and altogether reasonable: "Alice was beginning to get very tired of sitting by her sister on the bank, and of having nothing to do; once or twice she had peeped into the book her sister was reading, but it had no pictures or conversations in it, 'and what is the use of a book,' thought Alice, 'without pictures or conversations?'"[24] About illustrations, Churchill when young, surely agreed.

———————— ⨍⨍ ————————

Churchill was eager to get illustrations for his first book, *The Story of the Malakand Field Force: An Episode of Frontier War*. Writing to his mother, Lady Randolph Churchill, on November 17, 1897, Churchill announced that "the book is to be dedicated to Sir Bindon Blood whose photograph will form the frontispiece." Churchill also disclosed that he had "asked Major Hobday—a most skilful [*sic*] artist who witnessed all the operations—to illustrate it." Practical as he was always to be about the commercial aspects of publishing, he also asked his mother to find out for him "some details as to what the usual division of profit between author & artist should be."[25] But this became irrelevant because, as Churchill soon discovered and reported to his mother in a letter dated November 24, 1897, Lord Fincastle was writing his own account of the Malakand expedition and got to Hobday first: "I hear Ld Fincastle is also writing one and has received the pictures I had hoped to obtain."[26] Here was a sorry turnabout to a relationship that according to Churchill had started nicely enough a few months earlier when he and Fincastle "made great friends" and shared their affinity for exotic hats: "I tried on Fincastle's fez;—I look splendid!"[27] Setting their caps for authorship was not so friendly. Only three years older than Churchill, but already aide-de-camp to Major-General

Sir Bindon Blood, commander of the Malakand Field Force, Alexander Edward, Viscount Fincastle, was, like Churchill, a cavalry lieutenant also acting as a war correspondent. Fincastle wrote for the *Times*. Applying too late for that choice appointment, Churchill had to settle for the *Daily Telegraph* at what he considered an unsatisfactory compensation for writing such as his: "I recd [*sic*] today from the D.T. a cheque for Rs 1,238— about £80 at the current rate of exchange. I think they are most mean— and that the reward is altogether inadequate to the value or interest of the letters."[28]

Fincastle's lese majesty in embarking as a rival historian of the campaign is a leitmotif of Churchill's letters from India to Lady Randolph concerning *The Malakand Field Force* during the run-up to its publication: "He has not treated me with much consideration in the matter as he knew I was contemplating writing and might at least have informed me that he wanted to tell the tale." Churchill unconvincingly adds in this letter of November 24, 1897, that had Fincastle notified him he "would have given way" to concentrate instead on writing *Savrola* "as the novel filled & still fills my mind."[29] A few days later he complains again to Lady Randolph, warming to the subject of his rival's defects: "Fincastle has not altogether treated me civilly in the matter & he has neither answered my letters nor informed me of his intention to write an account. With many qualities he is not a good sort. I shall not give way."[30] Perhaps adding to Churchill's irritation was the fact that Fincastle had been awarded the Victoria Cross, whereas Churchill had to be content with a campaign medal and mention in despatches for making himself "useful at a critical moment."[31] While negotiating on his behalf with publishers, his mother tried to soothe Winston: "I think it is very tiresome about Ld Fincastle but I'm told he is a dull dog—you must be first in the field, that is all."[32]

Loss of the pictures still rankled when Churchill wrote to Lady Randolph on January 5, 1898: "Pictures I have not been able to get. Fincastle has secured those excellent ones I wanted."[33] Writing only two weeks later he mentioned the loss again, surely to vent his own exasperation, not because his very far from senile mother was likely to have forgotten the matter so quickly: "There are no pictures. They had already been secured." After this now familiar lament he proceeded to brisk instruction about the other kind of illustration (apart from the frontispiece photogravure) that remained available to him: "The maps should be shown to a skillful cartographer & carefully revised."[34] Scrupulous attention to securing accurate and expertly made maps of important stages of a campaign is a feature of Churchill's military histories. Cartography always remained dear to the heart of this ex-cavalry officer who had once excelled in riding about to sketch reconnaissance maps. Wherever maps could be useful he took pains to have them provided.

In the preface to his second military history, *The River War*, Churchill alerts readers to his care in assembling the most accurate available information for cartographic illustrations, to the importance of his maps (of which there are thirty-four in the two volumes), and to the importance of maps in general:

> The maps and plans are the most expensive—perhaps the most valuable—part of these volumes. For their topographical features I am indebted to the Director of Military Intelligence. The positions and movements of the troops are taken from the statements and diagrams of my various informants. I have every reason to believe them correct. It is of course absolutely impossible for anyone to understand a campaign or an action without continually referring to the map, and I trust that the reader will not be irritated by my repeated exhortations to him to do so.[35]

This insistence that attention to accurate cartography is the sine qua non of understanding campaigns and battles foreshadows the ascendancy of maps and charts in Churchill's later military histories. Attention to maps was a lifelong habit. He even had a "map room" at Chartwell (as few would have done in their house), and in the 1930s his first response to news from Europe was often to get out the maps. The thirty-four maps in *The River War*, however, compete for notice with seven full-page photogravure portraits of leading personalities involved in the Sudan campaign and with fifty drawings by Churchill's young fellow veteran of the Dervish war (also born in 1874), Lieutenant Angus John McNeill of the Seaforth Highlanders.

Despite—and perhaps because of—its profuse illustrations, Churchill's ardor for pictures had cooled while seeing into print *The River War*. In a letter to Lady Randolph dated from the Savoy Hotel in Cairo on April 3, 1899, Churchill disapproves of McNeill's work: "Mr McNeil [*sic*] has already gone back to England and is finishing up the sketches for the book. I do not think they are very good and Longman has reproduced them so small that you almost want a magnifying glass to make out what they mean. I shall be very curious to see what sort of pictures Jack Leslie has done."[36] If Churchill's "Uncle Jack" (Sir John) Leslie offered any pictures, they did not pass muster. Apparently faute de mieux—and probably at the publisher's advice that pictures would help sales or at least would be expected in such a book—McNeill's illustrations were put to use. Churchill acknowledges them in the *River War*'s preface with a polite but unenthusiastic single sentence that damns with faint praise: "I will not venture to pronounce upon the artistic value of the sketches with which Mr. McNeill has adorned the account: but I think that they are in every detail scrupulously accurate."[37] By relegating McNeill's pictures to mere adornments Churchill unmistakably implies that despite their scrupulous accuracy they are at best ornamental and thus (unlike the accurate maps) not indispensable aids to understanding his narrative. His refusal to say anything about "the artistic value of the sketches" leaves little doubt that he finds them mediocre.

No wonder. McNeill's illustrations are singularly unprepossessing. Only three, and those not the best, occupy an entire page. Although the rest are not quite so small and hard to make out as Churchill charges, they do break up his text without, in most cases, showing any scene closely or at all keyed to what Churchill writes about on or near the pages with pictures. Instead of adopting the usual nineteenth-century book illustrator's goal of aiming to depict as closely (or at least as imaginatively) as possible what is described in particular passages—often using sentences from a text as captions—McNeill provides what is more nearly an independent though related album of pictures showing typical sights en route to and including the Battle of Omdurman. McNeill's pictures complement Churchill's narrative but may have been seen by him as committing the cardinal sin of competing with it for attention and admiration. Henceforth he was wary about risking such competition.

No artist was ever again allowed by Churchill to provide a series of pictures for the debut of a book by him. The 1899 serialization of *Savrola* in *Macmillan's Magazine* had no illustrations. Nor did its first American and English editions in 1899 and 1900, although Churchill had tried to find an appropriate artist for at least a few pictures. It was not until 1908 that an illustrated edition of *Savrola* appeared with, however, only two pictures. These were probably supplied by the publishers without consulting Churchill, as happened with some of his other books after their first editions. His justly forgotten three-page short story "Man Overboard!" had three illustrations by Henry Austin when published in an 1899 issue of the *Harmsworth Monthly Pictorial Magazine*. Austin's melodramatic drawings are closely integrated with Churchill's narrative, and captioned accordingly with abbreviated versions of its text: "The Railing gave way, and he fell backwards into the sea with a splash"; "The light of the ship got smaller and smaller as he threw up his hands and sank"; and "Upright in the water, fifty yards away, was a black triangular object—a fin."[38] Like its protagonist, however, this story quickly sank out of sight, taking down with it Austin's pictures.

Steven Spurrier's five drawings illustrating "Fifty Years Hence" for its 1931 debut in the *Strand Magazine* were omitted when Churchill included this essay in *Thoughts and Adventures* the following year.[39] This book's only illustrations are a frontispiece photo of Churchill sitting brush in hand before an easel on which is one of his paintings in progress, and seven cartoons included to illustrate his essay "Cartoons and Cartoonists." Photographs illustrating *My African Journey*'s 1908 serialization in the *Strand Magazine* are mostly by Churchill and all closely related to his narrative.[40] When published as a book that same year *My African Journey*'s title page announced that it contains "sixty-one illustrations from photographs by the author and Lieutenant-Colonel Gordon Wilson, and three maps."[41] Photographs are captioned to indicate their subject but not the photographer. A few examples will suffice to suggest the ambience that the pictures enhance: "The Top of Murchison Falls"; "Nandi and Kavirondo Warriors at Kisumu"; "War-Dance at Kampala"; "Mr. Churchill on the Observation Ladder at Hippo Camp"; "Mr Churchill and Burchell's White Rhinoceros" (more helpfully captioned in the *Strand Magazine* "Mr. Churchill and a dead Burchell's White Rhinoceros," thus eliminating ambiguity over who shot the rhinoceros and its species); and for *My African Journey*'s frontispiece "Mr. Churchill and the Rhinoceros at Simba." There is small chance here of Wilson's photos deflecting attention from Churchill's account of Africa or (worse) from Churchill himself.

Equally firm integration of illustrations and text is apparent elsewhere. *Lord Randolph Churchill* (1906) is illustrated sparingly with photographs, cartoons, facsimiles of documents, and John Singer Sargent's sketch of Lady Randolph. *My Early Life* (1930) appeared with relevant photographs, plans, maps, a reprise of Sargent's sketch of Lady Randolph, a facsimile of the Boer poster offering a reward for Churchill's capture dead or alive, and as a sole example of war art, R. Caton Woodville's mediocre draw-ing (first printed in the September 24, 1898, issue of the *Illustrated News*) *The Charge of the 21st Lancers at Omdurman*. For the 1937 first edition of *Great Contemporaries* as well as its expanded 1938 edition with four more essays, only one photo of each person discussed is provided, although for prior magazine publication some essays were more profusely illustrated.[42] Churchill illustrated the first printings of *The World Crisis* volumes (1923–31) only with maps and charts. So too the six-volume first edition of *The Second World War* (1948–53) had maps but no pictures. With Churchill's approval its 1955 "Chartwell" edition was profusely illustrated with rele-vant photographs, a color frontispiece showing him in the uniform of an Elder Brother of Trinity House, and five other color frontispieces re-producing paintings of war scenes by various artists. In a note dated October 1, 1954, Churchill announces that "now a special edition is being published illustrated for the first time," thus putting his stamp of approval on the illustrations whether or not he selected them himself.[43] Repro-ductions of portrait paintings appear in the four-volume first edition of *Marlborough: His Life and Times* (1933–38), along with maps and facsimi-les of key documents. Here too maps are foremost among the illustrations because they enhance understanding of what Churchill considered most important about Marlborough's life: his campaigns.

———————— ❧ ————————

In *The Story of the Malakand Field Force* there are six maps. Two are multi-color foldout maps: "Map of N.W. Frontier of India, showing the Theater of the War" and "Map of the Operations in Bajaur." Four are black-and-white "sketch maps" of particular actions: "Sketch of the Malakand Camps"; "Rough Sketch of the Cavalry Action of 1st August"; "Sketch of the Mamund Valley—with plan of the Action of the 16th September"; and "Rough Sketch explaining the Attack upon Agrah, 30th September." Fincastle's *A Frontier Campaign: A Narrative of the Operatons of the Malakand and Buner Field Forces, 1897–1898* has sixteen illustrations but only one map: a far less helpful foldout monochrome map at a scale of one inch = four miles titled "Rough sketch map to show the operations in Swat, Bajaur and Buner." Using this map to follow Fincastle's narrative must have been hard for most civilians, and maybe for some Sandhurst graduates. Even without benefit of a course in military topography, readers can easily find much more information in the maps that Churchill supplied and directed his mother to have revised by an expert cartographer for *The Story of the Malakand Field Force*. In a letter to Lady Randolph before publication of either book about the Malakand campaign, Churchill hopefully anticipated comparisons to Fincastle's disadvantage: "I don't think Ld Fincastle has taken much trouble over his book. Some people have written one chapter, some another. Slipshod. But he never takes life seriously."[44] Churchill was either misinformed or (in a rare Falstaffian mood) inclined to exaggerate the number of his literary enemies. Fincastle had only one co-author, duly credited on the title page of *A Frontier Campaign*, which announces that it is "By the Viscount Fincastle, V.C., Lieutenant, 16th (Queen's) Lancers and P. C. Eliott-Lockhart, Lieutenant, 'Queen's Own' Corps of Guides."[45]

As for the elusive pictures whose loss Churchill took quite seriously enough, it must have been annoying to find approving mention of them a month later in a letter from Sir Bindon Blood even though his overall opinion of the rival book was more considerate of Churchill's sensibilities: "I also hear from Sir B.B. that his [Fincastle's] book is not good or well written though it contains many valuable facts and interesting pictures."[46] Wormwood and gall! Or so this report of "interesting pictures" may have seemed to Churchill, who had not yet seen Fincastle's book. Eventual inspection of it probably eased his mind about the pictures that got away. Only one of Fincastle's sixteen illustrations is signed by Hobday, the "most skillful artist" whose work Churchill admired and longed to secure: an ink drawing titled "Cavalry Reconaissance from Malakand." This shows in the foreground mounted British troops with lances upraised and dismounted troops firing at what in the picture's middle ground on the small page are tiny and indistinct enemy figures with a few flags, while in the background mountains rise above the hilly plain on which the action takes place, dwarfing the combatants.[47] The picture is not memorable but does allow appreciation of the terrain and the scope of this encounter involving about forty British troopers and a larger but (given the scale of the picture) uncountable number of enemies. Apart from this scene, Churchill's loss was not Fincastle's gain. Hobday reserved the rest of his drawings for his own book, *Sketches on Service during the Indian Frontier Campaigns of 1897*.[48] This is advertised on its title page as "Containing fifty-seven full-page engravings from original drawings, and fourteen photographic portraits of the commanding officers and their staffs."

Fincastle's other fifteen illustrations are by various hands: "Many . . . are due to Major Biddulph, 19th Bengal Lancers, Captain Hewett, Royal West

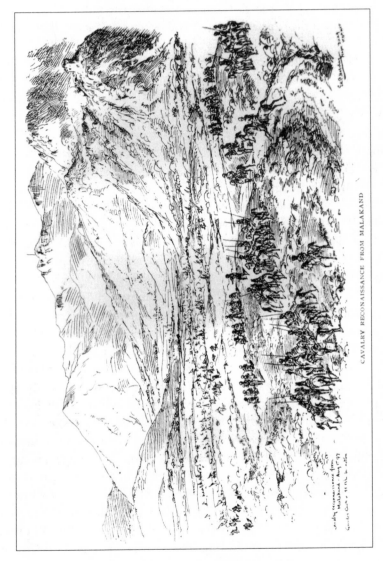

CAVALRY RECONNAISSANCE FROM MALAKAND

Figure 3. The one that got away: "Cavalry Reconnaissance from Malakand." A drawing by Major E. A. P. Hobday in *A Frontier Campaign: A Narrative of the Operations of the Malakand and Buner Field Forces, 1897–1898,* by Viscount A. E. Fincastle and P. C. Eliott-Lockhart. Private collection.

Kent, and Lieutenant Dixon, 16th Lancers, who by their kind contributions have endeavoured to lend an interest to a book which otherwise is merely a plain record of the part taken by the Malakand and Buner Field Forces in the recent Frontier Campaign."[49] Fincastle and Eliott-Lockhart's modesty about their "plain" narrative is altogether warranted. It is not analytical in its account of the campaign's strategy and blunders. Its explanation of the historical context is minimal. It makes little attempt to portray the mentality of frontier tribes or explain the clash of cultures sparking off their rebellion against British rule. Fincastle and Eliott-Lockhart sum up the rebellion as "the storm of fanaticism which ... was to sweep down the Swat Valley and hurl itself against our garrisons at Malakand and Chakdara."[50] Churchill devotes more thorough analytical attention to all these topics. He provides a more empathetic though hardly more approving explanation of the religious and secular motives of the rebellion. He places it as one among related conflicts in which "civilisation is confronted with militant Mahommedanism" with the result that "the forces of progress clash with those of reaction." His (and his implied reader's) side is of course that of progress and of Christianity as the superior faith: "The religion of blood and war is face to face with that of Peace." With irony worthy of his literary hero Gibbon (and of a kind absent from *A Frontier Campaign*), Churchill in his next sentence calls in question the English reader's likely assumption of moral superiority as an adherent of the less warlike faith: "Luckily the religion of peace is usually the better armed."[51]

Also in striking contrast to *The Story of the Malakand Field Force*, Fincastle and Eliott-Lockhart have only a few sentences describing the landscapes through which the army moved and on which it fought. Their descriptive terms are usually generic (e.g., "lofty snow-capped peaks in the distance"). Particular description was mostly left to those who contributed illustrations, perhaps because drawing was a popular pastime among the officers of this expedition (Churchill excepted). Of the "march up to Mingaora" through regions of the Upper Swat Valley "which had not been penetrated by a white man since the days of Alexander the Great," Fincastle and Eliott-Lockhart remark that "the numerous Buddhist ruins, and mountain landscapes showing lofty snow-capped peaks in the distance, gave plenty of occupation to both the amateur archaeologists and artists of our force."[52] Illustrations in *A Frontier Campaign* by some of these amateur artists depict typical moments during combat, landscapes with and without picturesque Buddhist ruins, and a few of the character types seen along the way. Among the latter are pictures of a fakir, a Malik (enemy tribal warrior), and a Sikh orderly smartly saluting. He is portrayed alone standing to attention facing the viewer holding the book, who is thus in the pleasing position of taking the salute. Among *A Frontier Campaign*'s military readers this scene surely stirred happy memories. Neither it nor the other pictures, including Hobday's, are notable as war art. But they are perfectly respectable book illustrations by the standards of the time.

No doubt Sir Bindon Blood was not alone in finding them of interest, perhaps especially so as a welcome relief from Fincastle and Eliott-Lockhart's "plain record." It is not clear from Churchill's summary of Sir Bindon's letter whether included among the pictures he found "interesting" was *A Frontier Campaign*'s frontispiece, which is a signed photograph of "Major General Sir Bindon Blood, K.C.B." This was the one picture that Fincastle and Eliott-Lockhart shared willy-nilly with Churchill, for whose book it also served (not autographed) as a frontispiece, with a more informative label eliminating any doubt about Sir Bindon's role in the campaign: "Major-General Sir Bindon Blood, K.C.B., Commanding Malakand Field Force." Hobday's *Sketches on Service* also features the same frontispiece portrait of Sir Bindon who, with admirable impartiality, apparently allowed publication of this image by any of his soldiers who requested it. He also graciously permitted Churchill to dedicate *The Story of the Malakand Field Force* to "Major-General Sir BINDON BLOOD, K.C.B., under whose command the operations therein recorded were carried out; by whose generalship they were brought to a successful conclusion; and to whose kindness the author is indebted for the most valuable and fascinating experience of his life."

Each frontispiece shows Sir Bindon as every inch the modern major-general circa 1890. With steel-gray hair and matching handlebar mustache, he stands in uniform gazing sternly ahead with eyes that are focused above the viewer as though concentrating on something far more interesting in the distance. His gloved left hand rests on his revolver holster and his gloved right hand rests on three bound volumes (perhaps war-diaries?). Unbuttoned and drawn back on his left side to reveal a crisp uniform and gleaming Sam Browne belt underneath, he wears the sheepskin coat then called a poshteen. With the sheep's wool facing inside, as usual for these coats, his poshteen is fur-trimmed and has elaborate ornamental designs embossed on its exterior. In a letter to Lady Randolph from India dated January 26, 1898, Churchill notes that receiving "Sir Bindon Blood's

Figure 4. "Major-General Sir Bindon Blood, K. C. B., Commanding Malakand Field Force." Frontispiece to Winston Spencer Churchill, *The Story of the Malakand Field Force*. This photo also appeared as frontispiece to Fincastle and Eliott-Lockhart's *A Frontier Campaign* and Major Hobday's *Sketches on Service During the Indian Frontier Campaigns of 1897*. Private collection.

photo . . . completes the materials" for his book. He adds: "I think the General looks vy [sic] fine in his 'poshteen' or warm coat wh [sic] all wear in the cold mornings on the frontier. I also remark with some amusement—that he is not superior to personal vanity. Who is?"[53] Who indeed? On this topic Churchill writes ex cathedra. But his observation was for Lady Randolph's eyes only. Churchill had no hesitation about risking whatever might smack of vanity in a twenty-four-year-old lieutenant fresh from Sandhurst hooking his literary star to Sir Bindon's reputation by dedicating a book to him and featuring a photo of him as, apart from maps, its only illustration.

──────── ☉ ────────

For *Savrola: A Tale of the Revolution in Laurania*, whose writing had been put aside while completing *The Story of the Malakand Field Force*, and to which he returned before his unwelcome and disillusioning association with McNeill's handiwork, Churchill wanted illustrations. He was perhaps all the more eager to commission them because of his failure to secure anything but a frontispiece and maps for his first book. Writing to Lady Randolph on June 1, 1898, from Bangalore with news that at last *Savrola* "is totally complete" he is emphatic about its need for pictures: "I must have some good illustrations."[54] In this letter he does not suggest any potential artists. In a letter dated the next day, probably in response to one received from Lady Randolph after the June 1st letter was written, Churchill is intrigued by the idea of securing illustrations from the famous French war artist and book illustrator Alphonse Marie de Neuville. With the letter of June 2, 1898, Churchill sent "the seven last chapters" of *Savrola*, an "altered contents table," and "a list of suggested illustrations." Unfortunately the list does not survive. In the letter Churchill remarks: "The de Neuville idea is worth thinking of. If he would draw the subaltern in mid air—£25 would vy [sic] cheap. It would be lithographed and reprinted by all the papers and from an advertising point of view would be an excellent business. Besides this it would add to the elegance of the book."[55] The idea of illustrations by de Neuville apparently came from Lady Randolph, or via her from *Savrola*'s publisher, Longmans, although Churchill is unclear on this point. Whatever its source, he knew enough about de Neuville's work to be exuberant about the publicity that would accrue from enlisting him. First, the moneymaking potential of a separately circulating scene from de Neuville's hand ("reprinted by all the papers") is highly appealing to the hardheaded business sense of the impecunious and extravagant young aspirant to literary fame and fortune. He suggests (or agrees) enthusiastically that "from an advertising point of view" the ideal episode in *Savrola* for de Neuville to illustrate is the exciting action of a daring escape from rooftop to rooftop under fire of young Lieutenant Tiro, who in the novel is one of the characters Churchill partly modeled on himself. Second, but far from an irrelevant afterthought, is Churchill's conviction that illustration by de Neuville "would add to the elegance of the book." Churchill here imagines in advance the kind of picture (or pictures) that de Neuville would provide if the artist's imagination, in turn, were fed with a narrative congenial to his special affinity for military subjects.

Churchill's conviction that such illustrations would make *Savrola* more elegant reflects not only his high estimate of de Neuville's art, but also widespread belief that illustration adds to the aesthetic appeal of any book if its pictures are at least of respectable quality. Illustrations, moreover, straddle the otherwise distinct categories of a book's contents and its quality as an aesthetic object. At the outset of his career Churchill was concerned to maximize the appeal of his books by making them attractive to look at as well as worthwhile to read. Of *The River War* he wrote to Lady Randolph on February 23, 1899, while he was finishing it up: "I propose to have it bound in blue & yellow . . . the colour and pattern of the medal ribbon which as you perhaps know is meant to represent the blue Nile flowing through the desert and hence is not unsuited to *The River War*. The bright colours will catch the eye and attract attention."[56] Here Churchill is equally concerned with a book's binding as symbolism and as advertising that will attract notice from potential buyers and readers. Churchill's publisher agreed. The two volumes of *The River War*'s first edition are indeed eye-catching. They are bound in dark blue-green with gilt decorations showing the Mahdi's tomb on each spine and a gunboat on each front cover. Perhaps this was some consolation to Churchill for his disappointment with McNeill's illustrations inside the book.

Savrola, however, had to make its debut without any illustrations because, unknown to Churchill or Lady Randolph when they corresponded about selecting an illustrator, Alphonse de Neuville had died thirteen years before, in 1885. Churchill did not find a substitute. Few if any available illustrators would have elicited from him anything like as much approval and enthusiasm as de Neuville had aroused. He was young Churchill's beau ideal of an artist. De Neuville's specialty was "military genre painting" characterized by "concern for topographical detail," precise depiction of uniforms and insignia, fondness for horses, "considerable talent for the rendering of horse and rider" in cavalry scenes, and a "gift for dramatizing the subject matter."[57] Actual and imaginary episodes of the Franco-Prussian War were his forte. He was also successful and much in demand as a book illustrator especially renowned for "graphically rendered scenes of Prussian brutality to accompany the texts of sensational novelettes" that inflamed French desire for revenge in the aftermath of the Franco-Prussian War.[58]

But de Neuville's work was not confined to that conflict. He copiously illustrated Jules Verne's *Twenty Thousand Leagues Under the Sea.* One of his best paintings, *La défense de Reorke's Drift* (The Defense of Rorke's Drift), shows a famous episode from the 1879 Zulu War in which, at the Battle of Rorke's Drift, about 120 British soldiers held out against thousands of Zulus fresh from their victory over some 1,700 British troops whom they killed at the Battle of Isandhlwana. On de Neuville's canvas, Zulu warriors are in the background mostly obscured by smoke from a burning building. In the foreground as the focus of attention in dramatic contrast to the dark smoke and indistinct Zulus are a small band of beleaguered British soldiers in vivid red coats defending their barricades. A few wear white pith helmets. Some wounded men are on the ground or being carried to shelter wearing only white shirts after their constricting red coats have been taken off. One soldier in center foreground comforts a white dog (or perhaps vice versa), thus illustrating English fondness for animals and de Neuville's kindred emotion. The white helmets, shirts, and dog also stand out in striking contrast to the dark mass of Zulus who blend anonymously into the smoky background. I do not know whether Churchill saw this glorification of the desperate though successful defense of Rorke's Drift by vastly outnumbered British troops. If so its attention to military details and its heroic presentation of British soldiers must have enhanced his admiration for de Neuville.

Surely Churchill saw at least reproductions of de Neuville's most well-known and widely circulated painting, *Les dernières cartouches* (The Last Cartridges). Another depiction of an actual episode, this one from the Franco-Prussian War, *Les dernières cartouches* was "the artist's most celebrated work, as well as the most famous painting dealing with the Franco-Prussian War. . . . here de Neuville isolated a handful of French soldiers during the battle of Sedan, making their last stand in a half-destroyed parlor in the village of Bazeilles."[59] In this interior scene a room in the foreground is occupied by seven soldiers. One is firing out of a window at the left through which a ray of light shines into the room's smoky atmosphere. Two soldiers standing near him gaze intently out the window from more sheltered vantage points. Two other soldiers crouched low behind him (one sitting on a crate) are busy taking stock of remaining weapons and ammunition. In the center a wounded (or perhaps dead) man lies propped up against a wall with a discarded rifle on the floor beyond his feet. At the extreme right another soldier stands disconsolately within easy reach of the rifle, but with his hands in his pockets, apparently out of ammunition. Visible in the center background through an open doorway to the next room are other soldiers highlighted by sunlight pouring through the (unseen) windows of that room. One man just beyond the doorway clutches with his right hand a wound in his left shoulder. The door between rooms is ripped off its hinges and propped against an alcove whose bullet-torn curtains are visible through panes of shattered and bullet-riddled glass in the upper half of the door. Unlike the defenders of Rorke's Drift, these French soldiers were defeated. But de Neuville equally glorifies their heroism in a scene that gains power from its evocation of a tragic outcome in a way that allowed *Les dernières cartouches* to establish "de Neuville's reputation as the painter of the anonymous but valiant soldier, fighting against the insurmountable odds which the French steadfastly believed had accounted for their defeat."[60] One art critic calls this aspect of de Neuville's oeuvre the Epic of Defeat.[61]

Whether or not Churchill's opinions about the Franco-Prussian War were influenced by such works, Churchill certainly took de Neuville's paintings as imaginative templates available for shaping both his memories and his manner of depicting scenes of combat. In *The Story of the Malakand Field Force*, Churchill sums up his account of how an outnumbered British contingent separated from the main force held out all night in the increasingly bullet and shell-torn ruins of a native village until relieved in the morning: "The whole scene, the close, desperate fighting, the carcasses of the mules, the officers and men crouching behind them, the flaming stacks of *bhoosa*, the flashes of the rifles, and over all and around all, the darkness of the night—is worthy of the pencil of De Neuville."[62] Churchill did not witness that defense against long odds. He was part of the relieving force that arrived in the morning. From the defenders, he

Alphonse de Neuville, *Les Dernières Cartouches* (1873). This poignant glorification of a heroic last stand by French marines at Bazeilles just before the Battle of Sedan during the Franco-Prussian War was de Neuville's most famous painting, and one of the most widely reproduced pictures in France up to 1914. His many similar combat scenes were almost equally well known. In *The Story of the Malakand Field Force* Churchill alludes to de Neuville's military art and takes such paintings as templates for narration of comparable episodes. De Neuville was also a profuse illustrator of books, including the first edition of Jules Verne's *Twenty Thousand Leagues Under the Sea*. After writing *Savrola* Churchill was enthusiastic about getting illustrations for it by de Neuville, but then discovered that the artist had died thirteen years previously. On canvas, however, Churchill never emulated de Neuville's methods of closely depicting soldiers in action. Apart from several pictures of the war-torn headquarters in Belgium where Churchill served during a World War I front-line interval commanding the 6th Battalion, Royal Scots Fusiliers, his own paintings, of which over five hundred survive, all show peaceful scenes, mainly tranquil landscapes. Picture courtesy of the Musée de la Dernière Cartouche, Bazeilles.

Winston Churchill: "Coast Scene on the Riviera," circa 1930. Courtesy of The Churchill Heritage. In the 1930s Churchill liked to paint Mediterranean seacoast scenes similar to the descriptions in *Savrola* of Laurania, the country he invented in that novel. It is as though he were drawn to seek analogs of his imaginary country in order to re-imagine it on canvas, although now depicting only its utopian physical beauty without any trace of its terrible political strife.

Winston Churchill: "View of Monte Carlo," circa 1930. Courtesy of the Churchill Heritage. Verbally creating a scene like this, Churchill in *Savrola* describes Laurania as his heroine, Lucile, sees it while looking out over the harbor from a balcony.

Winston Churchill: "Study of Boats," circa 1933. Courtesy of the Churchill Heritage. Had Churchill taken up painting earlier than he did, he might have supplied *Savrola* with passable illustrations of his own along the lines of this painting instead of trying, too late, to enlist Alphonse de Neuville. While writing the novel, however, Churchill thought the most effective illustrations would not be of Laurania's lovely waterfront, but of his tale's military action scenes, for which de Neuville would certainly have been an ideal illustrator.

reports, "Gradually we learnt the story of the night."[63] Churchill melds their separate eyewitness accounts into several paragraphs of seamless narrative told from what amounts to the viewpoint of an omniscient narrator. It is in the penultimate paragraph of this narration of the night's fierce action that he embeds by way of graphic summation his verbal painting of "the whole scene" in words that could be directions for—or a description of—a typical painting by de Neuville of outnumbered soldiers engaged in a desperate battle for survival. Churchill's explicit allusion to de Neuville calls up memories of his paintings in a way designed to stress the heroic significance of what the British troops endured and achieved. In Churchill's presentation theirs is a case of life imitating epic art. In turn the art identified here by Churchill supplies heightened drama and a well-understood paradigm of meaning to the actual "scene" that he describes. Resuming his narration in the final paragraph allotted to this episode, Churchill winds up with sentences of abstract analysis rather than emblematic images: "How much longer the battery and its defenders could have held out is uncertain. They were losing men steadily, and their numbers were so small that they might have been rushed at any moment. Such was the tale."[64]

To tell this "tale" of "the story of the night" Churchill begins at its conclusion by describing what he himself saw when he arrived with the relieving force at dawn. He does so in a way that provides another verbal equivalent of a de Neuville painting, although without explicit allusion to the painter:

> The village was a shambles. In an angle of the outside wall, protected on the third side by a shallow trench, were the survivors of the fight. All around lay the corpses of men and mules. The bodies of five or six native soldiers were being buried in a hurriedly dug grave. It was thought that, as they were Mahommedans, their resting-place would be respected by the tribesmen. Eighteen wounded men lay side by side in a roofless hut. Their faces, drawn by pain and anxiety, looked ghastly in the pale light of the early morning. Two officers, one with his left hand smashed, the other shot through both legs, were patiently waiting for the moment when the improvised tourniquets could be removed and some relief afforded to their sufferings. The brigadier, his khaki coat stained with the blood from a wound on his head, was talking to his only staff-officer, whose helmet displayed a bullet-hole. The most ardent lover of realism would have been satisfied.[65]

The "realism" of this scene to which Churchill calls attention is created in two ways. Firstly there is precise specification of details: a helmet with one bullet hole; a shallow trench; corpses of mules as well as men; five or six dead native troopers in the same grave; two officers among eighteen wounded men laying side by side in a roofless hut, one officer wounded in the left hand, the other in both legs, their wounds bound by "improvised" temporary tourniquets; a general with a bloodstained coat and head wound talking to what is apparently his only surviving staff officer; and all this is not brightly illuminated but visible in "pale light" which gives to the anxious and pain-wracked wounded men a "ghastly" appearance. Secondly this scene achieves "realism" by virtue of its grim subject matter—the death, wounds, and pain of battle—depicted with no attempt to omit or gloss over the unpleasant truth about war. This is very much in the mode of de Neuville.

"Realism" as a critical term in the 1890s when applied as Churchill applies it here had become an all-purpose word vaguely denoting painting, especially French painting, that focused on ugly and unpleasant aspects of life. "Realism" also denoted novels, especially in the tradition of Flaubert and Balzac, that similarly aspired to present in unflinching detail the seamier sides of society. Churchill deploys the term with twofold impact in his sardonic comment that by viewing the aftermath of that night's combat "the most ardent lover of realism would have been satisfied." Because the scene that he describes is so horrifying, he implies that those who ardently love such realism in art and literature may have a dubious taste for what ought to repel rather than attract. He also underscores the horror of real war by the ironic understatement of suggesting that even those most far-gone in their love of grim art and literature would have enough or more than enough if confronted by the actuality rather than merely its depiction.

Here as so often elsewhere in his writing, Churchill's own fascination with warfare goes along with unblinking attention to its terrible cost and sometimes doubtful value. He proceeds to describe the subsequent funeral with equal realism of attention to grim details though with more explicit moralizing about the lessons to be drawn from the scene:

> The funerals of the British officers and men, killed the day before, took place at noon. Everyone who could, attended; but all the pomp of military obsequies was omitted, and there were no Union Jacks

to cover the bodies, nor were volleys fired over the graves, lest the wounded should be disturbed. Somewhere in the camp—exactly where, is now purposely forgotten—the remains of those who had lost, in fighting for their country, all that men can be sure of, were silently interred. No monument marked the spot. The only assurance that it should be undisturbed is, that it remains unknown. Nevertheless, the funerals were impressive. To some the game of war brings prizes, honour, advancement, or experience; to some the consciousness of duty well discharged; and to others—spectators, perhaps—the pleasure of the play and the knowledge of men and things. But here were those who had drawn the evil numbers—who had lost their all, to gain only a soldier's grave. Looking at these shapeless forms, coffined in a regulation blanket, the pride of race, the pomp of empire, the glory of war appeared but the faint and unsubstantial fabric of a dream; and I could not help realising with Burke: "What shadows we are and what shadows we pursue."[66]

Churchill's description first evokes in the reader's mind by way of comparison another and more comforting kind of funeral scene replete with "the pomp of military obsequies" in which Union Jacks cover the fallen, volleys of rifle fire provide their final salute, and a monument marks their resting place to commemorate their memory. But here all this "was omitted." The dead were "silently interred." The sound of volleys, Churchill explains, might have "disturbed" the wounded. But instead of spelling out why, he involves readers by leaving it to them to imagine the possible reasons: that rifle shots could have awakened men who needed sleep; that inviting attention to an adjacent funeral might have increased the anxiety of men not yet sure whether they would survive their wounds. Readers will recall Churchill's account only a few paragraphs earlier of seeing wounded men whose "faces, drawn by pain and anxiety, looked ghastly in the pale light of early morning." He thus stresses that wounds in battle bring worry as well as pain. If there was any religious service or even a reading from the Bible, Churchill does not record it. Nor does he hint at the consolation of an afterlife or reward in heaven for "those who had lost, in fighting for their country, all that men can be sure of." Only this life is a certainty, Churchill states, and for them it is lost. He presents their fate as random and the soldier's life as a game of chance with high stakes: in "the game of war" they "had drawn the evil numbers."

In a scene mostly described negatively by noting what is *not* part of its composition—no flags, no firing squad, nor any other ceremonies ("obsequies")—Churchill describes only two visual features so that readers may envision (or an artist like de Neuville could paint) the particulars of what took place. First, readers are invited to imagine a large but unspecified number of military spectators around the graves because among the unwounded "every one who could, attended." Second, again without any specification of numbers but standing out more vividly and with more particularity as the centerpiece and focal point of Churchill's word painting, are "shapeless forms, coffined in a regulation blanket." These details are also partly defined by negation: no coffins, forms with no human or other recognizable shape. However exactly or vaguely Churchill's readers envision the appearance of British Army 1897-issue regulation blankets, their use as quasi shrouds and quasi coffins further obscures the individuality and even the human shape of those being buried because the blankets are all the same. Like the emblematic night battle scene "worthy of the pencil of De Neuville," and like Churchill's description of what he saw when he rode into the village the next morning, this bleak funeral scene is well designed to satisfy even "the most ardent lover of realism."

Churchill's wry allusion to lovers of realism implies an audience whose tastes run to novels or paintings or both because those genres had prominent schools of realism and appreciative followers of that mode. Such fiction and paintings therefore become the implicit templates by which readers are invited to measure what he describes and the way he describes it. Churchill's account of the funeral, however, evokes drama as another major template of his scenes. After cataloging what "the game of war" may bring to its participants ("prizes, honour, advancement, or experience . . . the consciousness of duty well discharged") if they are luckier than those who "had drawn the evil numbers," Churchill notes that for "spectators" of war (such as the readers of his book), there may be available "the pleasure of the play and the knowledge of men and things." The metaphor of war as a game (whether of chance or competitive sport) creates for "pleasure of the play" the primary meaning of satisfactions to be had by those who watch but do not participate in the "play" at card or other gaming tables, and also the pleasures available to those who watch the players of any sport. The second meaning of "play" is theatrical performance. "Pleasure of the play" for spectators thus also means the pleasures of watching a drama.

In Churchill's paragraph describing the funeral this secondary meaning of "play" is obliquely reinforced by words that distantly echo Shakespeare in Churchill's peroration recording (or professing to record) his own
state of mind while contemplating the burials: "Looking at these shapeless forms, coffined in a regulation blanket, the pride of race, the pomp
of empire, the glory of war appeared but the faint and unsubstantial fabric of a dream; and I could not help realising with Burke: 'What shadows we are and what shadows we pursue.'" The very accuracy of the
quotation from Burke's *Speech at Bristol on Declining the Poll* rubs in its
platitudinous moral in a rather heavy-handed and anticlimactic way. It
deflects attention from the biting points Churchill makes more subtly
(and therefore more effectively) by allusions that invite readers to recall
for themselves as a kind of implied companion piece to the sentence (and
the scene) the most famous passage in *The Tempest*. After entertaining
Ferdinand and Miranda with the masque that is a play within the play,
Prospero says:

> Our revels now are ended. These our actors,
> As I foretold you, were all spirits, and
> Are melted into air, into thin air;
> And, like the baseless fabric of this vision,
> The cloud-capped towers, the gorgeous palaces,
> The solemn temples, the great globe itself,
> Yea, all which it inherit, shall dissolve,
> And, like this insubstantial pageant faded,
> Leave not a rack behind. We are such stuff
> As dreams are made on; and our little life
> Is rounded with a sleep.[67]

Churchill's sentence indirectly but unmistakably evokes memories of Prospero's speech and its unnerving though beautifully stated point about the
evanescence of human life. Shakespeare's "baseless fabric" and "insubstan-
tial pageant" are combined and varied by Churchill in the phrase "unsubstantial fabric." Shakespeare's "we are such stuff / As dreams are made on"
becomes Churchill's characterization of the pride of race, the pomp of
empire, and the glory of war as appearing no more solid than a "faint . . .
dream." Here "faint" is a variation of Shakespeare's "faded" pageant, while
British (white) racial, imperial, and military glory momentarily dissolve

in Churchill's imagination just as in Prospero's (and Shakespeare's) vision the towers, palaces, temples, and earth itself "shall dissolve." Churchill's Shakespearean echoes in his account of the funeral provide a fleeting critique of empire and war as of no enduring value. The echoes also evoke for readers the sensation of regarding a scene in a play as well as (what the visual details evoke) a painting in de Neuville's mode of military realism.

Elsewhere in *The Story of the Malakand Field Force* Churchill more explicitly resorts to the metaphors of reading as playgoing and warfare as drama. Explaining that success or failure of the Malakand Field Force will have crucial consequences for British interests in adjacent parts of the empire, he remarks that "it might be well also to remember, that the great drama of frontier war is played before a vast, silent but attentive audience, who fill a theatre, that reaches from Peshawar to Colombo and from Kurrachee to Rangoon."[68] Contrasting the soldiers at war with their even more distant audience back in England, Churchill insists that "it is better to be making the news than taking it; to be an actor rather than a critic."[69] This remark is the moral Churchill draws from comparing the "scenes" at each end of the telegraph link between England and India:

> How different are the scenes. The club on an autumn evening—its members grouped anxiously around, discussing, wondering, asserting; the noise of the traffic outside; the cigarette smoke and electric lights within. And, only an hour away along the wire, the field, with the bright sunlight shining on the swirling muddy waters; the black forbidding rocks; the white tents of the brigade a mile up the valley; the long streak of vivid green rice crop by the river; and in the foreground the brown-clad armed men. I can never doubt which is the right end to be at. It is better to be making the news than taking it; to be an actor rather than a critic.[70]

Churchill's contrasting club and camp "scenes" are akin to paintings of indoor and outdoor scenes. His description of the club, however, reads more like stage directions for the start of a scene in a play, complete with sound effects: "the noise of traffic outside" and members "discussing . . . asserting." His description of the camp evokes a landscape painting divided between "foreground" and background, with colors specified: "bright sunshine . . . muddy waters . . . black . . . rocks. . . white tents . . . a long streak of vivid green . . . brown-clad . . . men."

In *The Story of the Malakand Field Force* Churchill's most general application of a theatrical metaphor is his variation on the familiar trope of life as a play, of which the most well-known version is Jaques' speech in *As You Like It* beginning "All the world's a stage, / And all the men and women merely players."[71] Churchill literalizes the metaphor as he tries to account for the puzzling phenomenon of courage under fire that allows "thousands of men, drawn at random from the population . . . to control the instinct of self-preservation." What makes such courage even more of a riddle for Churchill is its widespread manifestation across cultural divides: "Nor is this courage peculiar to any particular nation. Courage is not only common, but cosmopolitan." The explanation, according to Churchill, "appears to be this": "The courage of the soldier is not really contempt for physical evils and indifference to danger. It is a more or less successful attempt to simulate these habits of mind. Most men aspire to be good actors in the play. There are a few who are so perfect that they do not seem to be actors at all. This is the ideal after which the rest are striving. It is one very rarely attained."[72] Churchill thus takes as fundamental to individual psychology what in the jargon of our day we call (with equal literalization of metaphor) role-playing. In this view, acting a part as an "attempt to simulate . . . habits of mind" is far from carrying any stigma if it results in laudable conduct. On the contrary, it is praiseworthy, according to Churchill, even when motivated as he suggests it often is by "vanity, the vice which promotes so many virtues."[73] Conversion—or at least apparent conversion—of role to reality, of simulation to actuality, becomes Churchill's ideal. He thus defines and legitimizes his own goal of becoming the perfect actor in the theater of war or, later, of politics.

Churchill resorts to metaphors of painting rather than drama when defining the principles of composition that guided him while writing *The Story of the Malakand Field Force*. For its readers, these definitions involving analogies between painting and writing also provide suggestions about how they may understand the book's purposes as well as its methods. At the outset of chapter 8, "The Advance Against the Mohmands," there is "a change in the standpoint from which the story is told" as Churchill switches from "the impersonal style of history" to a narrative relying on his "own memory as well as well as on other people's evidence" because it is at this point that he himself joined the Field Force and became an eyewitness of its actions. Churchill here reminds his readers that "the original object with which this book was undertaken, was to present a picture of the war on the North-West Frontier to the Englishmen at home; a picture which should not only exist, but be looked at; and I am inclined to think that this end will be more easily attained by the adoption of a style of personal narrative."[74] Intrusion henceforward in the book of first-person accounts by Churchill as eyewitness will, he hopes, attract viewers to his "picture of the war." By reminding readers that a picture must after all not merely exist but be seen if it is to serve any social purpose, Churchill stresses the importance of his topic—frontier warfare—as one that "Englishmen at home" ought to understand and which, thanks to his "picture of the war" they will better be able to understand.

Churchill concedes that a danger of departing from "the impersonal style of history" is that "from the personal point of view . . . we are so prone to exaggerate the relative importance of incidents, which we see, over those we hear about, that what the narrative gains in accuracy of detail, it may lose in justness of proportion."[75] He argues, however, that possible gains in accuracy by adopting "the personal point of view" outweigh the dangers it incurs: "Many facts, too local, too specialised, too insignificant, for an historical record, and yet which may help the reader to form a true impression of the scene and situation, are thus brought within the compass of these pages. The account becomes more graphic, if less imposing, more vivid if less judicial. As long as each step down from the 'dignity of history' is accompanied by a corresponding increase of interest, we may pursue without compunction that pleasant, if descending, path."[76] The advantages of personal narrative which Churchill here specifies may also be taken as criteria for judging his (or any similar) book. Its ability via "accuracy of detail" to convey "a true impression of scene and situation" is one measure of its success, as it would be in any representational picture showing a landscape ("scene") or event ("situation"). Another and equally important measure of success is the degree to which it achieves the mode of realism marked by "graphic" and "vivid" particularity. This need not be the kind of social realism focusing on what is dreary and depressing that Churchill alludes to in his jab at the "ardent" lovers of realism. Here he refers more generally to modes of painting like that of seventeenth-century Dutch artists renowned for their minutely accurate depictions of clothing, buildings, ships, people, and landscapes.

In a later chapter Churchill explains that he has included an account of "what was after all only a skirmish" because "the picture of the war on the frontier is essentially one of detail, and it is by the study of the details alone, that a true impression can be obtained."[77]

Even when—indeed especially when—departing from the lofty impersonal style of "an historical record" toward a more journalistic mode, Churchill claims achievement of accuracy as the cardinal virtue of his book. Perhaps he is sensitive on this issue—or suspects that his readers will be—because, as he explains in a footnote, he was a correspondent covering this war before he even became one of its soldiers, much less its historian: "I . . . arrived at Malakand as press correspondent of the *Pioneer* and *Daily Telegraph*, and in the hope of being sooner or later attached to the force in a military capacity."[78] In his preface Churchill explains that he has included in his book revised versions of his "original letters" to the *Daily Telegraph*.[79] If such material and related personal memories of what he saw are steps "down from the 'dignity of history'" they are excusable, Churchill argues, not only because they increase fidelity to facts by adding more details but also because they may achieve an "increase of interest" so that the "descending path" becomes "pleasant." Here the measure of success is explicitly aesthetic: increase of interest provides pleasure, which in turn becomes a legitimate goal of his writing in itself and because it attracts an audience which the book's topic deserves.

There remains the problem of deciding which and how many details to include. After remarking that he has "devoted a good deal" of one chapter "to the account of the 'sniping' at Jar on the night of the 9th of October," Churchill speculates that "perhaps, a critic may inquire, why so much should be written about so common an incident." To mollify any such critic and any readers who have grown impatient, Churchill explains that he has described the night action at length "because this night firing, is so common a feature that . . . no picture of war on the Indian frontier, would be complete without some account of it."[80] The basis of this decision and similar ones is clear: any recurrent and characteristic aspect of the campaign deserves at least one detailed description which may serve to represent its features and also show its part in the larger "picture."

A more difficult problem is that of avoiding monotony while nevertheless conveying a sense of the tedium experienced by troops during most of their expedition: "The narration of the daily movements of troops, unmarked by variety of incident, is dull and wearying. Yet he who would obtain a true idea of the soldier's life on service, must mentally share the fatigues of the march and the monotony of the camp. The fine deeds, the thrilling moments of war, are but the high lights [*sic*] on a picture, of which the background is routine, hard work, and discomfort."[81] To justify including comparatively tedious accounts of dull intervals of marching and camping in between the more exciting narrations of "fine deeds," Churchill again resorts to the metaphor of painting a picture in which both background and "high lights" are necessary for a satisfactory composition.

To resolve the problem of how actually to accommodate the inclusion of both "dull and wearying" matters required for historical accuracy and those "thrilling moments of war" that are more likely to interest readers, Churchill in a Solomon-like mood splits his narrative and offers readers a choice of taking only one half. But he implies this is an offer they ought to refuse lest they miss one of "the most important" though not one of the most gripping parts of "the tale": "To record the actual movements of troops in a campaign is among the most important duties of one who undertakes to tell its tale. For the sake of clearness, of brevity, and that the reader who is not interested may find convenience in skipping, I shall at once describe the whole of the marches and manoeuvres by which Sir Bindon Blood moved his brigades across the Panjkora River, and after the Malakand Field Force is safely camped at Ghosam, the reader will be invited to return to examine the scenery, and remark the incidents of the way."[82] True to his promise, after having in his narration "brought the brigades peacefully to Ghosam," Churchill asks "the reader to return to the Malakand and ride thence with the Headquarter Staff along the line of march." By noting too that he "had the pleasure" of accompanying "Sir Bindon Blood and his staff," as they followed the route of the brigades, Churchill assures readers that his ensuing accounts of "scenery" have the authority of eyewitness testimony.[83]

———————— ∳ ————————

Landscape paintings of various kinds provide templates for Churchill's rendition of scenes along the way. One familiar genre that he evokes is that of paintings depicting a countryside with ancient ruins inviting meditation on the ravages of time: "The Valley at Sarai is about two miles wide, and the mountains rise steeply from it. On every ridge it is possible to distinguish the red brick ruins which were the dwellings of the ancient Buddhists. These relics of an early civilization, long since overthrown and

forgotten, cannot fail to excite interest and awaken reflection. They carry
the mind back to the times 'when the smoke of sacrifice rose from the
Pantheon, and when camelopards and tigers bounded in the Flavian am-
phitheatre.'"[84] Churchill's unidentified quotation here is from Macaulay's
famous tribute to the Roman Catholic Church as the one "institution . . .
left standing which carries the mind back to the times when the smoke
of sacrifice rose from the Pantheon." Macaulay also eloquently insists that
the Catholic Church is still strong, still growing around the world, and,
moreover, an institution that in the far future "may still exist in undimin-
ished vigour when some traveller from New Zealand shall, in the midst
of a vast solitude, take his stand on a broken arch of London Bridge to
sketch the ruins of St. Paul's."[85] Churchill assumes his readers will recognize Macaulay's phrase, remember its context, and probably recall as well
his invitation to imagine that future drawing by a New Zealander of a
depopulated London in ruins at a remote time when the British Empire
has vanished even more completely than the Roman Empire whose
decline and fall was chronicled by Churchill's other favorite historian,
Edward Gibbon. Unlike Macaulay's future London which is "a vast solitude," Rome in Gibbon's day as in Churchill's at least had a population
living amid the ruins of its imperial past. In addition to inviting us to
imagine the New Zealander's sketch, which would show a view of the
ruins of St. Paul's as seen *from* London Bridge, Macaulay also invites readers to imagine from some other vantage point the larger scene containing a solitary figure standing *on* "a broken arch of London Bridge" while
contemplating ruins of the city's Anglican and imperial past.

Macaulay's futuristic vision is emulated by Churchill as he goes on
to remark that viewing the Sarai Valley landscape with Buddhist ruins
will "also lead us to speculations of the future, till we wonder whether
the traveller shall some day inspect, with unconcerned composure, the
few scraps of stone and iron, which may indicate the British occupation
of India. Few indeed, the remains would be—for we build for immediate use, not future ostentation in these days, and if we should ever cease
to be a force in the world, all traces of us would soon be obliterated
by time."[86] Churchill's future Sarai Valley becomes a synecdoche of all
India under British rule, where building is "for immediate use, not future
ostentation." Like Macaulay, Churchill describes a scene including a solitary traveler contemplating aspects of the reader's present civilization in
a future state of decay. But Churchill's imaginary future Indian landscape

has no recognizable remnant of a building. Churchill does not meliorate the bleakness of his scene by including farms, villages, or any living person except his traveler whose destination is elsewhere. Nor is there even a hint of such religious comfort as Rudyard Kipling offered by the devotional framework of his melancholy poem on a similar theme, "Recessional," published in 1897 while Churchill was finishing *The Story of the Malakand Field Force*. In this famous elegy for an empire, Kipling surrounds with a prayer for God's mercy the dire statement that already "all our pomp of yesterday / Is one with Nineveh and Tyre!"[87] In Churchill's future Sarai Valley, after the British Empire has ceased "to be a force in the world" nature has taken over again. "The few scraps of stone and iron" remaining there inspire neither recollection nor prayer from Churchill's future traveler. Even at the outset of his career in the heyday of Victoria's apparently unshakeable empire, but fresh from his study of Gibbon's *Decline and Fall of the Roman Empire* and Macaulay's invitations to consider the vicissitudes of history over the centuries, Churchill is haunted by the possibility—if not the certainty—that the British imperium too will one day vanish as though it had never existed.

Churchill makes the best of this disquieting possibility by stressing the nobility of Britain's refusal to litter the countryside with useless monuments vaunting imperial magnificence. He goes on to remark of his future traveler unmoved by the "few scraps of stone and iron" that would remain: "Yet, perhaps, if that unborn critic of remote posterity would remember that 'in the days of the old British,' the rice crop had been more abundant, the number of acres under cultivation greater, the population larger and the death rate lower, than at any period in the history of India—we should not be without a monument more glorious than the pyramids."[88] Here at the very beginning of his writing career—and thus at his debut as a public figure entering debates over such political issues as frontier policies—Churchill tries out the rhetorical gambit adopted forty-two years later in his most famous and perhaps most influential sentence, the peroration to his June 18, 1940, address rallying the British to fight on after the fall of France: "Let us therefore brace ourselves to our duties, and so bear ourselves that, if the British Empire and its Commonwealth last for a thousand years, men will still say, 'This was their finest hour.'"[89] This sentence is more memorable not only because it is polished to nicer concision, but also of course because it deals with an issue of greater urgency than Churchill's youthful praise of what he claims

Britain accomplished in India. Nevertheless in the earlier sentence we can see the imaginative structure—the scaffolding of rhetoric, as he once called it in an essay of that name—that he later refined to perfection: an invitation to consider how the present will be regarded by the future and what, in the light of that consideration, ought to be most highly valued in present conduct. There is also in Churchill's "Finest Hour" peroration, as in the *Malakand Field Force* passage, a reminder that the British Empire's survival is contingent not inevitable: "*If* we should ever cease to be a force in the world" foreshadows "*If* the British Empire and its Commonwealth last for a thousand years." In both sentences Churchill's moral imperatives for the present remain equally valid whatever the ultimate fate of the British Empire.

Although romantic paintings depicting ancient ruins are a point of departure for Churchill's reflections on the Sarai Valley, the immediate model for his sketch of that scene in a distant future is not the related genre of paintings imagining present buildings after they have eventually fallen into ruins years ahead of the painter's and viewer's present time. Such futuristic scenes were less numerous, but their sporadic vogue may have encouraged Churchill's imagination of a distant future scene, or at least made some readers more receptive to it. The most famous among the first wave of these pictures is Hubert Robert's 1796 *Vue Imaginaire de la Grande Galerie en Ruines*, depicting ruins of the Louvre as they would appear to people living in a future Paris.[90] Another notable example is Joseph Gandy's 1798 *Architectural Ruins: A Vision*, "which showed the shattered dome of the Rotunda in the then-new Bank of England building."[91] More in the vein of Macaulay's passage evoking a future traveler from the antipodes sketching ruins is Gustave Doré's gloomy 1872 landscape *The New Zealander*, which shows in the background ruins illuminated by moonlight and in the foreground an artist drawing them. In 1893 Octave Saunier depicted *Paris en ruines*.[92] Whether or not Churchill had seen any of these pictures or similar ones, he explicitly alludes only to the more familiar literary precedent provided by Macaulay's passage inviting imagination of the ruins of St. Paul's in a future London.

When Churchill carries his narration beyond the Sarai Valley to arrival of the Malakand force at "the passes into the Utman Khel country" he also explicitly evokes a literary model for comparison, while nevertheless using the word "landscape" in a way that evokes its meaning of a painting of natural scenery while also conveying its other meaning of whatever scenery might be depicted in a landscape painting or taken in at a glance from some vantage point: "The landscape was one of the strangest, I shall ever see. On the opposite bank of the river were the dwellings of the Utman Khels, and in an area seven miles by three, I counted forty-six separate castles, complete with moats, towers and turrets. The impression produced was extraordinary. It suggested Grimm's fairy tales. It almost seemed as if we had left the natural earth and strayed into some strange domain of fancy, the resort of giants or ogres."[93] Churchill's very general comparison with Grimm's fairy tales invites readers to recall in an equally general way the fanciful giants, ogres, and other strange creatures populating those and similar stories that had become a staple of English childhood and thus of the English imagination. It is also an invitation to recall accompanying book illustrations by George Cruikshank and others. The images elicited by Churchill's description of "castles, complete with moats, towers, and turrets" can only be given particularity by recollections—that will not be the same for every reader—of medieval castles idealized in the realm of fairy tales by the stories and their illustrators. Utman Khel military architecture must have been less grandiose and handsome than such romantic images or even, for that matter, than the often imposing remains of actual medieval castles in England and elsewhere. Whatever the Utman Khel castles might look like in a photograph or accurate drawing, Churchill makes no attempt to describe them objectively beyond counting them and noting that all forty-six had "moats, towers, and turrets," although surely they did not each have the same configuration of these features. He stresses their subjective impact. The very oddity of their functional resemblance to the architecture of European castles, along with the fairy-tale quality of so *many* castles crowded in such a small area, invites the comparison that Churchill provides to convey their unsettling effect.

That effect is only momentary and partial. It *"almost"*—but not quite—seemed as though all the British soldiers of the Malakand force ("we") had deviated from "the natural earth" into a supernatural parallel planet existing only in "some strange domain of fancy." What Churchill describes to convey the quality of encountering this Utman Khel landscape is his experience of an unusual kind of déjà-vu in which a scene evokes not a false memory of having been to the same place before in real life but a memory of having been to a similar place before in the "domain of fancy" to which readers of Grimm's fairy tales had indeed previously traveled, although only mentally, while reading. That Churchill experienced and takes pains to report this moment of quasi déjà-vu shows that childhood encounters with fairy tales had vividly impressed themselves upon his own imagination, sometimes coloring his perceptions of what he saw.

The ensuing scenes which Churchill interrupts his narration to describe have affinities with more mundane landscape paintings. He closes chapter 9 ("Reconnaissance") with a set piece portraying the British camp after nightfall:

> To view the scene by moonlight is alone an experience which would repay much travelling. The fires have sunk to red, glowing specks. The bayonets glisten in a regular line of blue-white points. The silence of weariness is broken by the incessant and uneasy shuffling of the animals and the occasional neighing of the horses. All the valley is plunged in gloom and the mountains rise high and black around. Far up their sides, the twinkling watch-fires of the tribesmen can be seen. Overhead is the starry sky, bathed in the pale radiance of the moon. It is a spectacle that may inspire the philosopher no less than the artist.[94]

Despite inclusion of a few sound effects indicating slight movement within the camp ("shuffling of the animals and . . . neighing of the horses"), this description is essentially visual and static. It shows a peaceful interlude of warriors on both sides at rest when "the camp, if . . . it can be said to have a personality, shrugs its shoulders and, regarding the past without regret, contemplates the future without alarm."[95] Churchill portrays the camp at ease from a sufficiently distant though unspecified vantage point so that its entire setting can be taken in at once: a dark valley floor "plunged in gloom" interspersed with "red, glowing" remains of campfires and "regular lines of blue-white points" where arms are stacked; "black" mountains with "twinkling watch-fires" high on their slopes; and above "a starry sky, bathed in the pale radiance of the moon." Readers must infer that the moon is full or nearly so, and visible to a viewer of the scene. This description, like some of Churchill's previous ones, could serve as directions for a painter or book illustrator. Unlike the battle scenes, however, this and similar scenes are not designed to appeal to "the lover of realism" but to what Churchill elsewhere in *The Malakand Field Force* calls "the lover of the picturesque."[96] By this term he evidently means whatever is beautiful and/or exotic. As usual, he does not pause to rehearse the various definitions and critical theories that had proliferated at often bewildering length to explain concepts of realism and the picturesque. He assumes that the context within which he uses those terms will make their meaning clear enough, as in fact it does.

For Churchill, evocations of the picturesque are at once an opportunity and a problem. They may appeal to readers but run the risk of deflecting attention from more important military concerns. Because *The Story of the Malakand Field Force* falls partly into the genre of travel literature, Churchill must satisfy readers who expect accounts of exotic scenery. To omit such picturesque interludes would disappoint and perhaps alienate those who seek the usual pleasures of travel books. To include such material is a way of winning attention for the warfare that is the main substance of Churchill's narration while also often showing topographical difficulties the army had to overcome. Thus he introduces a description of the landscape to be seen from the top of the Malakand pass by remarking: "The view is one worth stopping to look at."[97] Churchill's description conveys both the aesthetically pleasing picturesque qualities of the landscape and its potential hazards for an invading army. Both aspects are apparent in his summary remark (after a detailed description) that a view of the pass from above reveals that the Malakand Field Force has "entered a strange land, as tangled as the maze at Hampton Court, with mountains instead of hedges."[98] While narrating the army's march away from the Utman Khel area that is reminiscent of Grimm's fairy tales, Churchill describes another pleasingly picturesque "view that repaid the exertions of the climb, even if it did not quench the thirst they had excited": "Far below us was a valley into which perhaps no white man had looked since Alexander crossed the mountains on his march to India. Numerous villages lay dotted about in its depths, while others nestled against the hills. Isolated forts were distinguishable, while large trees showed there was no lack of water."[99] This is an invitation not only to visualize the landscape seen by the British at this point in their campaign, but also to imagine the same landscape being crossed by Alexander and his troops. Churchill thus evokes as an implied but not particularized image a ghostly army of ancient Greeks marching alongside the British soldiers.

Churchill's most adroit rhetorical exploitation of expectations that his book will include picturesque moments comes early in *The Story of the Malakand Field Force* where he attempts to elicit sympathy for as well as understanding of the natives whose rebellion the British force was sent to quell. He starts an analysis of the rebels and their motives by portraying an imaginary scene aimed at readers who may have a romantic soft spot for picturesque natives even when, regarded unsentimentally, their customs are so at odds with English attitudes that, as Churchill coyly puts it, "of some of their manners and morals it is impossible to write":

> Yet the life even of these barbarous people is not without moments when the lover of the picturesque might sympathise with their hopes and fears. In the cool of the evening, when the sun has sunk behind the mountains of Afghanistan, and the valleys are filled with a delicious twilight, the elders of the village lead the way to the *chenar* trees by the water's side, and there, while the men are cleaning their rifles, or smoking their *hookas*, and the women are making rude ornaments from beads, and cloves and nuts, the Mullah drones the evening prayer. Few white men have seen and returned to tell the tale. But we may imagine the conversation passing from the prices of arms and cattle, the prospects of the harvest, or the village gossip to the great Power that lies to the southward, and comes nearer year by year. . . . Then the Mullah will raise his voice and remind them of other days when the sons of the prophet drove the infidel from the plains of India, and ruled at Delhi as wide an Empire as the *Kafir* holds today: when the true religion strode proudly through the earth and scorned to lie hidden and neglected among the hills: when mighty princes ruled in Baghdad, and all men knew that there was one God, and Mahomet was His prophet. And the young men hearing these things will grip their Martinis, and pray to Allah, that one day He will bring some *Sahib*—best prize of all—across their line of sight at seven hundred yards so that, at least, they may strike a blow for insulted and threatened Islam.[100]

Here Churchill first verbally paints for "the lover of the picturesque" a twilight scene whose foreground shows villagers gathered just after sundown by (to English eyes) exotic trees at a river's bank where the agreeably subdued light is "delicious." In the background are "the mountains of Afghanistan." The mullah droning through his ritual evening prayer does not seem to command much attention from either the women busy making ornaments or the men whose smoking and rifle cleaning seem equally desultory occupations as Churchill equates them. Natives could hardly be portrayed in a more favorable way than relaxing in a scene where at first mention even their weapons, described only generically as rifles, become merely picturesque props like the harmless hookas. The menace underlying this pastoral tableau is not conveyed by the visible details that Churchill includes at its outset, but by his statement that among actual witnesses to such apparently peaceful ceremonies of devotion "few white men have returned to tell the tale." He thus reminds European connoisseurs of the picturesque that they are well advised to seek out this variety only in books and paintings unless traveling with an army for protection.

Then Churchill animates the tableau as though it were a scene in a play. After inviting readers to "imagine the conversation" following prayers he adds another and more sinister visual detail inviting a double take: "the young men" all have Martini rifles. Successive models of this efficient weapon had been employed as standard-issue infantry and cavalry arms by the British since the early 1870s, although it was supplanted in 1898 by the even better Lee-Metford rifle. Churchill in his chapter of "Military Observations" on the expedition notes that it faced "an active and numerous enemy, armed with modern rifles."[101] Most of these, which he also refers to as "their excellent rifles," were Martinis, as he makes clear in another passage discussing "The question of the supply of arms to the frontier tribes."[102] Because "A good Martini-Henry rifle will always command a price in these parts of Rs. 400 or about £25," Churchill explains, "All along the frontier, and from far down into India, rifles are stolen by expert and cunning thieves." After dilating with evident relish on the ingenious smuggling methods employed, especially by "the Ut Khels, who . . . have made the traffic in arms their especial business" (in ways that do not provoke any further comparisons with Grimm's fairy tales), Churchill states that "the importance of the arms question cannot be exaggerated. The long-range rifle fire, which has characterised the great frontier war, is a new feature."[103] By remarking too in several passages the natives' good marksmanship and its devastating effects, Churchill leaves no doubt that Martinis in their hands are formidable. Thus the young men's prayer that Allah may grant them a nice clear shot at "some *Saihib*" is chilling. It is not to be taken as an empty threat from people with picturesque and ineffectual antique weapons.

But their devout longing to kill Englishmen is not presented by Churchill as inexplicable fanaticism. He makes their motives seem understandable and even in many respects laudable by summarizing the mullah's sermon recalling the great days of Islam "when mighty princes ruled in Baghdad." The mullah who only "drones the evening prayer" will "raise his voice" to attract attention while calling for a renewal of the time "when the sons of the prophet drove the infidel from the plains of India." We may smile at this very Churchillian mullah urging his people to live up to their glorious past by acting together to defy an invader and thus save (Islamic) civilization from a godless enemy. If the scaffolding of rhetoric here stands out in retrospect as one that, mutatis mutandis, was to serve Churchill and Britain well in 1940, the coincidence should not diminish appreciation for either his own more highly elaborated speeches addressing the German menace or his adroit invitation for readers of *The Malakand Field Force* to empathize with the viewpoint of Britain's Islamic opponents in 1898. Nowhere in that book does Churchill retract his assessment of them as "these barbarous people." Neither, however, does he allow that judgment to preclude an effort on his part—and by his readers—to understand what their attitudes may honorably have in common with European ideals: patriotic nationalism impelling them to fight invaders, desire to emulate their country's best days, and professions of piety. For readers of *The Malakand Field Force* the way to achieve this leap across a cultural divide is first to savor the pleasantly picturesque qualities of a scene and then but only then imagine what its subjects might be saying and how they might be thinking. As Churchill guides readers while they "imagine the conversation," he aims to elicit a shock of recognition when they discover that what seemed so picturesquely alien has much in common with themselves and their own humanity.

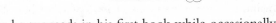

As he proceeds in his first book while occasionally sharing his composition problems with its readers, Churchill arrives at doubts about the landscape scenes he has sprinkled through its pages. Narrating "The March to Nawagai" in chapter 10, he launches into yet another familiar set piece account of a landscape. But he then has second thoughts on whether this sort of thing is worth doing:

It was already dusk when we returned from the reconnaissance. The evening was pleasant and we dined in the open air. All the valley was very dark. The mountains showed a velvet black. Presently the moon rose. I repress the inclination to try to describe the beauty of the scene, as the valley was swiftly flooded with that mysterious light. All the suitable words have probably been employed many times by numerous writers and skipped by countless readers. Indeed I am inclined to think, that these elaborate descriptions convey little to those who have not seen, and are unnecessary to those who have. Nature will not be admired by proxy. In times of war, however, especially of frontier war, the importance of the moon is brought home to everybody. "What time does it rise to-night?" is the question that recurs; for other things—attacks, "sniping," rushes,—besides the tides are influenced by its movements.[104]

At first a vocabulary of ordinary words serves to outline a scene that Churchill presents in successive stages. *Dusk* is followed by *evening*, at which point the valley is *very dark* while mountains in the background are *velvet black*. Rather than dwell upon the subtle distinction—perhaps as difficult for readers to visualize as it would be for painters to achieve— between *very dark* and *velvet black*, Churchill moves the scene and his readers on to moon rise, whose effect—beautiful, swift, illumination of the valley with "mysterious light"—he suggests in the same sentence wherein he renounces the impulse to provide any such description. Readers are given the basic ingredients for their own imaginations to work upon, but no more. Churchill's disinclination to echo, faute de mieux, words that "have probably been employed many times by numerous writers and skipped by countless readers" seems less a fear of falling into banal repetition of what others have written than awareness that he has used up his own vocabulary of "suitable words" for such descriptions. Without mentioning any of his predecessors, he guesses that the available repertoire has "probably" been drawn upon by many previous writers of what he calls while referring to his own book "a tale of travel or war."[105] His greater fear is of repeating himself. Perhaps too he hesitates here because what he must really describe if he is to convey the quality of that landscape is not how it looks at a particular moment but how the lighting and hence the scene changes as it is "swiftly flooded" by moonlight. Such effects are more the forte of cinema, then in its infancy, than of painting.

Churchill seldom expresses doubt about the ability of language—
especially as used by himself—to convey meaning. At issue in the foregoing passage is not the adequacy of language in general, or as an instrument
of historical narration and political rhetoric. The value to historians and
politicians of well-chosen and artfully disposed words was well understood from the outset of his career by the man who was later to receive
a Nobel Prize for his "mastery of historical and biographical description
as well as for brilliant oratory." In *The Malakand Field Force* he grapples
only with the much more limited question of how far words may do
what pictures can do by depicting admirable natural scenery in ways that
convey not merely its appearance but its beauty. It is only "*these* elaborate
descriptions"—i.e., of landscapes—that perhaps "convey little to those
who have not seen, and are unnecessary to those who have." Churchill
here is himself *inclined* to this pessimistic conclusion, but does not insist
on it unequivocally. If it is true, however, then it follows that "nature will
not be *admired* by proxy." The aesthetic response of admiration is at stake
here, not just topographical understanding required for military operations. Churchill does not pursue the corollary of his tentative conclusion
that "nature" can only be admired—apprehended aesthetically—at firsthand. Although his readers are taken to the brink of stating what logically follows, he refrains from going on to conclude that if nature cannot
be admired by proxy, then paintings of landscapes can only succeed in
arousing admiration for their own artistic qualities rather than for the
beauties of the scenery they depict.

Theoretical considerations of this sort were seldom articulated by
Churchill, although later in *Painting as a Pastime* his subtle analysis of the
process by which perceptions are translated to canvas earned the respect
of E. H. Gombrich. In *Art and Illusion* he quotes from *Painting as a Pastime*
a passage on "the part which memory plays in painting" because about
the differences between copying and suggesting a scene "no professional
critic has seen the nature of this problem more clearly than a famous
amateur artist . . . Sir Winston Churchill."[106] That order of insight, however, came only after Churchill took up painting. In *The Malakand Field
Force* he was content to wrestle with the problem for writers of how far
words could—or should—do the aesthetic work of pictures. After exper-
imenting with descriptive passages that he thought had used up the relevant vocabulary at his disposal for conveying "the beauty of the scene"
at various vantage points, he turns with evident relief from such attempts

to explain the military importance of moonlight "in times of war" as an aid to "attacks, 'sniping,' rushes." To understand such matters it is only necessary to know the relationship of topography to illumination and to the disposition of forces.

So too Churchill finds analogies with painting less helpful to the more exclusively analytical writing required when he arrives at his last chapter, "The Riddle of the Frontier." He introduces his final summing-up of political and military issues by stating the daunting problem that confronts—but of course does not stop—him as he seeks properly to conclude his narration by drawing what conclusions the war enforces: "When I reflect on the great number of diverse and often conflicting facts, which may be assembled under every head—military, economic, political or moral—and consider the accumulations of specialised, and technical knowledge, necessary for their proper appreciation, I am convinced that to compass the whole is beyond the mind of man."[107] Pushing forward after thus hopefully eliciting sympathy for the impossible task that he now undertakes, Churchill introduces a comparison with painting to further explain the difficulties under which he bravely labors while writing his last chapter—difficulties which may perhaps excuse any confusion it displays or arouses: "A point is reached where all relation between detail and proportion is lost. It is a picture of such great size that to see it all, it is necessary to stand so far off that neither colours nor figures are distinguishable. By constantly changing the point of view, some true perspective is possible, and even then the conception must be twisted and distorted, by the imperfections of the mental mirror."[108] Here the metaphor of writing as painting is used only as a way of underscoring the impossibility of really understanding the frontier situation in all its complexity. Perhaps recalling the discussion of magnitude in Aristotle's *Poetics*, Churchill remarks that a picture may be so large that its own size precludes apprehending how its parts are related: "All relation between detail and proportion is lost." Paradoxically, the big picture of frontier warfare and politics is too big even if—by implication especially if—it includes everything that ought to be included. The very accuracy of such a picture demands a scope that renders it impossible to see properly. Viewed from the distance required to regard it all "neither colours nor figures are distinguishable." This is a problem for spectators and readers.

It is also a problem for painters and writers deciding on the scope of their work, although here Churchill assumes that a picture or book should try to cover its topic thoroughly even at risk of sacrificing ease of apprehension. Although he later became a prolific essayist and in that genre a skillful miniaturist adept at concise character sketches, he remained attracted to the challenge of large-scale efforts. A favorite mode, very much in the Victorian tradition, was multivolume works of biography and history: two volumes for the River War, two volumes for Lord Randolph Churchill, four volumes for the Duke of Marlborough, six volumes for World War I, another six for World War II, and four for the English-speaking peoples.

In *The Malakand Field Force* Churchill's resort to the metaphor of mind as a mirror blurs his initial distinction between viewers and painters, readers and writers, by suggesting that only partial mitigation of the large-canvas difficulties can be achieved: "By constantly changing the point of view, some true perspective is possible, and even then the conception must be twisted and distorted, by the imperfection of the mental mirror." In Churchill's application of the traditional image of art as a mirror held up to the world, it is unclear whether the imperfect mental mirror belongs to the painter (author), the viewer (reader), or both. Authors and readers alike seem to be holding up mirrors in Churchill's confusing metaphor of their relationship to each other and to the reflected world they both try to see despite inevitable distortions. It is only authors (or painters) however, who have the power to change the point of view from which they portray what they see, and thus to control what their audience sees if they keep reading and do not skip. Earlier in *The Malakand Field Force* Churchill had commented less ambiguously about this issue of changing viewpoints when he explained how, where, and why he descends from "the impersonal style of history" to the "personal point of view" to present eyewitness accounts of scenes that will make the book "more graphic . . . more vivid."[109] The ambiguity and confusion of his last metaphor in *The Malakand Field Force* equating writing and painting shows the limitations of that metaphor as an aid to composition when dealing with analytical rather than descriptive passages. It also shows Churchill's determination to think and invite his readers to think often about writing in terms of painting. The imaginative process revealed is of progress from appreciation of the formal qualities requisite for a good painting to discovery of equivalent verbal techniques that will render appropriate aspects of an historical narrative "vivid," "graphic," "picturesque," "realistic," and even occasionally beautiful.

⌘

Paradigms from painting are also conspicuous in *Savrola*, where, however, they usually seem more like pictures of a stage set framed by a proscenium arch. The tableaux thus presented are immediately animated by dialogue and action reminiscent of scenes in a play. Churchill often describes a transformation as the sun rises or sets, or as other aspects of illumination change. Such scenes in *Savrola* are not static, although they are described in ways more akin to manipulation of lighting on stage during a play, or to a series of paintings, rather than to the effects that we now associate with cinema. Early motion pictures did not provide easily applicable templates for achieving analogous effects with words on a printed page, although Churchill in later works displays a propensity for what are now called tracking shots, in which the camera follows a character or group of characters over a long sequence of actions. Some of these sequences are summed up in rather abstract images that are in effect "freeze-frame" pictures that readers must animate in their own imaginations.

Thus in *Marlborough* there is an invitation to envision the "scarlet caterpillar" of British redcoats "upon which all eyes were at once fixed" in May of 1704 after it began "to crawl steadfastly day by day across the map of Europe" toward the Danube and the battle at Blenheim.[110] Similarly, in Churchill's account of the Battle of the Marne—"the greatest battle ever fought in the world" and one that "decided the World War"— he remarks that when the British army began its crucial advance into the German gap "the German aeroplanes see five dark 15-mile-long caterpillars eating up the white roads."[111] Most of Churchill's description of the battle itself is in the form of abstract analytical paragraphs explaining successive troop dispositions on both sides that are visualized only with equal abstraction by referring readers to three maps on which French, German, and British movements are symbolized by arrows: "The Marne (turn-about—6th Sept., 1914)"; "The Marne (What Happened to Kluck and Bulow, 5th–8th Sep., 1914)"; and "The Marne (German retreat Sept., 1914)." But to explain how the Germans actually received their order to retreat, or thought they had received it, Churchill tells how the head of German Intelligence, Colonel Hentsch, "a peripatetic focus of defeat, traversed and retraversed the entire line of the German armies. On the outward journey he gathered evil tidings, and as he returned he issued fateful orders." Churchill's tone is grim amusement as he narrates "this celebrated episode" of confusion among German commanders as to who authorized retreat and who had authority to do so. He follows the unfortunate protagonist's movements from the moment when "Colonel Hentsch got in his long grey car and went along the whole line of the Armies, stopping at each of their headquarters and finally reached Bulow's headquarters about dark."[112] Apart from the generic description of a "long grey car"—its length symbolizing Hentsch's status—and mention of the approach of night, Churchill's "tracking shot" of Hentsch provides only summaries of discourse and conjectures about what must have been said rather than further images. Nevertheless the effect is of a camera with sound recorder following as Hentsch moves along the German lines conferring with a general at each stop. *Marlborough* and Churchill's account of the Battle of the Marne were written in the 1930s when the technology of cinema was relatively advanced and the popularity of movies ensured that readers would appreciate any analogous effects achieved in writing.

Even when he wrote *The River War* Churchill had seen motion pictures and was alert to their possibilities—then very limited—as another source of pictorial imagery and of analogies to cinema that a writer could press into service. He notes among curious sights characteristic of the 1898 Sudan campaign the arrival among Kitchener's troops of "war correspondents equipped with ice machines, typewriters, cameras, and even cinematographs."[113] To explain what he and his fellow cavalry men subjectively experienced during the charge of the 21st Lancers at the Battle of Omdurman, Churchill evokes what he assumes will be his readers' familiarity with cinematograph screenings:

> Two impressions I will . . . record. The whole scene flickered exactly like a cinematograph picture; and besides, I remember no sound. The event seemed to pass in absolute silence. The yells of the enemy, the shouts of the soldiers, the firing of many shots, the clashing of sword and spear, were unnoticed by the senses, unregistered by the brain. Several others say the same. Perhaps it is possible for the whole of a man's faculties to be concentrated in the eye, bridle-hand, and trigger-finger, and withdrawn from all other parts of the body.[114]

Here Churchill makes clear that objectively there were sounds—yells, shouts, firing, clashing swords and spears—but that subjectively to himself and also to "several others" the encounter "seemed to pass in absolute silence." Moreover, because for Churchill "the whole scene flickered exactly like a cinematograph picture" it follows, paradoxically, that what an apparently objective camera (circa 1898) could have shown if recording the battle—silent, flickering images—would have been closer to a representation of his subjective perceptions of the cavalry charge than to a depiction of what it would have sounded and looked like to an observer at the event seeing it from a short (and safe) distance. Churchill implies that had one of war correspondents filmed it with his cinematograph, moviegoers would have experienced something more like the inner sensations of a participant than a detached portrayal of the scene. Rather than making explicit this implied reversal of the usual expectation that cameras show objective facts, however, Churchill merely evokes the reader's cinema experiences as one template for understanding a surprising feature of the psychology of close combat.

When Churchill much later wrote a chapter on "The Sensations of a Cavalry Charge" for *My Early Life*, he claimed that he could "describe exactly what happened to me: what I saw and what I felt" because "the impression is as clear and vivid as it was a quarter of a century ago."[115] Without any comparison to movies in this book, he reports merely that "the whole scene seemed to flicker." Perhaps because by 1930 flickering was no longer such a pronounced feature of cinema as to render a comparison helpful in understanding what Churchill experienced, he omits any equivalent to his earlier simile describing the experience as "exactly like a cinematograph picture." Perhaps because by 1930 movies were well into the transition away from silent films to talkies (*The Jazz Singer* appeared in 1927), Churchill does not mention as he had in *The River War* that during the charge "the event seemed to pass in absolute silence." Instead, he says in his autobiography "There was too much trampling and rifle fire to hear any bullets."[116] This is only to remark that the sounds of individual bullets passing by were drowned out by other noises. Thus when recalling his part in the Battle of Omdurman over thirty years afterwards, Churchill either forgot or decided to downplay one of the most striking aspects of his earlier account: that to a participant in the cavalry charge it unfolded as though it were a flickering silent film.

Explicit comparisons in *Savrola* are not to cinema but to the experience of watching a play. When Churchill's heroine, Lucile, observes from her room the construction of barricades and other preparations for battle in the street below, "she felt as though she was watching a play at the theatre, the window suggesting a box." After the fighting starts "the scene, filled with little foreshortened figures, still suggested the stage of a theatre viewed from the gallery."[117] In this and similar passages Churchill strives for a play-within-a-play effect. Accounts of combat in *Savrola* follow the unfolding action without attempting to suggest that such scenes of carnage present pretty pictures.

When describing more peaceful moments, however, Churchill strongly emphasizes the beauty of the interior and exterior settings that he depicts. Colors and forms are specified in ways designed to achieve the verbal equivalent of an appealingly harmonious painting or stage set, as when Churchill describes the panorama that Lucile sees while standing on a balcony of the Lauranian Presidential Palace:

> The scene which now stretched before her was one of surpassing beauty. The palace stood upon high ground commanding a wide view of the city and the harbour. The sun was low on the horizon, but the walls of the houses still stood out in glaring white. The red and blue tiled roofs were relieved by frequent gardens and squares whose green and graceful palms soothed and gratified the eye. To the north the great pile of the Senate House and Parliament buildings loomed up majestic and imposing. Westward lay the harbour with its shipping and protecting forts. A few warships floated in the roads, and many white-sailed smacks dotted the waters of the Mediterranean Sea, which had already begun to change their blue for the more gorgeous colours of sunset.[118]

This could almost be a description of one of the harbor scenes along the French Riviera that Churchill was fond of painting in the 1930s. His *Coast Scene on the Riviera*, for example, shows houses with surrounding trees and gardens in the foreground, a coastline ringed with houses in the middle distance, and hills receding into the background. His *View of Monte Carlo and Monaco* shows the harbor and waterfront houses as seen from a balcony that is depicted in the painting's foreground and which partially frames the waterfront visible in the background.[119] Other paintings provide a similar perspective of Monte Carlo and Monaco from the vantage point of a balcony which is partly depicted to frame the harbor scene.[120] Several of Churchill's waterfront and harbor paintings include boats.[121] None of Churchill's paintings exactly duplicates the landscape of his imaginary city of Laurania. What Lucile sees as she regards that city from the palace balcony, however, now seems a preview of scenes Churchill later loved to paint from balconies overlooking the Mediterranean.

Laurania is Churchill's utopia. It is his vision of the ideal city. But it is only utopian in its visual, architectural, and geographical aspects, not its politics. This good place which, like all utopias, is also no place outside its author's imagination, is located in a warm climate with a temperate winter "which has made the Lauranian capital the home of the artist, the invalid, and the sybarite."[122] We see through Lucile's eyes while she stands on the balcony looking at this city "of surpassing beauty," that there are "frequent gardens and squares whose green and graceful palms soothed and gratified the eye." Laurania is on the seacoast with a harbor that is beautiful as well as affording a safe anchorage and good facilities for cargo ships that allow seafaring commerce. It has for its "Parliament House" a "fine building" with an aspect of sombre importance" achieved by adornment with "the trophies and statues, with which an ancient and an art-loving people had decorated its facade."[123] There is a "great square" in front of the Parliament House. There is an impressive Presidential Palace to house the country's chief executive. Churchill also provides an imposing building for Laurania's mayor and city administrators: "The Municipal building was a magnificent structure of white stone, elaborately decorated with statuary and sculpture. In front of it, surrounded by iron railings and accessible by three gateways, stretched a wide courtyard, in which a great fountain, encircled by the marble figures of departed civic magistrates, played continually with agreeable effect."[124] What is striking about Churchill's Lauranians is that they are both "an ancient and an art-loving people." Whatever their political shortcomings—which the novel presents as severe—their creator endows them with admirable and undeviating good taste in the sphere of city planning. Their fountains, statues, and public buildings no less than the gardens and geographical setting (all in fact designed by Churchill) explain why Laurania is an ideal "home of the artist" as well as (a shade more ominously) "the sybarite."

There is a touch of sybaritic imagination at work when Churchill describes the "great reception-room" of the Presidential Palace almost as though issuing directives for an architect commissioned to design young Winston's own ideal prime minister's residence.[125] It would be like a utopian version of his imposing birthplace (but not patrimony), Blenheim Palace, rather than the more modest reality of 10 Downing Street:

The hall was spacious and well-proportioned. It was decorated in the purest style of the Lauranian Republic, the arms of which were everywhere displayed. The pillars were of ancient marble and by their size and colour attested the wealth and magnificence of former days. The tessellated pavement presented a pleasing pattern. Elaborate mosaics on the walls depicted scenes from the national history: the foundation of the city; the peace of 1370; the reception of the envoys of the Great Mogul: the victory of Rota; the death of Saldanho, that austere patriot, who died rather than submit to a technical violation of the Constitution. And then coming down to later years, the walls showed the building of the Parliament House: the naval victory of Cape Cheronta, and finally the conclusion of the Civil War in 1883. On either side of the hall, in a deep alcove, a bronze fountain, playing amid surrounding palms and ferns, imparted a feeling of refreshing coolness to the eye and ear. Facing the entrance was a broad staircase—leading to the state rooms whose doors were concealed by crimson curtains.[126]

Churchill includes here bits of imaginary history that are playful invitations for his readers to supply more details in their own imaginations if they care to envision "the envoys of the Great Mogul" or, drawing on their knowledge of English history for analogies, Laurania's battles on land and sea subsequent to "the peace of 1370." There is an invitation for readers to imagine for themselves a story (perhaps foreshadowing the outcome of *Savrola*?) about what is clearly for Churchill the utopian political ideal of an "austere patriot," who prefers death to even "a technical violation of the Constitution." Equally prominent, however, is Churchill's emphasis upon what for him are the palace's utopian aesthetics. Its interior public reception room is "well-proportioned." It is "decorated in the purest style" of its own country. Its floor is laid out in "a pleasing pattern." To describe the medium of this pattern Churchill uses the technical term "tessellated." He describes the historical scenes on the wall with equal precision as "mosaics." With a classical sense of proportion he provides on either side of the hall twin alcoves with bronze fountains playing amid plants to achieve for spectators "a *feeling* of refreshing coolness" that is perceived via "the eye and ear" instead of by virtue of any noticeable lowering of the actual temperature. The fountains *look* and *sound* pleasing. Their appeal is to aesthetic sensibilities involving sight and sound not to the merely physical pleasures of cooling off on a hot day. Churchill tops off the aesthetics of his design by placing across from the entrance a grand staircase leading up to doors "concealed"—which is to say highlighted—by "crimson curtains" that would provide a striking if gaudy contrast with the reception room's "pillars . . . of ancient marble." The public areas of the Presidential Palace are calculated to impress upon visitors Laurania's civilized refinement no less than its prosperity, the grandeur of its history which stretches back to the fourteenth century, and the reach of its diplomacy (which has attracted envoys from "the Great Mogul").

The inventor of Laurania takes equal pains to ensure that its "First Magistrate," whatever his political deficiencies or virtues, enjoys a utopian cuisine (à la Churchill) that lacks for nothing: "The generous revenue which it had long been the principle of the Lauranian Republic to bestow on her First Magistrate enabled the President to live in a style of elegance and luxury, and to enjoy the attractions of good silver, fresh cut flowers, and an excellent cook."[127] Warming to the subject of dining at the summit, Churchill takes readers away from the public reception rooms to admire the only somewhat less grandiose private dining room where at breakfast time in preparation for the arrival of Lucile and President Molara, her husband, a "table, which was set for two, was comfortably small and well arranged":

> The private breakfast-room of the Presidential palace was a small but lofty apartment. The walls were hung with tapestries; over the doors weapons of ancient type and history were arranged in elaborate patterns. The great French windows were deeply set in the wall, and the bright light of the morning was softened by heavy crimson curtains. Like the rest of the house it wore an official aspect. The windows opened on to the stone terrace, and those who passed through them experienced a feeling of relief in exchanging the severe splendours of the palace for the beautiful confusion of the garden, where between the spreading trees and slender palms the sparkling waters of the harbour were displayed.[128]

Here too Churchill stresses the aesthetic aspect of what he describes. Morning sunlight is "softened" and presumably given a red tint by "crimson curtains." The "splendours" of the room are "severe," especially by contrast with the informality of an English-style garden whose "confusion" is "beautiful." As in viewing a painting, Churchill invites readers to envision in the background of his garden scene "sparkling waters of the harbour" glimpsed between tree trunks. This passage combines a seaside landscape (the distant ocean viewed from a garden) with an interior of the kind Churchill later liked to paint showing dining rooms that he appreciated. Examples of the latter are his paintings *The Dining-room of Sir Philip Sassoon's house, Lympne c. 1930*, *The Banqueting Hall, Knebworth House 1920s*, *The Dining-room at Knebworth c. 1928*, and *The Dining-room at Chartwell with Miss Diana Churchill 1933*.[129]

---⟨∞⟩---

The only private dwelling in Laurania that Churchill describes is that of his protagonist and hero, Savrola. It is "a small though not inelegant house, for he was a man of means, in the most fashionable quarter of the town."[130] The entrance is at ground level into an apparently unremarkable room that Churchill does not describe. Perhaps—though Churchill does not say—it adjoins a kitchen and the quarters of Savrola's faithful old nanny and "foster-mother" Bettine (famously modeled on Churchill's own beloved nanny, Mrs. Everest). In the manner of London's Georgian town houses, Savrola's bachelor quarters are upstairs: "The apartments he lived in were on the second storey—a bedroom, a bathroom, and a study. They were small, but full of all that taste and luxury could devise." There is, for the period, ultramodern lighting: "The room was lit by electric light in portable shaded lamps."[131] At least in its most fashionable and wealthy quarter Churchill's ideal city is thus supplied with electricity. Its exterior public illumination remains more old-fashioned: "Lines of gas-lamps marked the streets and squares."[132]

Prominent in Savrola's study is the large "writing-table of a public man."[133] Walls are "covered with shelves, filled with well-used volumes," many of which Churchill enumerates as a kind of utopian reading list that is Savrola's (and Churchill's) "Pantheon of Literature": Schopenhauer, Kant, Hegel, "the Memoirs of St. Simon and the latest French novel," *Rasselas*, *La Curée*, the eight volumes of Gibbon's *Decline and Fall of the Roman Empire*, the *Decameron*, *The Origin of Species* ("by the side of a black-letter Bible"), *The Republic*, *Vanity Fair*, the *History of European Morals*, and "A volume of Macaulay's Essays." There are no paintings in Savrola's study, and only one work of art: "In the corner of the room stood a small but exquisite Capitoline Venus, the cold chastity of its colour reproaching the

allurements of its form."[134] Almost equally conspicuous though rather less
utopian than the books, sculpture, and modern lighting, "a half-empty
box of cigarettes stood on a small table near a low leathern armchair, and
by its side lay a heavy army-revolver, against the barrel of which the ashes
of many cigarettes had been removed."[135] Despite inclusion of an implausible love affair between Savrola and Lucile, the revolver is more emblematic of *Savrola*'s themes (and young lieutenant Churchill's interests) than
the statue of Venus. Its white marble would have been widely understood
in 1900 as symbolizing a Neoplatonic ideal of beauty detached from the
mundane realities of actual females. Their "allurements"—and perhaps by
implication those overly susceptible to them—are represented in the statue
mainly to be reproached by "the cold chastity of its colour." Savrola's
Venus, like his tepid romance with Lucile, bears out Churchill's remark in
a letter to Lady Randolph that his novel is deliberately "destitute of two
elements which are rather popular in modern fiction—*squalor & animal
emotions*."[136] Savrola's taste in art objects (of which he has only one even
though he is "a man of means") mirrors Churchill's decision as a novelist (although he wrote only one) to opt for a mode of romance rather
than realism.

The most unusual feature of Savrola's house is a door in his study
giving access to "a narrow, spiral stair which led to the flat roof" where
"a small glass observatory stood in one corner of this aerial platform, the
nose of the telescope showing through the aperture."[137] This is Savrola's
private retreat where "he loved to watch the stars for the sake of their
mysteries."[138] Among the mysteries that Savrola ponders is the question
of whether there would be any point to achieving utopian perfection
if somewhere—on Jupiter, for example—life were eventually to evolve
to a state in which "all the problems would be solved." He comes to the
"mournful conclusion" that it would not matter because on Jupiter—as
on earth—"the perfect development of life would end in death; the
whole solar system, the whole universe itself, would one day be cold and
lifeless as a burned-out fire-work."[139] In addition to dramatizing Savrola's
philosophical inclinations, Churchill gives equal emphasis to his protagonist's love of beauty. It is this as much as pursuit of intellectual "mysteries" that attracts Savrola to astronomy. When he arrives at his observatory,
"by a few manipulations the telescope was directed at the beautiful planet
of Jupiter, at this time high in the northern sky. The glass was a powerful one, and the great planet, surrounded by his attendant moons, glowed

with spendour. . . . Long he watched it. . . . At last he rose, his mind still far away from earth. . . . another world, a world more beautiful, a world of boundless possibilities, enthralled his imagination."[140] Although Savrola's intellect is engaged by the question of what the solar system's ultimate fate may imply, his "imagination" is captivated by the "splendour" and beauty as well as the "possibilities" of "a world more beautiful" than ours. Writing to his Aunt Leonie about *Savrola* before its publication, Churchill was confident that she would be as delighted as he himself evidently was with his characterization of Savrola: "You will like the hero—the Great Democrat, a wild sceptic with an equally powerful imagination."[141] In the novel, Churchill mainly associates Savrola's "powerful imagination" with the various kinds of beauty—of art, of landscapes, of Lucile—that, like "the beautiful" Jupiter, "enthralled his imagination."

Savrola's skepticism is apparent in his existential vision of "the whole universe" burning out sans religious consolation or purpose. He explains that scientific apocalypse in a gleefully nihilistic discussion with Lucile about theories of evolution: "All the universe is cooling—dying, that is— and as it cools, life for a spell becomes possible on the surface of its spheres, and plays strange antics. And then the end comes; the universe dies and is sepulchred in the cold darkness of ultimate negation." His skepticism is even more explicit in this conversation when he rejects the hypothesis of "a great Being" as "not scientifically or logically necessary to assume."[142] This may reflect Churchill's outlook while writing the novel. To his mother he professed himself "quite enthusiastic about it," adding "all my philosophy is put into the mouth of the hero."[143] To his Aunt Leonie Churchill explained that his forthcoming novel "appeals to all tastes from philosophical to bloodthirsty and is full of wild adventures and atheistic philosophy."[144] Appropriately for a tale about (and possibly by) "a wild sceptic," Churchill nowhere includes in his utopian city churches of any kind. If there are churches—as presumably there would be—they do not warrant mention. They play no significant role in events. Laurania's civic life is expressed in art, trade, war, and politics rather than worship. Its political system is utopian only in theory not practice. Laurania is a republic whose chief executive ("First Magistrate") is designated a president rather a than a prime minister. It is supposed to be governed by an elected parliament modeled on that of Britain circa 1900. But however glorious Laurania's past victories against external enemies may have been, its latest conflict is a bitter civil war whose conclusion in 1883 ushers in the harsh dictatorship of its victor, President Molinara. Laurania, Churchill's utopian place, contains only a political dystopia.

———————— ∽ ————————

As the novel begins, Molinara has violated the ancient constitution by drastically restricting electors' rights and thus the parliament's power, thereby provoking a crisis that results in bloodshed when his troops shoot down protestors. This precipitates *Savrola*'s main action: the rebellion and street fighting that culminate in the overthrow of Molinara's regime and his death. The novel's plot centers on Savrola's role as a leader—the "Great Democrat"—trying to restore democracy by organizing disparate power-hungry factions into effective opposition to "the Dictator" who "for five long years since the Civil War" has imposed on Laurania "the insult of autocratic rule."[145] This political plot is mildly spiced up by Savrola's love for Lucile, who at the end is free to join him in exile after Molinara's death when an ungrateful people have turned against Savrola, indifferent to "the illustrious exile who had won them freedom, and whom they had deserted in the hour of victory."[146] A perfunctory happily-ever-after epilogue reports that Savrola's return with "his beautiful consort" was eventually welcomed by the fickle populace and that "after many troubles, peace and prosperity came back to the Republic of Laurania."[147] But the novel's last "picture" of Laurania as Lucile and Savrola take a final look before leaving for exile is "a terrible one" showing the utopian place in ruins:

> At the top of the hill the carriage stopped. . . . Savrola opened the door and stepped out. Four miles off, and it seemed far below him, lay the city he had left. Great columns of smoke rose from the conflagrations and hung, a huge black cloud in the still clear air of the dawn. Beneath the long rows of white houses could be seen the ruins of the Senate, the gardens, and the waters of the harbour. The warships lay in the basin, their guns trained upon the town. The picture was a terrible one; to this pass had the once beautiful city been reduced.[148]

Although of course Churchill could not know it while writing *Savrola*, this "terrible" scene of wartime devastation foreshadows his 1916 paintings while serving on the Western front: most notably *"Plugstreet" under Shell-fire, Early 1916* and *Lawrence Farm, "Plugstreet," Advance Battalion HQ,*

Early 1916.[149] The writer who could not make, or find qualified artists to make, what he regarded as satisfactory illustrations for his histories of war in India and the Soudan or for his war novel, was himself later to become, though only briefly, a war artist.

It has often been remarked that Savrola is Churchill's idealized portrait of himself in the kind of heroic role that he hoped to play and later did play in real life: a "Great Democrat" fighting a "Dictator" to win freedom for his people. Also frequently remarked is the further but unwanted parallel of Churchill's dismissal by the British electorate after leading them through World War II, just as Savrola is "deserted in the hour of his victory" by the people of Laurania. It has been equally clear to students of Churchill's political methods that via his portrayals of Molinara and other dubious Lauranian politicians young Churchill explores the abuses of rhetoric in the public arena. He understood better than most that eloquence could be enlisted effectively in bad as well as good causes. *Savrola's* villain Molinara is not without virtues even though he uses them to pursue improper goals. He is intelligent, hardworking, brave, persevering in the face of adversity, a sufficiently tough-minded as well as courageous leader to emerge victorious from Laurania's civil war, and charming enough to have won Lucile's consent to marry him. He even—like Churchill later at Chartwell—is sometimes observed "staring into . . . water in which . . . fat, lazy, goldfish swam placidly."[150] During the civil war, however, Molinara's tough-mindedness also took such forms as deliberately sending potential rivals to their deaths in combat, breaking treaties, ordering the execution of prisoners, and torturing captured spies to obtain information. As dictator after the war he does not shrink from equally vile methods, including—"most odious of all"—an attempt to enlist Lucile in a plot to spy on Savrola.[151] For Churchill Molinara is a kind of "there but for the grace of God go I" figure. Savrola—or Churchill—gone bad would result in a person very much like Molinara. As for Macbeth, there is a tragic dimension of wasted potential apparent in Molinara's life and death. For readers—and probably also for Churchill—the tale may elicit a frisson of fear because no one is immune from falling into Molinara's mistakes and suffering his fate. His downfall is necessary but not an occasion for undiluted rejoicing. In killing him off, Churchill vicariously kills off that part of himself that might be tempted to go down the path of using great gifts to evil purposes. In *Savrola* he has imagined two possible alternative versions of himself in the future, and opted for the better one.

Another telling contrast that tips the scales against Molinara is his utter indifference to aesthetics. Unlike Savrola, Molinara has no use for beauty except when it may serve his political purposes. Walking through one of Laurania's "most beautiful and famous" gardens, Molinara is oblivious to its aesthetic appeal:

> The President . . . cared very little for flowers or their arrangement; he was, he said, too busy a man to have anything to do with the beauties of colour, harmony, or line. Neither the tints of the rose nor the smell of the jasmine awakened in him more than the rudimentary physical pleasures which are natural and involuntary. He liked to have a good flower garden, because it was the right thing to have, because it enable him to take people there and talk to them personally on political matters, and because it was convenient for afternoon receptions. But he himself took no interest in it. The kitchen garden appealed to him more; his practical soul rejoiced more in an onion than an orchid.[152]

This blindness to beauty is the least of Molinara's faults, and in itself no vice. Nevertheless Churchill dwells on it to enhance disapproval of his villain. Conversely, appreciation of beauty in art and nature is one of Savrola's endearing traits, as it is among Churchill's most engaging attitudes. His belated involvement with painting as an amateur artist is well known. It has been an increasingly prominent part of his legend ever since publication in 1921 of "Painting as a Pastime." What also deserves recognition, as I hope this chapter has demonstrated, is that from the outset of his career as an author in 1898 Churchill was equally though less obtrusively engaged with the aesthetics of art and with a search for writing techniques that could provide counterparts to the effects of paintings. He was no late convert to "the beauties of colour, harmony, or line."

IMAGINING SCIENCE:
CHURCHILL AND SCIENCE FICTION

Much has been written about the administrative side of Churchill's long and important involvement with science. As First Lord of the Admiralty in 1911 Churchill presided over great advances in warship armament, speed, and endurance that he describes in a very technical chapter of *The World Crisis* ironically titled "The Romance of Design."[1] Historians have noted other influential activities ranging from his encouragement of military aviation, tank development, and chemical warfare during the First World War through his concern as prime minister with radar, rockets, proximity fuses, asdic, atomic research, and other facets of what in his memoirs of World War II he fancifully calls "The Wizard War."[2] Well known are Churchill's singular friendship with his scientific mentor Professor Frederick Lindemann, and his role in the establishment of Churchill College at Cambridge University as a center for the study of science—upon continuing mastery of which, Churchill insisted in one of his last speeches, Britain's future depended.[3] Far less remarked is the imaginative core of Churchill's relationship with scientific ideas and their technological consequences. But even such phrases as "Wizard War" and "The Romance of Design" are telling clues to the fact that the possibilities of modern science stirred his vivid imagination no less than his powerful intellect.

Imaginative engagement with science was one of Churchill's fundamental traits. It is perhaps the feature of his mind and writing that best allows us to understand his remarkable flexibility in dealing with the staggering changes that he confronted in moving to the atomic age from his origins as a Victorian cavalry officer who rode in the charge of the 21st Lancers at the Battle of Omdurman in 1898, and whose entire curriculum at Sandhurst, as he ruefully noted long afterwards, consisted of "Tactics, Fortification, Topography (mapmaking), Military Law . . . Military Administration. . . . Drill, Gymnastics and Riding."[4] Had Churchill not on his own gone far beyond this education for Colonel Blimphood to grasp imaginatively the social as well as military implications of twentieth-century science, it is likely that the Battle of Britain, the Second World War, and with it world history, would have taken a very different and disastrous course. And that, as he warned in his most famous speech, could have plunged our planet into "the abyss of a new Dark Age made more sinister, and perhaps more protracted, by the lights of perverted science."[5] Far from clinging (as some charge that he did) to Victorian dreams of progress brought about by the march of science, Churchill was quicker than most to discard the underlying Enlightenment equation of reason, science, and utopia.

A key text is "Shall We All Commit Suicide?". This was first published in the September 1924 number of *Nash's Pall Mall* magazine and issued also that year as a separate pamphlet. Churchill adapted it within the conclusion of *The Aftermath* in 1929, reprinted it in his 1932 collection of essays *Thoughts and Adventures*, and finally in 1948 quoted it early in *The Gathering Storm*, volume 1 of *The Second World War*.

Churchill begins "Shall We All Commit Suicide?" with an irritating truth not universally acknowledged:"The Story of the human race is War. Except for brief and precarious interludes, there has never been peace in the world; and before history began, murderous strife was universal and unending."[6] He meliorates this Hobbesian vision of human relationships only to the extent of remarking that "up to the present time the means of destruction at the disposal of man have not kept pace with his ferocity."[7] Churchill devotes the rest of the essay to explaining why, thanks mostly to "Science on the Side of War," humanity confronts for the first time the possibility of annihilation: "It was not until the dawn of the twentieth century of the Christian era that War really began to enter into its kingdom as the potential destroyer of the human race."[8] After glancing at the new machinery of death employed in World War I, he provides a miniature alternative history by explaining how much more devastating the campaigns of 1919 would have been had the Armistice not intervened to prevent deployment of improved weapons—a topic on which there is in

The World Crisis an entire chapter entitled "The Unfought Campaign."[9] Churchill then speculates about the future of explosives:

> Have we reached the end? Has Science turned its last page on them? May there not be methods of using explosive energy incomparably more intense than anything heretofore discovered? Might not a bomb no bigger than an orange be found to possess a secret power to destroy a whole block of buildings—nay to concentrate the force of a thousand tons of cordite and blast a township at a stroke? Could not explosives even of the existing type be guided automatically in flying machines by wireless or other rays, without a human pilot, in ceaseless procession on a hostile city, arsenal, camp, or dockyard?[10]

After dwelling with equal prescience on future possibilities of chemical and bacteriological weapons, and on social conditions likely to foster such warfare, Churchill winds up by suggesting, not very hopefully, that "disasters compared to which those we have suffered will be but a pale preliminary" can only be averted by strengthening the League of Nations, which "raises feebly but faithfully its standards of sanity and hope."[11] What stands out in "Shall We All Commit Suicide?" is Churchill's inclination to imagine—and invite readers to imagine—future science and alternative pasts. Both are staples of science fiction. Both recur in Churchill's writing frequently enough to be characteristic features of his style, though not in every text.

—————— ∞ ——————

Churchill's only freestanding alternative history is "If Lee Had Not Won the Battle of Gettysburg."[12] This is a classic of the genre called in science fiction alternative or alternate history, and referred to by historians—often suspiciously—as counterfactual history.[13] Churchill presents his story as if it were written by someone living in a world where Lee *did* win the Battle of Gettysburg, thus precipitating (implausibly from our viewpoint) a sequence of events leading to the abolition of slavery, a Union of the English Speaking Peoples, and the prospect of a United States of Europe led by Kaiser Wilhelm II. Churchill's imaginary resident of that imaginary world speculates in vintage Churchillian prose about what dreadful things, including a terrible European war breaking out in 1914, might have happened had there *not* been a Confederate victory. Readers are thus invited to see from that surprisingly utopian perspective our *own* world as both dystopian and implausible. The narrator mentions, for example, a book written in 1909 by M. Bloch—but not accepted by leading military experts—predicting that a European conflict fought with modern weapons would be a long, bloody stalemate of trench warfare killing millions and leaving in its wake economic and political devastation. This alludes to Jean de Bloch's once-famous book *The Future of War*, which predicted with what proved remarkably accurate military detail the devastation that would attend a war between major European states, but which drew from this prediction the sadly inaccurate conclusion that such a war would therefore be avoided and would never take place.[14]

The brilliance of Churchill's essay lies in his decision to shift its narrative viewpoint so that readers must not only consider the possible consequences of a Confederate victory including alternatives to the bloodletting of World War I, but also imagine how inconceivable *our* world might seem if things had worked out differently. Emphasis is upon the contingency as well as the facts of history. Churchill powerfully exercises here that rare gift of political imagination which allowed him to portray dramatically different outcomes of a particular situation, whether the American Civil War or, later, the Battle of Britain. In Churchill's evocation of the very implausibility of what readers must nevertheless acknowledge to have been the stark reality of World War I's gigantic slaughter we may see a foreshadowing of the rhetorician who in 1940 rallied his country to the cause of civilization by inviting contemplation of the likelihood—too easily dismissed by many then and now—that a Nazi victory would plunge "the whole world . . . into the abyss of a new Dark Age." That chilling thought acquires much of its power by inviting imagination of one possible future as a kind of alternative feudal period whose tyrannies are accompanied and abetted by technological development more accelerated than anything actually achieved during the medieval era. In his "Finest Hour" speech, Churchill invites his audience to think of the worst possible outcome of Britain's fight against Hitler's Germany not as a unique situation incomparable with anything that has gone before but rather as an alternative past wrenched out of time to prevent and replace that desirable future in which "if we can stand up to him, all Europe may be free and the life of the world may move forward into broad, sunlit uplands."[15] Here and elsewhere Churchill's skill as alternative historian notably enhances the rhetoric that he so famously mobilized for war.

Most of Churchill's alternative histories are embedded in other texts, sometimes over several pages, sometimes in compressed form as in the sentence about a "new Dark age" in his "Finest Hour" speech. Here, for example is a paragraph in *The Aftermath* outlining how Britain would have fared had not Germany been defeated in World War I:

> Contrast for a moment the position which Germany occupies to-day [1929] with the doom which would have fallen upon the British Empire and upon Great Britain itself had the submarine attack mastered the Royal Navy and left our forty millions only the choice between unconditional surrender and certain starvation. Half the severity meted out by the Treaty of Versailles would have involved not only the financial ruin of our ancient, slowly built-up world organization but a swift contraction of the British population by at least ten million souls and the condemnation of the rest to universal and hopeless poverty. The stakes of this hideous war were beyond all human measure, and for Britain and her people they were not less than final extinction.[16]

In *The World Crisis* there is much speculation on how World War I might have ended more quickly with far fewer casualties had the Gallipoli campaign been fought more aggressively by admirals and generals on the spot, and had tanks been deployed initially en masse rather than dribbled onto the battlefield in quantities too small to be decisive. In Churchill's hands, as in much science fiction, alternative pasts are sometimes used not only to identify what he calls in *The Aftermath* "turning points" or (in a more classical mode) "hinges of Fate" and to suggest what depended on them, but also as invitations to think about utopian or dystopian futures.[17]

Churchill's chapter on "The Unfought Campaign" of 1919 is in a decidedly dystopian mode, culminating in a horrific Wellsian vision of an offensive that never was but might yet be, as Churchill once imagined it and now invites his readers to imagine it:

> My mind amid a vivid life of movement and activity always rested on one picture of the future: 10,000 fighting tanks, large and small, specially adapted to the ground they had to traverse, moving forward simultaneously behind the artillery barrage on fronts of assault aggregating 300 or 400 kilometres; behind them, working with

them, British, French and American infantry; and behind these again, 10,000 caterpillar vehicles unarmed and unarmoured, but each carrying forward across country, over fields and trenches, all the food, ammunition, kit and supplies of every kind which one platoon would require, while the roads remained clear and free for the advance of artillery and reserves.[18]

This "picture of the future" that Churchill says obsessed him while serving as munitions minister in 1918 stands as a prophetic warning that everything in it and more might *yet* take place in the reader's future if peace cannot somehow be established by political settlements better than those of the Versailles Treaty.

Before turning in *The Aftermath* to his blistering critique of Woodrow Wilson and other leaders at the Versailles conference who succeeded only in aggravating rather than removing conflicts that could lead to another and worse world war, Churchill indulges in a utopian alternative history presented in the venerable form of a dream vision: "one of the many Armistice Dreams."[19] In it Wilson, Clemenceau, and Lloyd George, instead of delaying as they did in the real world, meet promptly after November 11, 1918, and with better political preparation at home by Wilson than he achieved in reality. They decide that "the new instrument of world-order should be armed with the new weapons of science." They establish for that purpose a new "International Air Force" whose pilots—mostly World War I aces—will be, Wilson says enthusiastically, "the new nobility." This, Clemenceau suggests, will be in effect to revive "the old Orders of chivalry like the Knights Templars and the Knights of Malta to guard civilization against barbarism."[20] Shortly after this exchange Churchill ends his vision of a past that never was and a future that never will be with a conventional account of the dreamer—here himself—awakening again to dismal reality: "The spell broke. The illusion of power vanished. I awoke from my Armistice dream, and we all found ourselves in the rough, dark, sour and chilly waters in which we are swimming still."[21] Churchill's utopian vison of a new nobility of the air as enforcers of a new world order is if anything more Wellsian than H. G. Wells, though one thinks of *The War in the Air* (1908), *The Shape of Things to Come* (1933), and especially of *The World Set Free* (1914) with its aircraft, atomic bombs, and reconstitution of society after nuclear Armageddon. To read Churchill's Armistice dream is to understand better the utopian impulse underlying his eloquent

tributes in 1940 to the Few: "These young airmen. . . . going forth every morn to guard their native land and all that we stand for . . . of whom it may be said that 'Every morn brought forth a noble chance / And every chance brought forth a noble knight.'"[22]

⎯⎯⎯⎯⎯ ∞ ⎯⎯⎯⎯⎯

If the Armistice dream is Churchill's utopia lost, his and our impending dystopia is outlined with passages of Orwellian power in "Fifty Years Hence," an essay first published in the December 1931 *Strand* and included in 1932 along with "Shall We All Commit Suicide?" in *Thoughts and Adventures*. James W. Muller has rightly identified this essay as "a kind of acid test of Churchill's relevance" offering in addition to predictions "a diagnosis of the predicament of modern man."[23] Again Churchill's premise is that "this power called Science" has now accelerated the pace of change and come to dominate humanity in unprecedented ways: "None of the generations of men before the last two or three were ever gripped for good or ill and handled like this."[24] Accordingly the remote past is no guide to the future. Would-be prophets must discard methods employed by historians in favor of scientific extrapolation:

> There are two processes which we adopt consciously or unconsciously when we try to prophesy. We can seek a period in the past whose conditions resemble as closely as possible those of our day, and presume that the sequel to that period will, save for some minor alterations, be repeated. Secondly, we can survey the general course of development in our immediate past, and endeavour to prolong it into the near future. The first is the method of the historian; the second that of the scientist. Only the second is open to us now, and this only in a partial sphere. By observing all that Science has achieved in modern times, and the knowledge and power now in her possession, we can predict with some assurance the inventions and discoveries which will govern our future. We can but guess, peering through a glass darkly, what reactions these discoveries and their application will produce upon the habits, the outlook and the spirit of men.[25]

This remarkable passage deserves wider currency. It shows Churchill's acute awareness that the modern period—thanks largely to science—is in crucial respects an unprecedented break in the continuity of human history and accordingly demands new modes of historiography, including the occasional practice of *future* history: accounts (as best they can be constructed) of what has not yet happened.[26] He was prolific as a conventional historian. But in "Fifty Years Hence" Churchill applies to the task of writing future history a scientific and science fictional mode of imagination via extrapolation rather than a conventional historian's usual method of looking to the past for archetypes.

What results is portrayal in "Fifty Years Hence" of two alternative futures made possible by science: one utopian, the other dystopian. Churchill's utopia is an amusing pastoral vision of teeming cities transformed into uncrowded countrysides whose inhabitants enjoy gardens and glades, "wireless telephones and television," vat-grown chicken breasts, and other "synthetic food." Because this is, after all, a Churchillian utopia, readers are assured that the "the pleasures of the table" will remain available without resort to food in the form of unappetizing pills: "That gloomy Utopia of tabloid means need never be invaded. The new foods will from the outset be practically indistinguishable from the natural products, and any changes will be so gradual as to escape observation."[27] But this gardeners and gourmets paradise is less persuasively elaborated than Churchill's Orwellian nightmare of humanity falling into spiritually empty materialism and ultimately displaced altogether by a posthuman race of bioengineered android slaves serving a power-hungry despotism.

This dystopian vision is introduced by an allusion to Karel Čapek's *Rossum's Universal Robots* (1920), where the term "robot" was first used, although referring in Čapek's play to biological androids rather than to the mechanical robots more common in later usage of his term.

> A few years ago London was surprised by a play called *Roosum's* [*sic*] *Universal Robots*. The production of such beings may well be possible within fifty years. They will not be made, but grown under glass. There seems little doubt that it will be possible to carry out in artificial surroundings the entire cycle which now leads to the birth of a child. Interference with the mental development of such beings, expert suggestion and treatment in the earlier years, would produce beings specialized to thought or toil. . . . A being might be produced capable of tending a machine but without other ambitions.[28]

Unusually alert as Churchill was to the possibilities of real science, even if a little off here in his estimate of when artificial gestation might be fully realized, for him Čapek's science fiction classic was no mere political parable or fanciful prophecy unrelated to reality. In Churchill's imagination *Rossum's Universal Robots* was a stimulus to an even more sobering exercise of future history with an important moral for the present. Churchill's sketch of a horrific state that scientifically controls for its own totalitarian purposes both the physiology and the mentality of its people strikingly anticipates Aldous Huxley's elaboration of that prospect in *Brave New World*. Because Huxley's novel was published early in 1932, shortly after the deut of "Fifty Years Hence" in the December 1931 *Strand Magazine*, Churchill evidently arrived independently as well as slightly ahead of the novelist at the same core conceit of people biologically and psychologically conditioned by their government in ways that eliminate human freedom and even what was commonly taken to be human nature. Churchill treats the idea concisely and somberly. Huxley's longer work is a comic masterpiece that points an equally somber moral. *Brave New World* has achieved enduring fame thanks to its hilariously effective satire as well as the ever-increasing relevance its warning shares with that in Churchill's essay. In satire and science fiction, Churchill is far from Huxley's equal. Nevertheless it is remarkable that as a writer Churchill was alert to the same intellectual and artistic currents that prompted *Brave New World*, and well able to try his hand to good effect at related forms of writing.

In "Fifty Years Hence" Churchill unmistakably alludes, although not by name, to another science fiction classic: Olaf Stapledon's 1930 novel, *Last and First Men*:

> I read a book the other day which traced the history of mankind from the birth of the solar system to its extinction. There were fifteen or sixteen races of men which in succession rose and fell over periods measured by tens of millions of years. In the end a race of beings was evolved which had mastered nature. A state was created whose citizens lived as long as they chose, enjoyed pleasures and sympathies incomparably wider than our own, navigated the inter-planetary spaces, could recall the panorama of the past and foresee the future. But what was the good of all that to them? . . . No material progress, even though it takes shapes we cannot now conceive, or however it may expand the faculties of man, can bring comfort to his soul.[29]

Like Čapek's science fiction play, Stapledon's panoramic future history stimulated Churchill's literary and moral imagination as he considered what might lie ahead for humanity. The key to all futures, Churchill suggests, will be atomic energy: "Nuclear energy is incomparably greater than the molecular energy which we use today. . . . There is no question among scientists that this gigantic source of energy exists. What is lacking is the match to set the bonfire alight, or it may be the detonator to cause the dynamite to explode. The Scientists are looking for this."[30] Twenty-four years later, during his second term as prime minister, Churchill quoted this prediction at the outset of his March 1, 1955, speech to the House of Commons on the hydrogen bomb, by way of illustrating his long-standing interest in atomic energy.

Under the pressure of war, Churchill had been among the first to facilitate the transition from prediction to reality. After Professor Lindemann in an August 1941 memo confirmed the feasibility of producing atomic bombs within the immediate future, thus raising among other specters that of a Nazi bomb, Churchill as prime minister vigorously supported the atomic research program code-named Tube Alloys.[31] He later authorized full British cooperation with America's Manhattan Project for producing useable bombs. At the Quebec conference with President Roosevelt in August 1943 Churchill negotiated an agreement on atomic cooperation calling, among other provisions, for mutual consent to any use of atomic bombs against third parties. This clause was rather casually honored en route to Hiroshima and Nagasaki, was not widely known in or outside the United States government, and to Churchill's dismay was given up in 1948 by Clement Attlee.[32] Under his Labour government, however, Britain moved independently to secure its own atomic bombs to serve, along with those of the United States, as a deterrent against attack by the Soviet Union. Although Churchill well understood the menace posed by these new additions to the arsenals on both sides of the Cold War, he understood too that it was the leap to thermonuclear weapons—the hydrogen bomb—which finally placed humanity in danger of abandoning control of its destiny and perhaps actually destroying itself. We might indeed all commit suicide, as he explained to the House of Commons in his March 1, 1955, speech on defense: "The atomic bomb, with all its terrors, did not carry us outside the scope of human control or manageable events in thought or action, in peace or war." But with advent of the hydrogen bomb "the entire foundation of human affairs was revolutionized, and mankind placed in a situation both measureless and laden with doom."[33] Churchill's earlier predictions about nuclear energy had become fact— and far short of fifty years hence.

In that same 1955 speech Churchill outlined for Parliament not only the horrific consequences should nations use their hydrogen bombs, but a hopeful possibility that their very destructiveness would deter use: "Thus it may well be that we shall by a process of sublime irony have reached a stage in this story where safety will be the sturdy child of terror, and survival the twin brother of annihilation."[34] After piously hoping that under the umbrella provided by mutual terror a better day might eventually dawn, Churchill concluded with words that have often been taken out of context as his final credo: "Meanwhile, never flinch, never weary, never despair."[35] It is good advice, but neither easy to follow nor easily arrived at. After mentioning the unparalleled "blast and heat effects" of hydrogen bombs, Churchill noted the even more sinister consequences of radioactive fallout: "This would confront many who escaped the direct effects of the explosion with poisoning, or starvation, or both. Imagination stands appalled."[36] In a 1954 speech commenting on release of information about American thermonuclear test explosions in the Pacific, Churchill had also remarked the unsettling confrontation of imagination with fact: "The hydrogen bomb carries us into dimensions which have never before confronted practical human thought and have been confined to the realms of fancy and imagination."[37] Churchill understood that in the awesome applications of atomic energy, realities had at last outstripped even his powerful imagination. There was little comfort in this appreciation of its limits as a guide to the future.

But in "Fifty Years Hence" Churchill had not merely tried to imagine the future basing his predictions on extrapolation from "all that Science has achieved in modern times, and the knowledge and power now in her possession." He also engages the reader's moral imagination by suggesting that, given the likely course of scientific developments, their future social outcome—whether utopian or dystopian—will depend on humanity's psychological and moral qualities. On this issue Churchill is realistic and certainly a good (and equal-opportunity) prophet: "The nature of man has remained hitherto practically unchanged. Under sufficient stress—starvation, terror, warlike passion, or even cold intellectual frenzy, the modern man we know so well will do the most terrible deeds, and his modern woman will back him up."[38] As in "Shall We All Commit Suicide?",

Churchill urges his readers to consider the consequences of clinging to old attitudes. He argues eloquently that human survival depends on setting aside selfish materialism in favor of developing our capacities for "Mercy, Pity, Peace and Love."[39] That was Churchill's policy. It is neither his fault nor his preference that, despite many efforts over the years as a peacemaker, he was destined to be famous not as an advocate of mercy, pity, peace, and love but as the prime minister who could only offer blood, toil, tears, and sweat.[40]

In "Fifty Years Hence" Churchill's all too well justified foreboding culminates in an apocalyptic vision of science misapplied by tyrannies for dehumanizing purposes:

> In a future which our children may live to see, powers will be in the hands of men altogether different from any by which human nature has been moulded. Explosive forces, energy, materials, machinery will be available upon a scale which can annihilate whole nations. Despotisms and tyrannies will be able to prescribe the lives and even the wishes of their subjects in a manner never known since time began. If to these tremendous and awful powers is added the pitiless subhuman wickedness which we now see embodied in one of the most powerful reigning governments, who shall say that the world itself will not be wrecked, or indeed that it ought not to be wrecked? There are nightmares of the future from which a fortunate collision with some wandering star, reducing the earth to incandescent gas, might be a merciful deliverance.[41]

Here Churchill is sublime. Readers are taken in imagination beyond our planet's problems to its end. This fearful vision is placed within a moral framework that invites us against all our instincts and all our vanity to consider that end as a possible blessing. This variety of what I call the science fictional sublime is rare in Churchill's writing but nevertheless altogether characteristic. It is no late development.

As I remarked in chapter 3 above, an invitation to consider future catastrophes on an astronomical scale appeared in *Savrola*, which Churchill began writing in 1897 and published serially in *Macmillan's Magazine* in 1899 before its appearance as a book later that year. You'll recall that in one episode its protagonist Savrola, an idealized self-portrait of the young author, gazes at Jupiter through a telescope then thinks of "the incomprehensible periods of time that would elapse before the cooling process would render life possible on its surface, of the slow, steady march of evolution, merciless, inexorable," and arrives at a "mournful conclusion": even if biological evolution there leads to some kind of extraterrestrial utopia, eventually and inexorably "the cooling process would continue; the perfect development of life would end in death; the whole solar system, the whole universe itself, would one day be cold and lifeless as a burned-out firework."[42] This sublime meditation might almost be a précis of the far future scenes of a dying planet in an expiring solar system at the end of H. G. Wells's *The Time Machine* (1895). In *Savrola* Churchill provides in concise form an elegant variation on one apocalyptic theme of that great scientific romance: the prospect that, thanks to the iron determinism of thermodynamics, human history, and thus all individual achievements, will ultimately be rendered meaningless by the oblivion into which they will be plunged by the final extinction of life everywhere. If that is to be the case, both works invite their readers to wonder, then what, sub specie aeternitatis, is the point of ambition or achievement? Why should a politician—or for that matter anyone—live strenuously?

The passages of utopian and dystopian speculation that I have singled out reveal major imaginative affinities linking Churchill with science fiction. His quarrels with one of its founders, H. G. Wells, have often been remarked. They expressed especially acrimonious disagreement about capitalism and the British Empire, which Wells disliked and Churchill defended, and about what Churchill rightly saw as Wells's naive approval of the Soviet Union.[43] Too often overlooked amid these fierce political exchanges is an underlying friendship that had at its core a mutual imaginative appeal. They corresponded. They occasionally met for lunch. To extend opportunities for such meetings Churchill even proposed Wells for membership in the Other Club.[44] Their views sometimes coincided. In an Open Letter to Labour voters, Wells (to the dismay of his usual political allies) supported Churchill's 1908 campaign for election to Parliament as an Independent Liberal candidate. By that time he and Wells "had for some years been in lively and friendly correspondence."[45] After blithely taking credit for tanks as "an old notion of mine" worked out in "the *Land Ironclads* (published in the *Strand Magazine* in 1903)," Wells praised Churchill for attempting to make them an effective battlefield reality: "These obvious weapons were forced upon the army by Winston Churchill against all the conservative instincts of the army."[46] In *The World Crisis* Churchill notes that although the idea of an armored land vehicle had a long history and could not be credited to any one individual including himself, it was nevertheless true that H. G. Wells "in an article written in 1903, had practically exhausted the possibilities of imagination in this sphere."[47] Probably "The Land Ironclads" (a short story, not an article) mainly provided ratification of directions in which Churchill's own powerful imagination was leading him to envision more clearly than most of his contemporaries such military implications of science. Here too it was a matter of imaginative affinities rather than influence.

Unlike some other English leaders during the first years of World War I, Churchill escaped criticism in Wells's 1916 novel about its horrors, *Mr. Britling Sees It Through.* In 1923 Churchill and his friend Brendan Bracken prevailed on Wells to write an article on the future of the British Empire.[48] In the 1930s both Churchill and Wells warned against the catastrophic possibilities of another world war that science would make even more devastating than the first one. Perhaps in a gust of emotional response to their mutual though very different attempts to stave off that disaster, Wells's 1937 novel *Star Begotten* announced itself "Dedicated On a Sudden Impulse To my Friend Winston Spencer Churchill."[49] Despite the apologetic tone Wells created by announcing that his dedication was impulsive rather than a carefully considered gesture, Churchill wrote effusively to Wells: "It gives me real pleasure that my early admiration of thirty five years ago for your wonderful books should have come to rest in our later times in a harbour of personal friendship."[50] But Churchill politely avoided public comment on *Star Begotten's* bizarre theme of hidden Martian rays stimulating the development of earthly intelligence. Wells applauded Churchill's defiance of Hitler in 1940, and rejoiced—rather more than Churchill—at the latter's quick embrace of an British alliance with the Communist rulers of the Soviet Union after Germany's 1941 invasion of Russia.[51] Despite divergences that were the more usual public hallmark of their relationship, Churchill and Wells respected each other's abilities. Above all, when they disagreed on issues of the day, each could enjoy the imaginative pleasure of appropriating the other as a famous figure conveniently available for depiction as a symbolic bête noire that, hopefully, their readers would love to hate.

To Wells, Churchill was sometimes a hero but more often a deliciously vivid bogeyman standing for all that was reprehensibly regressive in English society. To Churchill, Wells was a great English writer who nevertheless was too often the very archetype of a gullible intellectual taken in by the blandishments of Communism and, to boot, a notoriously ungrateful exemplar of that very opportunity to rise from obscurity to fame and riches that Churchill thought was due to freedoms guaranteed by the traditional English political and social order. Each, for the other, could be the stimulus to florid rhetoric that attempted the persuasiveness of an ex cathedra tone achieved by resort to vaguely biblical imagery. Churchill's sharp critique of Wells's enthusiastic account of his 1920 visit to the Soviet Union provoked from Wells the countercharge that Churchill "has smeared his vision with human blood. . . . This vision of his is no more and no less contemptible than some misshapen idol esteemed by the tribe, to which we may presently see our children sacrificed."[52] Here is Winston as Moloch. Churchill, commenting in 1931 on how Wells had prospered as people bought his books regardless of their often unfriendly ideology, remarked that "The young H. G. Wells struck the brazen front of bad old England as Moses smote the rock with his rod, and there gushed forth an abundant golden stream."[53] Here, at first glance more benignly, is H. G. as Moses the miracle worker. But, creating a double take, there is also a sarcastic hint of Wells as a decidedly unholy young Moses producing if not worshiping the ingredients for a golden calf.

In his 1922 novel *Men Like Gods*, Wells gives Churchill a starring role as its warmongering, imperialist villain, very thinly disguised as Rupert Catskill, the secretary of state for war. Churchill's private secretary Edward ("Eddie") Marsh makes a cameo appearance as Freddie Mush. They are among a small group of people transported to a far-future alternative world when a scientific experiment there gets out of control. The accidental tourists from our 1920s find themselves unwelcome atavisms in a utopian society whose peaceful socialistic virtues Wells invites readers to admire while deploring the attempt of Catskill and his English allies to make it, in effect, yet another of Britain's colonies by embarking on a "crusade to restore the blessings of competition, conflict and warfare to Utopia."[54] In the course of the novel's exciting action, Wells misses no opportunity to heap similar scorn on what he thus caricatures as Churchill's ideology. Catskill is nevertheless portrayed as a rather engaging person who is always energetic, always interesting, and never merely malicious. Imagination is the attribute of Catskill's dynamic personality to which Wells recurs as a leitmotif accounting for what is most praiseworthy as well as most reprehensible in Catskill's conduct.

At the outset of *Men Like Gods*, when the group from our world abruptly find themselves on a strange road in a landscape very different from the one they had just been driving through, they halt to take stock. To one who wonders why they don't just continue to their destination, the answer is: "Because . . . Rupert insists that we are in some other world. And won't go on."[55] He is right, although none of the others is endowed by Wells with a sufficiently quick imagination to grasp their peculiar situation. With nice irony, he then makes one of the group criticize the quality that has allowed Catskill alone to understand their predicament correctly: "He has always had too much imagination. He thinks that things that don't exist *can* exist. And now he imagines himself in some sort of scientific romance and out of our world altogether. In another dimension. I sometimes think it would have been better for all of us if Rupert had taken to writing romances—instead of living them."[56] Of course, by an amusing self-reflexive stroke on the author's part, Catskill is indeed "in some sort of scientific romance." Wells here criticizes Churchill's imagination as running amok in the real world but simultaneously accords him the accolade of suggesting, however backhandedly, that he too might have been a notable writer of science fiction. A speech that Catskill makes (in the Churchillian manner) is praised as having "that imaginative touch which makes for eloquence."[57] Where Catskill the eloquent rhetorician and imaginative science fiction writer manqué goes astray is in having "an incurable craving for fantastic enterprises."[58]

Deflection of Catskill's imagination to scripting real-world exploits instead of writing romances is accounted for by a public school education that has molded him as a model British imperialist. Although Mr. Barnstaple (the H. G. Wells surrogate in *Men Like Gods*) concedes that Catskill is "fundamentally a civilized man," his schooling is found wanting:

> "You have a very good imagination," Mr. Barnstaple reflected. "The trouble is that you have been so damnably educated. What is the trouble with you? You are be-Kiplinged. Empire and Anglo-Saxon

and boy-scout and sleuth are the stuff in your mind. If I had gone to Eton I might have been the same as you are, I suppose."

"Harrow," corrected Mr. Catskill.

"A perfectly *beastly* public school. Suburban place where the boys wear chignons and straw haloes. I might have guessed Harrow."[59]

Apart from the slap at Harrovian hairstyles and hats, this inventory of what is most deplorable at public schools is a conventional socialist critique. It is surprising only for inclusion of sleuths alongside boy scouts among the models held responsible for Catskill's infantile attitudes and "puerile imaginations."[60] It is true that Sherlock Holmes made his debut in *A Study in Scarlet* the year before Churchill entered Harrow in 1888, and then solved that initial series of increasingly famous cases chronicled by the faithful Dr. Watson and collected together as *The Adventures of Sherlock Holmes* in 1891, the year after Churchill left Harrow. But as Churchill was never among the outspoken admirers of the Great Sleuth, Wells seems here mainly to be taking a pot shot at what for him was the rival genre of detective stories.

A summary of Catskill's life unmistakably identifies him as Churchill while singling out imagination as the quality that has made him dangerous: "He has lived most romantically. He has fought bravely in wars. He has been a prisoner and escaped wonderfully from prison. His violent imaginations have caused the deaths of thousands of people."[61] In *Men Like Gods*, Wells charges that with less imagination, or imagination otherwise employed than in warlike imperial enterprises, Churchill would have been more admirable because more useful in moving society toward the kind of socialist utopia that in this novel Catskill tries to destroy. Even so, portraying Churchill as Catskill fascinated Wells, who "himself remarked later that Churchill had threatened to run away with the book, giving lovely speeches and starting wars, that he 'had to stun him' to get the novel under control."[62]

Perhaps to avoid the danger of Churchill again hijacking the author's imagination, Wells keeps him offstage in *Meanwhile*, his 1927 novel set at the time of the 1926 General Strike. A letter from one of the characters to his wife presents Churchill's efforts against the strike, including his editing of the government's antistrike newspaper, the *British Gazette*, as merely the unbalanced antics of a man who craves action, any action: "As might be expected Winston has gone clean off his head. He hasn't been as happy since he crawled on his belly and helped snipe in Sidney Street. . . . He careers about staring, inactive, gaping, crowded London, looking for barricades."[63] While serving as home secretary Churchill had gained a reputation for impulsive activity because of his imprudent appearance at the scene of the 1911 Sidney Street police shootout with anarchists. But in fact he did not himself take part in the gunplay during the "siege of Sidney Street." The letter's unfair but amusing comment on Churchill is illustrated with a droll sketch by Wells showing a stick figure of Churchill pointlessly running down a street lined with puzzled spectators. It is titled "Winston doing Something." Wells has his letter writer dismissively sum up both the strike and Churchill's response to it: "The essence of it is, miners locked out, transport workers of all sorts striking, printers striking, Winston probably certifiable but no doctors can get near him to do it, soldiers and police going about with loaded guns looking for a Revolution that isn't there . . . and the general public, like me, agape. All London agape."[64] Although the charge of lunacy is put in a lighthearted way, for Wells it was indeed "the essence" of what he saw as the mental disease of Churchill's incurable imaginative craving for fantastic warlike or quasi-warlike enterprises.

Oddly, the accusation that Churchill was "certifiable" from the viewpoint of a socialist utopian is less mistaken than the conclusion drawn by Wells that were Churchill accordingly locked safely away from all political action England would benefit. The flaw in Wells's reasoning is that we do not live in a sane world, as George Orwell remarked in his 1941 essay "Wells, Hitler and the World State." Orwell there charges that Wells "was, and still is, quite incapable of understanding that nationalism, religious bigotry and feudal loyalty are far more powerful forces than what he himself would describe as sanity."[65] Writing this devastating critique of Wells while Hitler was at the height of his conquests, Orwell echoed and amplified the imagery of Churchill's 1940 warning in his "Finest Hour" speech that unless England, then fighting alone, could resist Hitler, "the whole world" would "sink into the abyss of a New Dark Age."[66] Orwell took Wells to task for not grasping that "creatures of the Dark Ages have come marching into the present, and if they are ghosts they are at any rate ghosts which need a strong magic to lay them." Amid such regression toward unreason, Orwell finds that "Wells is too sane to understand the modern world."[67] Churchill certainly understood it, however certifiable he may have been according to the narrow definition of Wellsian sanity.

Churchill could therefore put the kind of imagination that Wells disliked to effective political use in staving off that relapse into Fascist barbarism and madness that Wells in the less effectual realms of utopian fantasy was also striving to defeat.

———————— ✆ ————————

Despite their political disputes, Churchill lavishly praised Wells as an "unquestionably great English writer." This magnanimous phrase is from Churchill's essay on H. G. Wells in the *Sunday Pictorial* of August 23, 1931, where, after castigating again (and as usual) Wells's political views, Churchill turns to invite appreciation of "the gifted being to whose gay and daring fancy and to whose penetrating vision so many of us owe so much." This now almost entirely forgotten panegyric deserves a reprise as much for the accuracy of its literary judgement as for the light it sheds on what caught Churchill's imagination.

I am a great reader of Wells. It must be more than thirty years ago that I first discovered his *Select Conversations with an Uncle* or read in the pages of the *Strand Magazine* his *Queer Side of Things*. I responded at once to his intellectual stimulus and literary dexterity; and when I came upon *The Time Machine*, that marvellous philosophical romance, not unworthy to follow at some distance, but nevertheless in the train of, *Gulliver's Travels*, I shouted with joy. Then I read all his books. I have read them all over since. I could pass an examination in them. One whole long shelf in my small library is filled with a complete edition. . . . Here is entertainment and frolic. Here are shrewd ideas of peace and war. Here are prophecies of the future, not a few of which we have lived to verify and endure.

Wells the magician, the seer, saw quite clearly, nay in meticulous detail, all that flying meant, as soon as the first man could fly. He visualised and portrayed the hateful developments which now make it a matter of course even among the signatories of the Kellogg Pact (if a war should most improperly and incorrectly arise) that the bombing of undefended cities and wholesale slaughter of men, women and children would be perpetrated. He saw from the beginning of this new discovery that it would lead the twentieth century to accept with a helpless shrug barbarities of which Marius and

Julius Caesar would have been ashamed, and which even Genghis Khan would have thought unbecoming.

Wells described with incredible accuracy exactly how the Great War would come. He painted beforehand the opening scenes and impressions in the streets, in the cottage homes, in the suburban train, in the mammoth hotel, in the pleasure city. Nothing was hidden from him. He knew that hell was going to break loose and knew exactly what it would look like and feel like when it did. But he became still more definite. . . . He described the "Tank" long before such engines had been conceived, even in the primitive form in which they were used in the Great War. He imagined the great land-battleship, the irresistible Juggernaut, driving through towns and villages as through a field of standing corn—a type which Armageddon itself could not achieve, but which will certainly some day play its part in the struggles of races or of doctrines.[68]

Churchill's enthusiasm reveals mental and stylistic affinities, shared tastes and concerns, even more than influences. These are the tones of someone who has discovered a kindred spirit, not someone whose life or writing was greatly *changed* as a result of the encounter. Churchill's appreciation of Wells's writings was no passing fancy. The lasting impression made by *The Time Machine* on Churchill's imagination is attested by a conversational remark recorded in 1947 when he was over seventy years old: "Wells is a seer. His *Time Machine* is a wonderful book, in the same class as *Gulliver's Travels*. It is one of the books I would like to take with me to Purgatory."[69] It is pleasant to know that in Churchill's view even the burdens of Purgatory may be lightened by a choice library including at least one science fiction classic.

The *Sunday Pictorial* essay also goes on to express preference for Wells over Jules Verne on grounds that Wells belongs mentally to the twentieth century even though he (like Churchill) got started as a writer late in the Victorian fin de siècle milieu: "Jules Verne delighted the Victorians. He told them about all the things they hoped they would be able to do. He showed them the possibilities of science applied to the nineteenth century. Wells took up his work in the twentieth, carried it much further in a far more complex scene; and Wells saw the bloody accomplished fact, illustrating his pages while their ink was wet."[70] In this matter of Wells versus Verne, as on so many other more weighty issues, Churchill shows himself at home if not altogether happy in the post-Victorian world. His sympathies are for writers, whatever their chronological roots, who remain a vital part of the twentieth century. The subtleties of elite avant-garde modernists like T. S. Eliot, Henry James, and James Joyce had notoriously little appeal for Churchill. But he was much more responsive to—and familiar with—those science fiction masters like H. G. Wells, Karel Čapek, and Olaf Stapledon who, arguably in a century so dominated by the applications of science, dealt with themes of more pressing urgency and greater philosophical moment. Churchill's ability and willingness to adopt the forms of science fiction as they did, though in smaller and more scattered doses, is another and insufficiently appreciated sign of that versatility, skill, and power as a writer that won him the 1953 Nobel Prize for Literature. Moreover, Churchill's imaginative affinity with many techniques, themes, and writers of science fiction, the literature of the scientific imagination, is a significant measure of his openness to the future, of his capacity to imagine the social consequences of science, and thus of his remarkable ability not only to survive in but to shape for the better the twentieth century.

TIME AND IMAGINATION
IN *MARLBOROUGH*

Isaiah Berlin rightly insisted that "Churchill's dominant category, the single, central, organising principle of his moral and intellectual universe, is an historical imagination so strong, so comprehensive, as to encase the whole of the present and the whole of the future in a framework of a rich and multi-coloured past."[1] But Churchill's historical imagination also worked the other way around very often, by enclosing present and past in the framework of an imagined future. Recall his most famous sentence. After warning in June 1940 that British failure to stand up to Hitler would plunge the world "into the abyss of a new Dark Age made more sinister, and perhaps more protracted, by the lights of perverted science," Churchill stated his immortal imperative: "Let us therefore brace ourselves to our duties and so bear ourselves that, if the British Empire and its Commonwealth last for a thousand years, men will still say, 'This was their finest hour.'"[2] Churchill does not equate history with progress. He characterizes an all too likely regressive future by recourse to a familiar stereotype of medieval horrors summed up in the phrase "Dark Age." He then radically shifts his audience's temporal perspective by inviting imagination of how they themselves may be—or at least should be—characterized a thousand years hence.

This surprising imaginative leap forward in time entails a shift in psychological as well as temporal point of view. The first half of Churchill's conclusion urges a community of speaker and audience to act resolutely together in the present: "Let *us* therefore brace *ourselves* to *our* duties and so bear *ourselves* that . . ." By next inviting imagination of people in a distant future looking back at the result of his exhortation, the rest of Churchill's sentence compels this British community of 1940 to regard themselves momentarily from an outside as well as from a temporally distant perspective. They must think of themselves not in terms of *our* finest hour, or of *ourselves* or *us*, but of *their* finest hour. They must also regard their present as though it were already other people's past. In striking contrast to Hitler's vain assurances of a thousand-year Reich, Churchill emphasizes the unpredictability of history, which may or may not involve a long duration for the empire: "*If* the British Empire and its Commonwealth last for a thousand years." It is within the framework of a long but uncertain future that Churchill dismisses his audience to contemplate their conduct, their present predicament, and humanity's precarious journey from the Dark Age to perhaps the brink of a new Dark Age.

In its shifting of temporal and psychological viewpoints the peroration of his "Finest Hour" speech epitomizes aspects of Churchill's imagination that are fundamental to much of his historical writing, including *Marlborough*. First, Churchill embeds his narrative in a double temporal framework. Past events are viewed in the light of their future while events contemporary with writing and reading of the book are viewed from the perspective of the past which it recounts. Readers are invited to see Marlborough's lifetime within the framework of its future, and to regard their own present from the perspective of its past as manifested in the attitudes and actions of Marlborough's day. All history views the past in the light of the present and vice versa, but not in the same ways or to the same degree. Churchill's methods of doing so are a significant measure of his imagination. Second, Churchill's strong sense of the contingency of history inclines him to include passages of alternative or counterfactual history: discussions of what might have happened. Along with a preponderant narration of real history—actual events authenticated by documentation—Churchill includes briefer but crucial flights of imaginary history. In this chapter I start by considering his recourse to counterfactuals in *Marlborough*. Then with reference to its announced and unannounced purposes I remark important aspects of Churchill's presentation of time as the matrix within which actual and alternative history must be apprehended by readers. Finally, in the light of these features of his narrative methods I invite reconsideration of *Marlborough*'s literary merits.

——————— ∞ ———————

Historians disagree about counterfactual history. Some relegate it to the realms of fantasy best left to novelists. Others regard it as indispensable.[3] In his valedictory lecture at Oxford, Hugh Trevor-Roper identified appreciation of alternatives as the necessary act of imagination at the heart of all worthwhile history: "The historian's function is to discern . . . alternatives, and that, surely, is the function of imagination. . . . If we are to study history as a living subject, not merely as a coloured pageant, or an antiquarian chronicle, or a dogmatic scheme, we must not indeed lose ourselves in barren speculations, but we must leave some room for the imagination. History is not merely what happened: it is what happened in the context of what might have happened. Therefore it must incorporate, as a necessary element, the alternatives, the might-have-beens."[4] Although Churchill often suggested history's intriguing or illuminating might-have-beens, he never debated the pros and cons of counterfactual history. But he understood its difficulties. In "A Second Choice," an essay taking up the question of whether if it were possible it would be desirable to live one's life over again armed with foreknowledge of how things turned out the first time, Churchill remarks that one cannot be sure that other actions would have resulted in better outcomes. By reviewing turning points of his own career ranging from leaving his pistol behind on the armored train and consequently being captured during the Boer War to his decisions about Gallipoli, Churchill argues the futility of trying to assess definitively what advantages or disadvantages would have attended altered chains of circumstances created by acting differently at crucial moments during an alternative life. In this essay he dwells on what is most problematic in speculation about "a world whose structure and history would to a large extent diverge from this one." Churchill's examples show how for the would-be counterfactual historian (he does not use that phrase) "imagination bifurcates and loses itself along the ever-multiplying paths of the labyrinth."[5] Appreciation of such difficulties, however, did not hobble Churchill's imagination.

As I remarked in chapter 4 while tracing Churchill's affinities with science fiction, counterfactuals are a characteristic though not omnipresent feature of his writing. They are especially prominent in his attempts to explain the nature of causation in history and individual lives. Early in *The Second World War*, for example, he states that in the first volume of this history it is his "purpose . . . to show how easily the tragedy of the Second World War could have been prevented." To do this is to imply throughout the actual history an alternative history of a more peaceful world in which "it was a simple policy to keep Germany disarmed and the victors adequately armed for thirty years, and in the meanwhile, even if a reconciliation could not be made with Germany, to build ever more strongly a true League of Nations capable of making sure that treaties were kept, or changed only by discussion and agreement."[6] In another volume of *The Second World War* Churchill provides a counterfactual sketch of the war as it might have unfolded had France not agreed to an armistice with Germany in 1940 but instead carried on the war from Africa and other parts of its empire while maintaining its alliance with Britain. He introduces what he calls "this ghostly speculation" by remarking that "although vain, the process of trying to imagine what would have happened if some important event or decision had been different is often tempting and sometimes instructive." He speculates on Germany's possible responses to continued French belligerence while conceding that "it is still more shadowy to guess what Hitler would have done." Churchill nevertheless argues forcefully that an inevitable feature of the conterfactual world that he here outlines is that "France would never have ceased to be one of the principal belligerent allies, and would have been spared the fearful schism which rent and still rends her people."[7] At the outset of his labors on *Marlborough* in 1930, as I also remarked in chapter 4, he published one of the enduring classics of counterfactual history in the realm of belles lettres: "If Lee Had Not Won the Battle of Gettysburg."[8] In practice though not at the level of debates over historiography, Churchill was one of the very few in his day to side with those historians who find counterfactuals not merely or primarily entertaining, but instructive and accordingly worthwhile imaginative exercises for those who would understand the past.

In the opening paragraphs of his preface to the first volume of *Marlborough* Churchill stresses what Marlborough accomplished, summing up the book's thesis by remarking that the Duke's "victorious sword established upon sure foundations the constitutional and parliamentary structure of our country almost as it has come down to us to-day."[9] Readers are also invited to imagine (though only for the duration of a sentence) an alternative world in which Marlborough did not prevail: "The triumph of the France of Louis XIV would have warped and restricted the development of the freedom we now enjoy, even more than the domination of Napoleon or of the German Kaiser."[10] This, like Churchill's allusion to a "new Dark Age," is very compressed and abstract. Nevertheless it is an effective miniature counterfactual. As at the peroration of his "Finest Hour" speech, Churchill leaves ample room for readers to exercise their imaginations. Everyone will have an idea, however inaccurate, of the horrors of the "Dark Ages," and thus be able to imagine how terrible a new Dark Age could be. Similarly, readers will know enough about Napoleon and the Kaiser (in their capacity as bogeymen) to respond with a shudder at Churchill's hint of a more repressive England as it would have been without his hero's achievements. Churchill does not paint this grim picture in detail. But he provides a sufficient sketch so that readers can grasp at the outset what was at stake in the long tale they are about to follow: establishment thanks largely to Marlborough of the free England in which they reside versus the possibility that if France under Louis XIV had won they might have been born into a society more "warped" and "restricted" than even domination by Napoleonic or Prussian regimes would have created. Here is the stuff of bad dreams.

For Churchill while First Lord of the Admiralty during World War I, as later during his early days as prime minister, a more specific recurring nightmare was the prospect of a successful invasion of England. However dreadful to contemplate, the possibility had an irresistible imaginative appeal to military minds of a literary cast. George T. Chesney had demonstrated this in 1871 with publication of *The Battle of Dorking*, his bestselling and much-imitated account of a forthcoming German invasion and defeat of Britain.[11] This story that inaugurated the still-thriving genre of future-war tales evidently stuck in Churchill's mind while leaving him—as it was intended to leave all British readers—with an urge to provide a happier outcome in reality by beefing up Britain's defenses so no actual invasion could succeed. Churchill was more than once in a position to do so. In the realm of fiction Churchill never took up his pen to provide for publication a more cheerful freestanding version of Chesney's theme showing an invasion repelled or forestalled. In 1913, however, while First Lord of the Admiralty Churchill prepared for the Invasion Committee of the Committee of Imperial Defense scenarios of successful German invasions of England. This kind of exercise was in fact often indulged by journalists and others during the run-up to World War I, inspired by imitations of *The Battle of Dorking* and by the immense popularity of Erskine Childers's 1903 spy thriller about the discovery of German naval preparations to invade England, *The Riddle of the Sands*. One of Churchill's invasion scenarios was titled "The Time-Table of a Nightmare." Another was called "A Bolt from the Grey."[12] In *The World Crisis* Churchill describes these as "imaginative exercises couched in a half-serious vein, but designed to disturb complacency by suggesting weak points in our arrangements and perilous possibilities." He remarks that "they show the kind of mental picture I was able to summon up in imagination of the tremendous period which was so soon to rush upon us."[13] These and similar memoranda later in his career illustrate the fact that statesmen and military planners must always practice a kind of future history that might be called prospective counterfactuals. Only thus can the possible consequences of choices be contemplated in advance. For those in the military, war games afford training in counterfactuals. Statesmen are in no less need of such training, though usually without any equally systematic method of obtaining it. As historian, Churchill provided himself with further self-education in counterfactuals imagined from the perspective of a statesman better than most at seeing choices and convinced by hard experience that choices matter.

In *Marlborough*, Churchill provides an alternative past rather than future history of an invasion repelled by Marlborough in the summer of 1690. Churchill speculates on what might have happened had Louis XIV agreed to James's request to send an actually available "excellent French army of over twenty thousand men" to England against Marlborough's scant resources of "about six thousand regular troops and the hastily improvised forces of the nation":

> There seems no doubt that in July and August 1690 this was the right strategy for France. Had it been adopted Marlborough's task would have been peculiarly difficult. He would have had to face the disciplined veterans of France with a mere handful of professional troops aided by brave but untrained masses, ill-armed and with hardly any experienced officers. Such a problem was novel to the military art of those days; but it was not necessarily beyond the resources of his flexible genius. He would probably "have thought of something," and our history might have dwelt with pride upon a battle of Dorking or a battle of London as the first example of the power of hardy, stubborn yeomanry and militia supported by the population against regular forces.[14]

Churchill's imaginary past Battle of Dorking undoes the ignominious future defeat at that town portrayed by Chesney.

In its allusion to *The Battle of Dorking* Churchill's cameo counterfactual history of an invasion thwarted by Marlborough in 1690 is another reminder of his familiarity with Victorian science fiction that I noted in chapter 4 above. The allusion is insufficiently particularized to reveal whether he had read Chesney's tale or merely knew of it by title and reputation, although considering the story's fame during Churchill's youth, his military interests, and his reading habits, it is likely he knew it firsthand. In any case, the passage, which now seems to verge on unintentional prophecy, also reveals the deep roots of his post-Dunkirk confidence—or at least hope—that a Nazi invasion might be dealt with by those apparently unpromising land forces available after the fall of France. The combination of a rescued British Expeditionary Force and ragtag embryonic Home Guard could almost be described by the phrase "a mere handful of professional troops aided by brave but untrained masses, ill-armed and with hardly any experienced officers." While this phrase does not do justice to the Home Guard's well-trained World War I veterans or the numbers evacuated from Dunkirk, a better fit is provided by Churchill's reference to "the hastily improvised forces of the nation" and to "the power of hardy, stubborn yeomanry and militia supported by the population against regular forces." The invaders of 1940 would not have been "disciplined veterans of France" but disciplined veterans of Germany. Even the time of year—late summer—is eerily prophetic. But of course this is only apparent in hindsight. Churchill in writing the passage had no intention of providing a forecast. And in the fraught summer of 1940 Churchill actually based most of his confidence on the power of the navy and the RAF to ward off an invasion.

Neither, however, does this account of how Marlborough might have dealt with an invasion that never happened primarily serve Churchill's usual purpose of including counterfactuals to identify what he calls "turning points" or "hinges of fate": events whose possible outcomes one way or the other have immensely important but very different consequences.[15] Churchill does not spell out whether a successful French invasion of England in 1690 would have ended the conflict in favor of France. He only suggests that although from a military standpoint the French *should* have invaded, if they had done so Marlborough would "probably" have defeated them. This outcome, to be sure, would have staved off the ultimate result of a decisive French victory mentioned by Churchill in the preface to volume 1 of *Marlborough*: an England with "warped" and "restricted" liberties. But defeat of a French invasion in 1690 would not have meant victory for England in its war against Louis XIV, only a continuation of the long conflict recounted in *Marlborough*. Churchill's emphasis is less on the consequences of victory or defeat of the imaginary invasion of 1690 than on the more limited tactical question of whether such an incursion could have been repelled by a mixed array of soldiers and populace resisting "regular forces."

His belief that invasion might indeed have been thus defeated, thereby allowing Marlborough to score a military first that real history denied him, is evidently based on Churchill's conviction that actual later instances exist demonstrating "the power of hardy, stubborn yeomany and militia supported by the population against regular forces." Perhaps Churchill had in mind some aspects of the American Revolution or the Boer War. He does not say who actually did take advantage of what history denied to Marlborough: an opportunity of providing "the *first* example" of such power. Clearly, however, the wish that it had been Marlborough (thereby affording British historians yet another reason for regarding him "with pride") reflects Churchill's longing for at least vicarious experience of a distinctive kind of victorious battle against long odds.

But the passage is more than utopian yearning for a glorious episode that never happened. It reflects one of the ways in which writing *Marlborough* was an occasion for Churchill to continue and extend his own thinking about warfare. Commentators have often remarked this aspect of his work along with the irony of Churchill's later opportunity as prime minister and defense minister to apply his ideas in practice. J. R. Jones, for example, concludes that "the work which Churchill put into the examination of Marlborough's military and diplomatic leadership of the Grand Alliance proved to be an invaluable education for his own direction of Britain's war-effort in 1940–45."[16] Manfred Weidhorn notes that "presenting the world with a portrait of heroism, Britain with a reminder of her mission, and himself with a model and 'prophecy,' this exercise unwittingly prepared him for the imminent six-year war against Nazism."[17] Churchill's counterfactual history of England invaded in 1690 shows that he not only thought about Marlborough as a model, learning from close study of what he did, but also took occasion to reflect on what might have been done in some situations as well as (by implication) what should or could be done if parallel occasions arise in the future. As though to lay down a premise for himself and for readers about to contemplate an account of Marlborough's career as a school for strategists, however, Churchill also remarks early in *Marlborough* that "the success of a commander does not arise from following rules or models. . . . every great operation of war is unique."[18] Having provided this caveat, Churchill does not hesitate to include counterfactual scenarios to serve along with episodes of actual history as a template for thinking about future military contingencies for which no exact prescriptions can be written in advance or derived from the past.

In the murkier realm of psychological rather than military possibilities Churchill rejects counterfactuals. After reviewing Marlborough's devious relationship with the Jacobites to prove that in the end all his apparently friendly communications gained them nothing they could not otherwise have obtained, Churchill adds:

> Nor can we at this stage pursue the hypothesis of what he would have done if this or that had happened. If, for instance, upon the demise of Anne, James III had landed after declaring himself Protestant and being acclaimed by England, as William III had been after Torbay, would Marlborough have felt bound to die for the house of Hanover? The Jacobites could not tell at the time, and we certainly cannot to-day.
>
> We must confine ourselves to what actually happened. Every account, every record, summed up, shows that the Jacobite Court were for a quarter of a century flattered, duped, baffled, and in the event ruined by an inscrutable and profound personality.[19]

Even while explaining the futility of speculation where motivation is so well concealed, Churchill paradoxically illustrates his point by concisely providing an intriguing scenario of what James III *might* have done in 1714 to tip the balance, perhaps decisively, against a Hanoverian succession. Churchill implies too that had James turned English public opinion in his favor by converting to Protestantism and arriving in England to press his claim, Marlborough would have faced a major and perhaps a difficult decision. Or maybe for him the dilemma would have been easily enough resolved. Which would it have been? If as Churchill insists we cannot say, neither is it easy for his readers to refrain from trying at least momentarily to answer that question after the hypothetical has been so teasingly posed in the very process of Churchill's denial that there is any point to posing it.

Insofar as readers draw upon their memories of what has been written about Marlborough to this point in the biography in order to decide for themselves which way he might have jumped, and insofar as, like Churchill, they conclude that available evidence does not provide a clear answer, credibility is gained for his subsequent sentence defending Marlborough's actual fidelity to the Protestant cause. Here Churchill's small flight of counterfactual history—suggesting the one act by James III that might finally have swayed England toward a Jacobite succession when Anne died—serves to underscore both the importance and the limits of what can be said about Marlborough's relationship with the Jacobites.

After recounting how the 1696 conspiracy to murder King William failed, Churchill reverts to counterfactual history as a way of bolstering his case for Marlborough's essential loyalty to the Protestant succession:

> Even if the plot had not miscarried, James had no chance of regaining his lost crown across the murdered corpse of William. The leading Ministers were in the closest contact with Marlborough, and long forethought had taught them to link their future with Anne. No panic or disorder would have followed the bloody deed. Within the compass of a single day, swept upward by a wave of national indignation, Anne would have mounted the throne and Marlborough would have gripped the Army. Not a shot would have been fired. Not a dog would have barked. The new organism of government would have presented itself far stronger than the former combination. No doubt after a few months Marlborough would have again been found sending soothing messages to Saint-Germains explaining that in the temper of the nation it had been impossible for him to act otherwise, that his love for His Majesty and the debt he owned him, of which he would ever be sensible, made it his duty to preserve his Sacred Person from the certain destruction which would have awaited him on English soil; but that in other circumstances a day might come when he would be able to prove in a manner which none could doubt his unchanging devotion to the royal cause. He might well have added a few words of caution upon the importance of the Jacobites making no movement in England when the atmosphere was so unfavourable, and against a Government under the sovereignty of King James's loving daughter and so strongly supported by his ever—at heart—faithful servant. And it is very likely James

would have passed the news on to Louis to show him that hope was not even yet extinct; and history would have quoted it as proof of Marlborough's treachery to Anne. This is but a speculative epitome of the realities.[20]

Here Churchill explicitly uses fiction to convey facts. Anticipating and trying to defuse objections to his soaring flight of speculation in this paragraph, he winds it up by emphatically though paradoxically insisting that it is "but a speculative epitome of the realities." The idea underlying this phrase, that fiction may convey truth, is of course a classic defense of fiction. The only novelty is Churchill's surprising and somewhat defensive resort to the statement to justify his inclusion within an historical narration of a manifestly fictional passage very clearly presented as such. This assertion that realities may be epitomized via speculation is as close as Churchill comes to a theoretical explanation of the utility to historians of counterfactuals.

The realities alluded to here are mainly political: a stable and strong "organism of government" that would doubtless—so Churchill claims—have responded to an assassination by maintaining its power and would even have gained strength by profiting from a "wave of national indignation." Psychological realities are involved only to the extent that the assumed support for Anne would have depended on a continuation of attitudes amply demonstrated prior to the conspiracy—and sufficiently recounted in Churchill's previous pages to render his hypothesis plausible. Here Churchill does not need any psychological analysis accounting for or even describing the inner mental states behind the outward conduct which is postulated: "No panic or disorder would have followed the bloody deed. . . . Anne would have mounted the throne and Marlborough would have gripped the Army." Churchill pursues his hypothesis to a comic anticlimax (echoing a famous comment on how easily Oliver Cromwell had expelled the Rump Parliament in 1653): "Not a shot would have been fired. Not a dog would have barked." Whether taken literally or metaphorically, this amusing image of all the dogs in England reduced to silence by Anne's accession hammers home Churchill's argument that the 1696 conspiracy against William did not matter in the long run. Even its success would not have altered the course of British politics. Its discovery was certainly an interesting moment, especially for those concerned, but no turning point in national or world history. Although Churchill's conclusion is negative, the passage is nevertheless characteristic of his resort to counterfactuals to decide whether a particular event—or its absence—was crucial in shaping the future.

Churchill's précis of imaginary letters from Marlborough to the Jacobite court is a tour de force of stylistic imitation. As readers can tell from previous accounts of actual communications of the sort, especially in his chapter on "The Jacobite Illusion," Churchill duplicates the tone and substance of such missives so perfectly that his précis rings true, adding verisimilitude to the entire counterfactual passage. Readers must agree on the basis of what they have encountered earlier that this is exactly how such letters would have been written. The précis is also very funny. It parodies the (to our eyes) excessively elaborate courtly style of late seventeenth-century formal correspondence between such elevated personages. It catches the duplicity (in a worthy cause) revealed by such glaring disparity between professions of love and solicitude for James and actual unwavering service to Anne. With a deftness worthy of Restoration comedy, Churchill highlights Marlborough's artistry in gulling James, James's vulnerability to being gulled, and his pathetic though hardly less duplicitous announcement of the gulling correspondence to Louis XIV "to show him that hope was not even yet extinct." Churchill's comedy here takes on a satiric edge. His satire is not directed at Marlborough, but at the gulled, ineffectual Jacobites and more generally at an absurd political situation that encouraged such hypocritical correspondence.

By presenting the imaginary exchange here in a comic light, Churchill also furthers his continuing effort to defend Marlborough against charges that his relationship over the years with the Jacobites amounted to treason. Earlier and later in *Marlborough* Churchill argues that England was well served not betrayed by Marlborough's contacts with the Pretender's court. The précis, by emphasizing in its very compression what is most ridiculously and obviously insincere in such exchanges, transfers them from the arena of solemn assessment for evidence of treachery to the stage whereon is played out for our amusement a comedy of manners. By encouraging readers to laugh at Marlborough's deft gulling of James, Churchill tries to prevent such correspondence from being taken with high seriousness. Readers see that it was all part of the game, no more, and a part that ought to elicit our applause at Marlborough as a kind of loyal con man par excellence. We momentarily see the warrior and diplomat as picaro not traitor.

In the comic turn given to the last part of this paragraph of alternate history yet another satiric stroke is aimed at historians hostile to Marlborough. Churchill again directs laughter at those whom he derides in an earlier chapter as "the long succession of historians who follow each other like sheep through the gates of error."[21] Lacking appreciation of the glaring and hilariously successful insincerity of Marlborough's unctuous professions of devotion to James, such historians would have cited communications after assassination of William "as proof of Marlborough's treachery to Anne." Thus in a final burst of comedy, Churchill remarks the obtuseness of imaginary historians who would have misinterpreted the same *kind* of evidence that actual obtuse historians have misused to condemn Marlborough wrongly. This hit at Macaulay and like-minded traducers of Marlborough who are not merely satirized but refuted at length elsewhere in the book is all the more effective for Churchill's restraint in not bothering to name names here.

Of far more consequence is a chapter titled "The Unfought Waterloo," where Churchill contends that a major turning point in history was Dutch failure to authorize an attack Marlborough's forces were poised to deliver on August 18, 1705. Churchill argues that an engagement pressed home then as Marlborough urged would have been victorious and would have guaranteed a bright future for Holland, whereas the decision *not* to fight led inexorably to that nation's eclipse:

> Thus set the star of the Dutch Republic. . . . Time is inexorable. Had Marlborough won the unfought battle of Waterloo in August 1705, all the French power in the Netherlands would have been thereby annihilated. . . . Marlborough would have acquired that supreme authority which he always lacked to plan the campaign of 1706. He would have been there to execute the great projects which we shall presently unfold, unless even better had presented themselves. The year of victory, 1706, might also have been the year of peace. But the Dutch wore out Fortune with their sluggish precautions. . . . Not all their courage, their sacrifices, and their dauntless constancy could appease the insulted gods. Long and bloody years of struggle lay before them. They were to see their cherished Blue Guards mown down under their own prince at Malplaquet. . . . They were to exhaust their wealth in a seemingly interminable series of campaigns. Their sea-power and their share in the New World

were to pass insensibly, but irresistibly and soon, to England. In the end . . . England, now so fierce and ardent, would sicken of an endless war, desert her allies, and leave them to their fate. But if the valiant Republic . . . was to be deprived of its fruition in modern times, condemned for ever to be a minor Power while rivals grew so great, this was the fatal scene. Here by the cross-roads of bodeful Waterloo, as earlier upon the heaths of Peer, the destinies of Holland turned.[22]

In the chapter that concludes with this glimpse of a bright future lost forever by Holland, Churchill explains the military basis of Marlborough's confidence that an attack would have been successful and that accordingly ending the war eight years before it actually ended would have been among the remarkable benefits of victory. Churchill's case is partly based on assumptions about what Marlborough could and would have done if success on August 18, 1705, had allowed him to achieve at last "that supreme authority" which in reality he "always lacked." What he might have accomplished with such power is only hinted at in Churchill's allusion to "the great projects which we shall presently unfold." As readers continue through *Marlborough* they duly encounter these projects and what prevented their realization. Churchill's explanations augment the credibility of the counterfactual that at the conclusion of "The Unfought Waterloo" he interweaves with his poignant proleptic sketch of the Dutch Republic's decline and fall.

The chapter's rhetoric is organized around Churchill's deft exploitation of the geographical coincidence that Marlborough's army confronted the French but did not fight them at the very scene of Napoleon's final defeat. In his chapter title and concluding allusion to "the cross-roads of bodeful Waterloo" Churchill draws upon every reader's knowledge that here where no clash took place on August 18, 1705, there was fought on June 18, 1815, a battle everywhere acknowledged as one of world history's decisive turning points. It is hard to imagine a reader of *Marlborough* who would not know about Napoleon's Waterloo. Churchill's implication is illogical but inescapable: here if anywhere one might well expect to find (because at a later time one does find) the locale of a crucial encounter. This is not good logic but it is great drama.

Churchill mobilizes all the connotations of 1815 in aid of his case that something fateful was bound to occur at that location: the *cross-roads*

of *bodeful* Waterloo. "Cross-roads" may be taken literally, as a glance at
Churchill's accompanying map will ensure. But the word also alludes
metaphorically to the site as a locus of crucial decision. "Bodeful" is one
of Churchill's effective archaisms. It is a rare word indeed, used here to
characterize the place as "containing omens" or "presaging," while including too the sense of "foreboding" or "ominous." By these denotations
together with his prior allusions to the Dutch wearing out "Fortune"
and their inability to "appease the insulted gods," Churchill implies that
Waterloo is a place of destiny. He suggests that it is a scene where fortune
and the gods play their role in human affairs. The suggestion is only to be
taken figuratively but it is all the more effective for that. Churchill's archaic
tropes heighten and dramatize his case that inaction at Waterloo in 1705
was the mistake that ruined Holland. However readers react to Churchill's
quaint allusions to fortune, the gods, and an ominous place of omens, it
is impossible to read his account of "The Unfought Waterloo" without
having in mind as a kind of psychological palimpsest events that occurred
at the same location in 1815 and their manifold consequences. By the title
and conclusion of his chapter on "The Unfought Waterloo" Churchill
compels his readers to sustain a double temporal perspective: his narrative
of 1705 is overlaid with evoked but unrecounted memories of 1815.

In his chapter titled "The Thwarted Invasion" Churchill draws similar attention to the crucial importance of something that did not happen:
"We must regard the refusal of the Allies to accept Marlborough's scheme
for the invasion of France at this juncture as one of the cardinal points of
the war."[23] As for the unfought Waterloo of 1705, after outlining the basis
of his conviction that Marlborough's plan would have succeeded had
he been authorized to carry it through, Churchill sketches the counterfactual history that would have ensued: "If his strategy had prevailed, not
only would Ghent have been freed, but all the French armies and garrisons would have been recalled to defend the capital and to confront the
invasion. Great battles would have been fought in the heart of France, and
victory would have provided in 1708 that triumphant peace which after
so much further bloodshed the grand Alliance was still to seek in vain."[24]
Here Churchill resists the temptation to dwell on details of this delicious military reverie. His readers are left to imagine for themselves all
the particulars and even the number of those "great battles" that "would
have been fought in the heart of France." He also leaves readers on their
own to envision the nature and precise consequences of that "triumphant

peace" that might have been achieved in 1708 had Marlborough's allies been as bold as he.

In Churchill's chapter on "The Lost Peace" of 1709 even greater imaginative scope is allowed for readers to fill in details of a momentous unrealized alternative to actual European history when he suggests how Marlborough might have averted the French Revolution and its violent aftermath. This chapter's title and substance provide yet another prominent invitation to consider what might have happened alongside what did happen. Churchill prints in italics Marlborough's remark in a letter to Godolphin that were the war to end victoriously for the Allies "*The queen shou'd then have the honour of insisting upon putting the ffrench [sic] Government upon their being againe govern'd by the three Estates which I think is more likely to give quiet to Christendome, then the taring provences from them for the inriching of others.*" Of this suggestion Churchill observes:

> This is one of the most revealing insights which we have into Marlborough's statecraft. The idea of substituting for the despotic rule of France a Parliamentary regime had long commended itself to him. It is a strange speculation how the course of history would have been changed if he had been able to enforce his policy upon France. The French Revolution might have accomplished itself gradually and beneficently in the course of the eighteenth century, and the whole world would have moved on to broader foundations without paying the awful price in war and horror. There might have been no Napoleon! To pursue such thoughts beyond their earliest suggestions is vain; but Marlborough's words show how far in this respect he stood ahead of his times—and our own."[25]

I doubt that Marlborough's suggestion tells us as much about his statecraft as about his fleeting political fantasies. Marlborough never reiterated that statement. It is so speculative that it can hardly be taken as a proposal likely to have been actually put forward among peace terms or even proffered as informal though serious advice to the French had the war then ended. If not quite the articulation of so settled a goal as to warrant being described as a "policy" that Marlborough aimed "to enforce upon France," however, the suggestion does reflect a yearning for peace and parliamentary forms that with the advantage of hindsight lends itself to elaboration in the mode of utopian counterfactual history.

This Churchill provides by his memorable invitation to imagine (if we can) a world without Napoleon. The idea is so startling that Churchill presents it only as a possibility not a certainty, and accentuates it with an exclamation point: "There *might* have been no Napoleon!" Perhaps Churchill's conviction that exceptional people put their stamp upon events inclines him to concede implicitly that no matter what happened there might still have been such a man with such a bloody career. In any case, a world without Napoleon or his like would have meant a France that evolved peacefully toward more beneficial and democratic institutions while spared the "awful price in war and horror" that brought him to power and marked his career. In such a world Bonaparte would have existed but would have remained in obscurity. Hence its alternative twentieth century would have been a world without knowledge or memory of Napoleon and his wars, and in that sense a world with no Napoleon.

Churchill's rueful acknowledgment that "to pursue such thoughts beyond their earliest suggestions is vain" reflects at once his stern rejection of utopian fantasies as politically pointless and his conviction nevertheless that to understand history it must be viewed not only in the light of how it actually could have happened otherwise but also occasionally by comparison with an ideal though impossible vision of how things *should* have transpired. Thus Churchill as historian reminds us that to understand reality we must also sometimes glance at Utopia.

Another notable instance of Churchill's utopian impulse to compare reality with a better but unattained world is the last sentence of *Marlborough*, which by its placement inevitably serves as a summing-up of the book's lessons. In this conspicuous place Churchill takes leave of his readers by urging them not only to recollect Marlborough's impressive achievements but to imagine a far better alternative world closer to a utopian ideal of strength, happiness, and progress that its hero *would* (not might) have achieved had he been accorded the trust he deserved: "He had proved himself the 'good Englishman' he aspired to be, and History may declare that if he had had more power his country would have had more strength and happiness, and Europe a surer progress."[26] The folly of diluting a supreme commander's power is an important lesson reiterated throughout *Marlborough*. It is one that Churchill himself later took to heart on becoming prime minister cum defense minister. His concluding insistence on this lesson by evocation of counterfactual history echoes and emphasizes his statement at the outset that he hopes "to show that [Marlborough] was not only foremost of English soldiers but . . . one who only needed an earlier and still wider authority to have made a more ordered and a more tolerant civilization for his own time, and to help the future."[27] Though posed in very general terms, these invitations to imagine how Marlborough might have done even more and *what* he might have done are revealing affirmations of Churchill's own guiding values. Whatever Marlborough's motives may have been, and whatever he might have done with more authority, the better world toward which his biographer insists he tried to steer England and Europe is certainly Churchill's own vision of utopia: a place where a powerful leader and a strong nation strive to bring about "a more tolerant civilization" not only for present happiness but to help the future. Here again Churchill presents a very wide temporal perspective oriented toward the future. In the context of the 1930s, surely, it was no idle question whether a man aspiring to leadership and urging rearmament stood for power in the service of toleration. Few did.

——————— ∞ ———————

Churchill only announces some of his goals. He had little need to explain or apologize for writing *Marlborough* as an act of family piety and a contribution to keeping himself afloat financially. His subtitle proclaims that the work is a "Life and Times": part biography, part history of an era. Churchill makes clear that he focuses on military and political history because they illuminate his subject's life and vice versa, and because both help account for the character of England in the twentieth century. *Marlborough* is partly a narrative of events in chronological sequence and partly a series of what amount to legal briefs sometimes taking the form of analytical arguments about the validity of documentary evidence and sometimes (as in the chapter "Avarice and Charm") taking the form of a character sketch built up of anecdotes from many different times. Of Churchill's use of the biography to present a case for the defense of Marlborough, Robert Eden astutely remarks that "the whole enterprise depends on one orator's force of imagination; the world becomes a courtroom only because Churchill sees it vividly before him; the reader believes that the trial is proceeding, and is an urgent matter of public duty, only because Churchill is sure that the future depends on how John Churchill is presently judged, that the cause fully deserves the best of his intellect and oratory."[28] It was indeed a feat of the imagination to sustain interest in Marlborough during the 1930s, a decade beset by more pressing matters than arriving at a final verdict on a man who died in 1722. Although the rise of dictatorships spurred an interest in perennial questions about the role played by great (or at least unusual) men in shaping events, it did not self-evidently follow that turning to Marlborough might provide new answers. Nor did those questions as applied to him altogether resolve the dilemma of what to include in his biography.

Churchill's three primary criteria for selection of material are relevance to proper appreciation of Marlborough's character, relevance to understanding the political and military currents in which he swam, and relevance to understanding his role in preserving England's "constitutional and parliamentary structure."[29] Churchill glances at social and cultural history mainly insofar as they help further his explicit purpose of redeeming Marlborough's reputation by refuting charges brought by contemporary detractors and enshrined in history by Macaulay. The most serious accusations are of treason, embezzlement, warmongering, avarice, and exploitation of women. Churchill's counterattacks interrupt the narrative flow. They partly account for expansion of the work from an envisioned two volumes to four which demand a heavy investment of reading time and place great burdens upon the reader's memory. Paradoxically, however, the counterattacks also increase *Marlborough*'s force and political impact as Whig history, thereby contributing to Churchill's major unannounced goal: enhancement of his own political prospects.

At stake in Churchill's plea for reversal of Marlborough's conviction by Macaulay was far less Marlborough's reputation than Churchill's own standing, and accordingly facilitation of his path to office with all that depended upon his leadership. It is not easy to decide exactly how far publication of the biography swayed public opinion toward Churchill. Victor Feske concludes that in the 1930s, thanks largely to *Marlborough*, "With his personae as historian and politician merging into a single identity in the public mind, by the end of the decade Churchill could pose as a spokesman for the nation, defender of liberalism against totalitarianism, and disinterested critic of the policies of Baldwin and Chamberlain."[30] Certainly insofar as Marlborough's character was redeemed he could serve as an exemplary vehicle of what Churchill, doing his vigorous best for the Whig interpretation of history, presented as England's contribution to the world's progress toward civil liberties, parliamentary democracy, and freedom from domination by any one power.[31] Acceptance of Marlborough as a hero of this version of history—and of Churchill as a comparable proponent of British freedom and British power—in turn depended on presentation of parallels between England's situation in Marlborough's day and in the parlous 1930s. This Churchill does with increasing explicitness throughout *Marlborough*.

Louis XIV becomes an archetype of Hitler, no less than Napoleon. Marlborough's wars are described as a World War. The Grand Alliance is described as an earlier League of Nations, thereby enforcing Churchill's moral that collective action is the key to national salvation in the 1930s just as it was in Marlborough's day: "We see a world war of a League of Nations against a mighty, central military monarchy, hungering for domination not only over the lands but over the politics and religion of its neighbours."[32] Churchill deplores England's recurring inclination after military victory "to cast away its fruits" by failure to remain united and strong: "Now after Ryswick, as at Utrecht, as at Paris in 1763, as after the Napoleonic wars and Waterloo, and as after Armageddon, the island mainspring of the life and peace of Europe broke; and England, amid a babel of voices, dissolved in faction, disbanded her armies, and sought to repay the spites and hardships of war-time upon the men who had carried her through."[33] "Plus ça change" is the sad moral of this and similar remarks. Far from exemplifying the simplistic Whig interpretation of history famously condemned by Herbert Butterfield for presenting the past mainly as a way of ratifying as well as accounting for the present, Churchill's identification of such parallels suggests that history all too often displays cycles rather than progress and accordingly stands more frequently as a warning than as model or prologue to better present days.[34] Wherever he notes parallels between present and past, however, Churchill narrows the reader's sense of temporal distance from the events narrated and the people who populate his pages.

As well as thereby making it easier to understand how current political lessons may be derived from such ancient history, Churchill also enhances and exploits every reader's sense of closeness to the past in order to refute some of the charges against Marlborough. It is in the area of manners and morals that he is most liable to hasty adverse judgment in the twentieth century, as in the nineteenth, because at first glance more recent attitudes will seem quite different and much better. Hardest to accept are Marlborough's early career as a courtier and his liaison with Barbara Villiers, Duchess of Cleveland. His first steps up the career ladder at court were smoothed by his sister Arabella's affair with the Duke of York. His next steps were assisted by money from Barbara. Equally awkward to explain is Marlborough's morally dubious though undeniably dextrous extrication from his entanglement with Barbara in order to marry Sarah. All this must somehow be made to square with acceptance of his courtship of Sarah, their love letters, their marriage, and their apparent fidelity thereafter as a grand romance to be admired as we admire, say, Romeo and Juliet. So far as concerns court customs such as the keeping of an official mistress by royalty, Churchill duly remarks the necessity of taking into account *Autres temps, autres moeurs*. In some ways the past is indeed a foreign country, he implies, and to be absolved accordingly. But Churchill's prevailing strategy is to remind readers that the twentieth century is no better and to suggest that only the most unsophisticated—among whom few readers would wish to be counted—are really shocked by such peccadillos among consenting adults. Irony is his usual mode on these issues: "There was undoubtedly an easy commerce of the sexes, marked at times by actual immorality. . . . We in this happy and enlightened age must exercise our imagination to span the gulf which separates us from those lamentable, departed days. Securely established upon the rock of purity and virtue, ceaselessly cleansed by the strong tides of universal suffrage, we can afford to show tolerance and even indulgence toward the weaknesses and vices of those vanished generations without in any way compromising our own integrity."[35] In such matters there is, in short, no significant difference between then and now. Residence in the twentieth century affords no basis for stepping forward to cast the first stone at Marlborough's relationships with women. Churchill's witty variations on this point are hardly invalidated by recent history.

Churchill also employs irony with equal relish to note ways in which the past is genuinely different though not necessarily inferior. He remarks, for example, that among "the differences of feeling and outlook which separate the men and women of these times from ourselves" is the importance they accorded religion: "It played as large a part in the life of the seventeenth century as sport does now."[36] Such observations also forestall any inclination to assume that our customs are the proper measure of past conduct. In comparisons it is often the present that Churchill finds wanting. But he does not romanticize the past. It was frequently brutal, he suggests, but we are worse:

Although perhaps four hundred villages were burned, the devastation of Bavaria was neither so sure nor so widespread as that which France had inflicted upon the Palatinate a quarter of a century before. It was, of course, incomparably less efficient than the destruction wrought by the Germans in their withdrawals from France and Belgium in our own times. But we must make allowances. Explosives were then in their infancy, and fire often leaves cottage walls standing. Moreover, Marlborough would not allow the beautiful trees to be cut down, as was systematically done in the orchards of Northern France in 1917. Thus the policy was not applied with the thoroughness which our broader civilization has achieved.[37]

In such passages scattered throughout *Marlborough*, though most frequent in its earlier pages as Churchill provides orientation to Marlborough's era and deals with his initial sexual and financial relationships, readers are encouraged to adopt a complex view of how the past both resembles and differs from the present. Churchill suggests that each may on occasion be used to measure the other's shortcomings. Thus about attitudes toward pain, punishment, and death then and now he remarks:

These were the ages of Pain. Pain, when it came, was accepted as a familiar foe. No anaesthetic robbed the hospital of all the horrors of the torture-chamber. All had to be endured, and hence—strangely enough—all might be inflicted. Yet in some ways our forerunners attached more importance to human life than we do. Although they fought duels about women and other matters of honour, instead of seeking damages from the courts, and although death sentences were more numerous in those days, they would have recoiled in lively horror from the constant wholesale butcheries of scores of thousands of persons every year by motor-cars, at which the modern world gapes unconcernedly.[38]

About treatment of discharged veterans after the War of the League of Augsburg Churchill comments:

The reductions were carried out in the most brutal manner, the war-bitten veterans and the Huguenot refugees who had fought so well being summarily flung on the streets and treated as rogues and vagabonds on the first provocation. . . . An orgy of insult and abuse in which all classes of the civil population heartily joined began around all uniformed men, the half-pay officers, and especially those who had already been disarmed and turned adrift and had no means of support. . . . The gibbet and the lash were meted out with ruthless vigour on all who fell into the clutches of the law. Such was the process of demobilization in the seventeenth century.[39]

Such passages do not sustain criticism that Churchill idealizes the past. He does, however, point to ways in which the twentieth century has regressively abandoned some of the customs that meliorated life in Marlborough's time, such as prompt efforts after battles "to rescue the wounded, instead of leaving them to perish inch by inch in agony in No Man's Land."[40]

With devastating Swiftian irony in another memorable passage mocking the idea of progress, Churchill contrasts protection accorded law-abiding enemy aliens during wartime then with their treatment during World War I:

Of course, nowadays, with the many improvements that have been made in international morals and behaviour, all enemy subjects, even those whose countries were only technically involved, even those who had lived all their lives in England, and the English women who had married them, would, as in every other state based on an educated democracy, be treated within twenty-four hours as malignant foes, flung into internment camps, and their private property stolen to assist the expenses of the war. In the twentieth century mankind has shaken itself free from all those illogical, old-world prejudices, and achieved the highest efficiency of brutal, ruthless war.[41]

The history of World War II offers nothing to diminish the relevance of this rebuke. What emerges from such passages is Churchill's conviction (often manifested in his other writings) that in each era human nature remains in the main equally deplorable and essentially the same, although customs vary and science now gives wider scope for the exercise of humanity's worst impulses.

———————— ∞ ————————

Like all historians, Churchill had to find narrative techniques for dealing with the gulf of time separating his subject from his readers. He had to strike an appropriate balance between the opposite but not incompatible methods of bringing the past forward by showing that it differed only superficially from the present and of stressing key differences that illustrate the past's remoteness and heighten every reader's sense of encountering alien attitudes that cannot be measured by present standards. The first step was to specify the temporal location and the composition of his audience. Churchill professes to write neither for posterity nor for professional historians, though no doubt he hoped for favorable attention from both: "I have attempted the task of making John Churchill intelligible to the present generation."[42] Here "present generation" may incompletely but not inaccurately be taken to mean the British electorate of all ages during the 1930s along with, more generally, readers elsewhere in the empire and in the United States. Churchill addresses those whom Samuel Johnson called common readers by allying himself with "the new school of writers who are reconciling scientific history with literary style and popular comprehension."[43] The temporal viewpoint of the narrative, as of its readers, is the twentieth century.

One consequence that Churchill remarks is the foreshortening of time when viewed in retrospect. He warns that in historical narratives this phenomenon creates an inherent tendency to elicit misjudgments:

> To understand history the reader must always remember how small is the proportion of what is recorded to what actually took place, and above all how severely the time factor is compressed. Years pass with chapters and sometimes with pages, and the tale abruptly reaches new situations, changed relationships, and different atmospheres. Thus the figures of the past are insensibly portrayed as more fickle, more harlequin, and less natural in their actions than they really were. But if anyone will look back over the last three or four years of his own life or of that of his country, and pass in detailed review events as they occurred and the successive opinions he has formed upon them, he will appreciate the pervading mutability of all human affairs. . . . Each individual decision is the result of all the forces at work at any given moment, and the passage of even a few years enables—nay, compels—men and peoples to think, feel, and act quite differently without any insincerity or baseness.[44]

By inviting readers to reflect on their own awareness of the difference between the subjective pace of lived and recollected experience, Churchill tries here, at the outset of his chapter on "The Personal Cleavage," to prevent unwarranted condemnation of those—including and especially Marlborough—whose shifting loyalties to William and James may at our remove in time seem to have fluctuated with inexplicable or immoral haste. The remark is part of Churchill's case for the defense. As another part of his argument on Marlborough's behalf in this chapter Churchill stresses areas of discontinuity between past and present by explaining at length why "the events of the Revolution had created conditions in England to which no parallel exists in later times."[45] His explanation of how retrospective narrative accelerates the apparent speed with which narrated events succeed one another ventures into the artistic dimension of historical narrative. This dimension includes all aspects of writing that Churchill, avoiding as usual entanglement with any explicit theory of aesthetics, fleetingly refers to as the "literary style" that may be reconciled with "scientific history."

He leaves no doubt that in his view questions of time are paramount in making his portrayal of Marlborough achieve verisimilitude as well as accuracy. Both are at issue in observing that historical narratives by virtue of their retrospective viewpoint inevitably depict people "as more fickle, more harlequin, and less natural . . . than they really were." "Harlequin" is used in the sense of "variegated," i.e., not of a piece, not consistent. In this sense it is roughly synonymous with "fickle," thus emphasizing the point made by that word. "Harlequin" in its more general sense of resembling a figure from pantomime comedy—more caricature than portrait—anticipates and thereby also emphasizes the sense of "less natural." To seem unnatural is to lose plausibility. To the extent that characters seem "less natural . . . than they really were"—caricatures from a harlequinade—the narrative in which they appear, along with its arguments for or against those characters, will seem less credible. The conduct described will seem less probable, thus diminishing the narrative's verisimilitude and in that way weakening the rhetoric of its defense of Marlborough as well as the accuracy of its portrait of him.

Elsewhere in *Marlborough* Churchill reveals how he solved narrative problems involving discrepancies between the temporal flow of narrated events and the pace of narration. Although none of his explanations dwell at length on the aesthetic issues involved, he gave them more than passing attention in deciding how to present the available material. He also wanted to be sure his readers understand and appreciate his method of narration. With a characteristic metaphor applying the vocabulary of painting (whose medium is space) to the art of narration (whose medium is time), Churchill states his premise that "in a portrait or impression the human figure is best shown by its true relation to the objects and scenes against which it is thrown, and by which it is defined."[46] To present figure against ground, however, Churchill must present a backdrop that often "broadens until . . . it covers the entire history of our country and frays out extensively into the history of Europe."[47] There is accordingly a risk that figure and ground will reverse so that the account of Marlborough is overwhelmed by an account of British and European history per se. Nevertheless by situating Marlborough in his own time and place, that is to say firmly at a remove of over two centuries from readers of the biography, Churchill hopes also, despite all difficulties, "to recall this great shade from the past, and not only invest him with his panoply, but make him living and intimate to modern eyes."[48]

Here is *Marlborough*'s aesthetic sine qua non. Readers must apprehend the protagonist as *living*: vitally present in their here and now. They must also apprehend him as *intimate*: not merely present but close. If Marlborough remains a remote figure the biography cannot sufficiently engage its readers to accept either its subject *or its author* as of much relevance to current issues. Marlborough would remain dead and gone. Churchill would dwindle to a mere antiquarian: no very good prospect to lead a nation in peril. Marlborough cannot of course actually be brought forward, as Churchill's trope acknowledges. The historian must be an illusionist summoning from the past to put before every reader's eyes not Marlborough, only his ghost—his essence, his spirit. But how?

A remedy for the temporal foreshortening created by retrospective narration would be to put in everything available, thereby slowing down the reader's pace to provide the closest possible approximation to the tempo of written-about time. The more pages there are recounting a given interval the longer readers must dwell on that interval and the greater accordingly will be their sense of the time involved. For Marlborough's early years a dearth of material prevents this approach. The first published volume of the biography covers the fifty-two years from 1650 to 1702 in a little under five hundred pages. The following three volumes cover twenty more amply documented years in a little over fifteen hundred pages. The ratio of reading time to read-about time shifts significantly toward the unattainable (and undesirable) limit of 1/1. The effect is to minimize those difficulties that Churchill attributes to retrospective foreshortening of written-about time.

But the writer then has an opposite problem: "Whereas the records of Marlborough's earlier life are singularly scanty, we now enter a period where information is baffling because of its abundance."[49] Churchill henceforward has more than enough material to slow the narrative pace, as indeed he does. More pages are devoted to smaller intervals of narrated time. But he must also be selective to achieve his aesthetic goal of making Marlborough seem alive and close. It would defeat that purpose simply to shovel in material from printed and manuscript collections of "ponderous official correspondence" amounting to "considerably over a million words."[50] Churchill's basis of selection is to choose private over public letters, and correspondence written in medias res not afterward: "I have sought rather to throw a new light upon Marlborough's character and toils by using whenever possible his own words which have remained up till now unknown, written under stress of events from camps and quarters to those who were dearest to him and were also his most trusted colleagues."[51] Churchill's solution is in effect though surely not by conscious derivation to adapt to his purposes the methods of Boswellian biography and the epistolary novel developed by Samuel Richardson.

Richardson's *Clarissa* (1747–48) earned its place as a landmark in the development of fiction by a combination of two features designed to avoid adverse consequences of retrospective narration. By "retrospective narration" I mean here an account of events from a perspective significantly later in time than the events recounted. First, Richardson's story is told entirely in the form of letters between its characters, thus altogether eliminating the voice and stance of a narrator looking back on events in which he himself played no part. Nothing stands between readers and characters. Second, and even more crucially, the letters concerning each episode are supposed to be written at the time with the outcome unknown to participants, rather than afterward. Richardson explained the advantages of what he called "writing to the moment" and "instantaneous Descriptions" by remarking that "*much more* lively and affecting . . . must be the Style of those who write in the height of a *present* distress; the mind tortured by the pangs of uncertainty (the Events then hidden in the womb of Fate); *than* the dry, narrative, unanimated Style of a person relating difficulties and dangers surmounted, can be; the relater perfectly at ease; and if himself unmoved by his own Story, not likely greatly to affect the Reader."[52] Churchill could not eliminate himself as narrator looking back with detachment on events distant in time. Nor would he or any responsible historian want to abandon the role of interpreter and judge. History would dwindle to compilation and arrangement of documents. But Churchill does see the advantages of including many letters "written under the stress of events." They create immediacy by allowing readers to grasp without intermediary narration how things appeared to participants at the time. Uncertainties, hopes, and "the stress of events" may thus be more readily experienced vicariously. In *The World Crisis* (as later in *The Second World War*), Churchill had included contemporary documents, especially his own, mostly to avoid charges that he had never appreciated at the time what became apparent to historians and others looking back after the outcome of events was known.

Novelists use the technique of "writing to the moment" to heighten suspense as to the outcome during a first reading, and perhaps create dramatic irony on a second reading (or recollection of the novel upon completion) when the characters' expectations can be compared with the event. Historians must usually assume that most readers will know before picking up a book at least the general outline of its "plot": who won the wars recounted, whether the main personalities succeeded or failed in their endeavors. Taking no chances about such foreknowledge, however, Churchill includes enough explicit foreshadowing of his plot so that readers first time through—and for most there will be no second reading of so large a book—can appreciate the various ironic disparities between its ultimate outcome and appearances or expectations at particular moments in the tale.

Early in the book Churchill defines *Marlborough's* overall plot as comic in the sense of having a happy outcome—and moreover an unforeseeably happy outcome—for both its protagonist and his country. Marlborough, as Churchill reminds or informs readers by quoting Sarah (and elaborating on the point), was "to rise from the lowest Step to the Greatest."[53] His is a comedy of advancement from impecunious obscurity to fame, power, and riches, although not without moments of adversity and a final fall from the summit. To heighten appreciation of the dramatic ironies involved in his fall, Churchill also departs from the mostly chronological order of his narrative to look ahead from the moment of Sarah's kindness to her relative Abigail Hill and explain how Sarah "by indulging her most generous sentiments of compassion . . . prepared for her own undo-ing and her husband's fall at the moment when the consummation of all his victories and toils seemed so near."[54] By calling this "a classic instance of how far romance lags behind reality" Churchill invites favorable com-parison of his true story with the most appealing fiction. In this way too the one-time novelist indicates his awareness of how the historian may resort to a novelistic technique—here foreshadowing that heightens appreciation of dramatic irony—and use it to better effect than writers of romance because reality, properly presented, may be more gripping than fiction.

England's rise as Churchill foreshadows it is also remarkable for its unpredictability beforehand, however inevitable it may seem in retrospect:

> No dreamer, however romantic, however remote his dreams from reason, could have foreseen a surely approaching day when, by the formation of mighty coalitions and across the struggles of a gener-ation, the noble colossus of France would lie prostrate in the dust, while the small island, beginning to gather to itself the empires of India and America, stripping France and Holland of their colonial possessions, would emerge victorious, mistress of the Mediterranean, the Narrow Seas, and the oceans. Aye, and carry forward with her, intact and enshrined, all that peculiar structure of law and liberty, all her own inheritance of learning and letters, which are to-day the treasure of the most powerful family in the human race.[55]

The trumpet tones of this statement of his Whig thesis and appeal to all the English-speaking peoples ensure that Churchill's readers will not only appreciate *his* patriotic endorsement of England's laws, liberties, learning, and literature along with *his* contribution to English literature, but will keep in mind this comic plot of national (and for Marlborough personal) triumph when reading letters written under "the stress of events" *with-out* foreknowledge of that victorious outcome. Thus Churchill attempts to combine the advantages of retrospective narration (and there are many) with the Richardsonian immediacy achieved by inclusion of letters writ-ten to the moment.

Like *Marlborough*, James Boswell's *Life of Johnson*, the archetype of modern biography, has for its main purpose a defense of the protagonist against previous adverse portraits. Just as Churchill intends above all to dispose of Macaulay's accusations against Marlborough, Boswell announces that his work, if it succeeds, "will, by a true and fair delineation" vindicate "the character and conduct of my illustrious friend" Johnson from "the injurious misrepresentations" of Sir John Hawkins and Mrs. Thrale.[56] Boswell is accordingly more concerned with selecting evidence bearing on Johnson's character than with providing a chronicle of events by heaping on all available material. Boswell's great innovation as a biographer was to achieve a closer look at a person's private life than anyone had ever before attempted. He does this by including material that allowed readers not only to understand events intellectually via authorial analysis and narration but also to undergo an experience corresponding to the temporal flow and duration of the reported episodes: "Indeed I cannot conceive a more perfect mode of writing any man's life, than not only relating all the most important events of it in their order, but interweaving what he privately wrote, and said, and thought; by which mankind are enabled as it were to see him live, and to 'live o'er each scene' with him, as he actually advanced through the several stages of his life."[57] To live over each scene is to proceed at something more like the slow pace of experienced duration than the foreshortened time of analytical or narrative retrospection. This is the formula of modern biography. Churchill follows it.

If we take him at his word, and there is no reason to doubt him, Churchill did not start off with the Boswellian model in mind or later decide on *The Life of Johnson* as a template for *Marlborough*. He never mentions Boswell. But Churchill arrived at the Boswellian formula after wrestling with the problems presented by availability of so many documents. He reports an abandoned effort to make his own narration loom larger by cutting down on quotations from Marlborough's "secret, intimate correspondence" with Sarah and Godolphin: "I have sedulously endeavoured to reduce them, in the interests of the narrative, but in so many cases they *are* the narrative, and tell the tale far better than any other pen."[58] He states in the preface to the third published volume of *Marlborough* that in it he has followed "the method of the earlier volumes" by trying "as far as possible to tell the story through the lips of its actors or from the pens of contemporary writers, feeling sure that a phrase struck out at the time is worth many coined afterwards."[59] In his preface to the fourth published volume Churchill again calls attention to the quotations by affirming that he has "followed the method used in earlier volumes of always endeavouring to make Marlborough speak whenever possible."[60] Such references to speech are mostly metaphors alluding to quoted correspondence because, as Churchill laments, nothing like extensive reportage of actual conversation exists: "This was before the age when everybody kept diaries or wrote memoirs. . . . The age of military diarists and memoir-writers had not begun."[61]

Churchill does provide a few bits of actual dialogue as recorded mostly in the reports of ambassadors: "It is in the dispatches of Goes, Wratislaw, and other envoys that we can most plainly hear Marlborough speak."[62] From the episode of Marlborough's imprisonment in the Tower there is a transcript of highlights from the "dramatic" interrogation of his accusers Blackhead and Young which gives us "an intimate and invaluable picture of the methods of those days."[63] There are even some imaginary speeches clearly labeled as such and intended to make various attitudes or episodes seem more immediate by dramatization. With all the zest of a playwright poking mild fun at a favorite creation (or a parent starting to worry about his own children's prospects), Churchill makes up old Sir Winston's anxious rebuke to John at the prospect of his romantic but impractical marriage to the impecunious Sarah.[64] There is an imaginary conversation between Godolphin and King William that Churchill presents, tucked away in a footnote, as "probably more true to life and reality than the monstrous assumptions which historians have adopted."[65] Here again is Churchill's conviction that fiction may convey truth. For the sake of drama and immediacy he changes "from reported into direct speech" a conversation between Marlborough and King James taken, Churchill explains, from a dubious source in which "the colloquy has obviously been embroidered" although "it was almost certainly not invented."[66] This is a nice distinction between embroidering and inventing. It would not be easy to say just where the former stops and the latter begins. "Almost certainly" is a masterfully comic hedging of the historian's bet on veracity for the sake of verisimilitude. Such fictionalized passages are rare. They reveal something about a side of Churchill's literary imagination which evidently tempted him but that he seldom indulged after completing *Savrola*. His fictions most often take the form of counterfactual history embedded in factual narrative rather than imaginary dialogue or fully developed stories. What *Marlborough*'s rare bits of invented dialogue mainly reveal is Churchill's acute awareness that for his purposes it was crucial to find means of achieving temporal and psychological immediacy.

How far Churchill succeeded is a question best answered by a counterquestion: could anyone have done more? I doubt it. The letters included are well chosen to show as much as Marlborough ever cared to reveal. His was a personality marked, as Churchill wryly concedes, by impenetrable reserve. It was often necessary to mask his feelings and intentions. The letters to Sarah are doubtless sincere but seldom very revealing on topics apart from politics. Their professions of undying love and yearning for reunion during intervals of separation after marriage ring changes on a very limited repertoire of clichés that are the common property of people who feel deeply but don't aspire to new or interesting expression and don't need to. Marlborough's letters during their courtship, mostly undated but arranged by Churchill in plausible order to tell a tale of ups and downs with a happy storybook ending in marriage, read alas more like third-rate romance: "If you are unkind, I love so well that I cannot live, for you are my life, my soul, my all that I hold dear in this world; therefore do not make so ungrateful a return as not to write."[67] Confronted with such melodramatic professions by Marlborough that Sarah's unkind refusal to correspond would be the death of him, there will not be a wet eye in the house. But that is not Churchill's fault.

On military and diplomatic matters, Marlborough's letters included in the biography are at once more interesting, more revealing of his responses to situations, genuinely informative about important issues, and more appealing invitations to experience moments of closeness if not exactly intimacy with a great commander at some of history's crucial turning points. But even brought within his tent, as it were, we are inclined by the remarkably business-like tone of even his "secret, intimate correspondence" to keep a respectful distance. In person he could charm contemporaries. But his written words read centuries later display less warmth, intimacy, and appeal than impressive intellect and force of will. Readers are more likely to respond intellectually than emotionally, which is no very bad thing when attempting to understand a life that—so Churchill argues—crucially shaped the world in which we still live.

Other aspects of the narrative take readers away from intimate contact with Marlborough in the direction of analytical apprehension with all the advantages of the distance afforded by retrospection. There are facsimile documents, but most are hard to decipher. It is tempting to glance at them and move on. A few merely illustrate important moments such as Marlborough's report of victory at Blenheim. All the facsimiles to some extent bring the past forward. In contemplating them, however, readers are brought less close to Marlborough than, in most cases, to Churchill's impressive analytical arguments on his behalf, for which the facsimiles provide confirmation. We acquit the client but admire the counselor.

Maps of battles and campaigns are another prominent feature of the narrative to which Churchill calls attention: "Great pains have been taken with the diagrams and maps."[68] As Churchill intended, these are immensely helpful in understanding the progress of Marlborough's wars. The maps provide a series of snapshots taken successively that allow readers to picture the temporal sequence of military action. Like the brilliantly lucid battle narratives in which they are embedded, however, the maps keep readers firmly at a temporal and psychological remove from intimate involvement with the smoke, dust, confusion, and agony of the battlefields. We are told of all these but mostly regard them from afar via retrospective analysis. Churchill's chapter on "The Structure of the War" includes a kind of genre scene inviting imaginative as well as analytical understanding of what Marlborough's battles must have been like: "In prolonged severe fighting the survivors of a regiment often stood for hours knee-deep amid the bodies of comrades writhing or for ever still. In their ears rang the hideous chorus of the screams and groans of a pain which no anaesthetic would ever soothe."[69] This invitation to imagine what such battles sounded and felt like to participants is also an appeal to remember and fill in imaginatively the experiential details of battlefield realities while reading more analytical accounts of each engagement. But for reasons that Freud has explained, readers are more likely to forget such painful details without narrative reiteration by the author. Churchill had little choice, however, because, as he explains, "we are singularly lacking in stories of his campaigns from those who served in them."[70] To engage intimately rather than analytically with the battles in the course of narrating each one would have been to employ the methods of novelists like Stendhal and Tolstoy. This was more fictionalizing than Churchill cared to include in history. It is a pity that better eyewitness accounts were not available for Churchill to weave judiciously into his narrative because he was himself a master of presenting such reportage from the viewpoint of those on the field, as he demonstrated in *The Story of the Malakand Field Force*, *The River War*, his Boer War books, and *My Early Life*.

In any case, Marlborough's letters, together with Churchill's indispensable context of artfully arranged narration and explanation, do "recall this great shade from the past." How far he seems "living and intimate" will I suppose depend to a considerable extent on each reader's sense of what they require for liveliness and what they must know about a person to feel on intimate terms with him. The grand paradox of Churchill's task, as he acknowledges, is that Marlborough was not someone who at all encouraged or welcomed intimacy from his contemporaries beyond the very small circle of his Cockpit, political, and military associates. Nor did he care about the future. He wrote nothing directed to posterity. He made no effort by way of memoir or otherwise to explain himself to later generations. He was therefore a singularly uncooperative subject for a historian bent on recalling him from the past. Churchill in this respect could not have been more different from his hero. Churchill's eye is almost always as much on the future as on the present and on the past.

Whatever *Marlborough* does for its protagonist, the book still lives. Not only Churchill's prior and subsequent career, but its own virtues, make *Marlborough* of enduring interest to its future audiences. Had it been written by someone other than Churchill, or had his career not been what it was, that interest would be less. The inescapable fact for any reader now taking up *Marlborough* is that it *was* written by a person whose own accomplishments and attitudes warrant close study. It deserves more than ancillary attention because its narrative remains a living and intimate portrait of its author. Although hardly a vehicle for confessional or autobiography, in its pages are recorded a very generous sampling of Churchill's thoughts on topics ranging from politics, strategy, and other aspects of public life to love, marriage, and sex. We find many of the things that make him (and we with him) laugh. We see what rouses him to indignation. The myriad character sketches tell us what he admired and what he despised in people, and in what terms he understood human psychology. The catalogue of direct and oblique self-revelation could be extended to illustrate the fact that for all its skillful deployment of techniques that take us close to Marlborough, the major and omnipresent character in *Marlborough* is its narrator.

Churchill's narrative techniques for dealing with past time bring Marlborough forward sufficiently, and make him live sufficiently, so that there is a degree of real poignancy when those who have invested enough of their time to read some two thousand pages about Marlborough take their leave of him at the end. There is a sadness about his last years that Churchill succeeds in conveying because he has in the previous pages managed about as well as anyone could have to make Marlborough live in our imaginations. We care when we read of his death. But just as what is most compelling throughout the long narrative is the play of Churchill's intellect upon the facts of Marlborough's life and times, what is most compelling in that account of the end is not the passing of Marlborough but the intimate glimpse we have of an aging Churchill contemplating the passage of time that inevitably brings mortality: "It is foolish to waste lamentations upon the closing phase of human life. Noble spirits yield themselves willingly to the successively falling shades which carry them to a better world or to oblivion."[71]

ENVOI:
CHURCHILL'S DREAM

Churchill recalls that when he "acquired the chief power in the State" as prime minister on May 10, 1940, he felt "a profound sense of relief" when he "went to bed at about 3 a.m." after that momentous day: "I thought I knew a good deal about it all, and I was sure I should not fail. Therefore, although impatient for the morning, I slept soundly and had no need for cheering dreams. Facts are better than dreams."[1] Far from dismissing dreams as worthless, this remark implies that they may sometimes have their uses. Churchill only states that once in power recourse to wishful dreaming was unnecessary to sustain his morale even amid grim circumstances as the Battle of France began. He did not *then* need cheering dreams because authority to take charge combined with confidence that he would succeed was sufficiently encouraging to dispel gloom. Elsewhere he remarks his "happy gift of falling almost immediately into deep sleep."[2] That such sleep was dreamless, or at any rate not followed by recollection of dreaming, is implied in Churchill's account of his wartime slumbers: "During all the war soon to come and in its darkest times I never had any trouble in sleeping. In the crisis of 1940, when so much responsibility lay upon me, and also at many very anxious, awkward moments in the following five years, I could always flop into bed and go to sleep after the day's work was done. . . . I slept sound [*sic*] and awoke refreshed, and had no feelings except appetite to grapple with whatever the morning's boxes might bring."[3] Churchill's physician Lord Moran, however, records in his diary occasions during the war when Churchill requested sleeping pills, and in an entry dated November 30, 1954, even states "that for ten years he has not had natural sleep apart from sedatives."[4] Moran also records several postwar days when Churchill on waking recounted vivid dreams and wondered what they might mean.[5]

Whatever the accuracy of Moran's assertions, Churchill himself did not choose to describe any wartime nights when sleep was elusive or accompanied by dreaming. He reports an interval of agonized wakefulness while working in bed (as was his morning custom) on December 10, 1941, after a telephone call informing him that the battleships *Prince of Wales* and *Repulse* had been sunk by Japanese aircraft: "As I turned over and twisted in bed the full horror of the news sank in upon me."[6] He does record in dramatic—one might say melodramatic—detail what he claims was his one prewar night of insomnia, when for a while "the dark waters of despair overwhelmed" him after Anthony Eden resigned as foreign secretary to protest Chamberlain's appeasement policy:

> But now on this night of February 20, 1938, and on this occasion only, sleep deserted me. From midnight till dawn I lay in my bed consumed by emotions of sorrow and fear. There seemed one strong young figure standing up against long, dismal drawling tides of drift and surrender, of wrong measurements and feeble impulses. . . . he seemed to me at this moment to embody the life-hope of the British nation, the grand old British race that had done so much for men, and had yet some more to give. Now he was gone. I watched the daylight slowly creep in through the windows, and saw before me in mental gaze the vision of Death.[7]

Here Churchill contrasts with his "vision of Death" the "strong young figure" of Eden, symbolizing Britain's moral and political life in its best and most vigorous condition. In Churchill's "mental gaze" Eden is displaced by Death as night gives way to dawn and daylight slowly illuminates the bedroom. Churchill does not specify whether his "vision of Death" took the traditional form of a skeleton clothed in black and wielding a scythe. The image remains abstract, allowing readers to imagine what they will as to its substance, although its meaning is unambiguous. He describes a waking reverie, a kind of conscious imagining, not recollection of a nightmare.

If cheering dreams or vexing nightmares ever accompanied Churchill's sleep, he did not dwell on them in writing or transcribe their images on canvas. His paintings depict actual not fictitious landscapes, interiors, and people. Despite the quasi-impressionistic styles that Churchill developed to escape from banal realism, almost all his paintings are of identifiable people and places viewed in daytime. There are no dreamscapes. As an orator and author no less than as a painter, he preferred engagement with the daytime world of reality even when its facts assumed the menace, worse than any nightmare, of totalitarian regimes and world wars. Apart from one novel, a few short stories, and his obscure though interesting efforts at scriptwriting for Alexander Korda's studio, Churchill concentrated on genres that elevate fact over fiction: history, biography, memoir, essay, travel book, political speeches, and journalism including much early work as a war correspondent. Nevertheless he certainly appreciated and had occasional recourse to those waking and consciously shaped reveries that take various forms of fiction. Among them are his only freestanding essay in alternative history "If Lee Had Not Won the Battle of Gettysburg," many brief passages of counterfactual speculation embedded in longer works, and memos outlining future military or political actions. Some of these memos are on if not well across the blurry boundary separating realistic contingency planning from utopian dreaming. Churchill's counterfactual sketches of alternative history—of what might have happened—embedded in his histories often amount to miniature retrospective utopias or dystopias. The only one he explicitly labels as a dream vision, however, is his "Armistice dream"—categorized by him as "one of many Armistice Dreams"—in *The Aftermath*, where Churchill imagines how Wilson, Clemenceau, and Lloyd George could better have managed the settlement with Germany after World War I.[8] As I noted in chapter 4, Churchill's account of this "dream" and the sleeper waking from it adopts the convention of a literary dream vision that is well understood not to be a report of any actual dream.

Nor does Churchill profess to report an actual dream in his most poignant short story, "The Dream," in which he describes a conversation at his studio in Chartwell between himself and the apparition of his long-dead father, Lord Randolph Churchill. Reserved for posthumous publication when there would be no opportunity to question its author about the eerie episode recounted, and revised through several drafts following its inception in late 1946 or early 1947, this tale of an uncanny encounter is itself a kind of communication from the dead to the living. It is Churchill's last testament in the realm of imagination.

⌘

His working title for the manuscript was simply "Private Article." His family as well as friends allowed to read it and make suggestions called it "The Dream," and it was thus headed when finally published in the *Sunday Telegraph*, January 30, 1966, almost exactly a year after his death on January 24, 1965. A version of the conversation with Lord Randolph's shade was first told by Churchill to his son Randolph and his daughter Sarah at a family meal "in late 1946 or early 1947." When asked by Randolph whom he would invoke to join them if he could summon any one from any era, Churchill replied, "Oh, my father, of course." Of Churchill's ensuing account outlining the story, his son remarks: "It was not plain whether he was recalling a dream or elaborating on some fanciful idea that had struck him earlier. But this was the genesis of the story."[9] The title chosen by his family for publication is close enough to the mark as a signal of the tale's genre, and is certainly more memorable than "Private Article." Churchill's avoidance of any conventional category as a label for the manuscript while he polished it reflects not only his usual indifference to niceties of literary pigeonholing and his frequent difficulties in picking a title, but perhaps also an effort to keep this work ambiguously hovering between the realms of fact and fiction as befits a ghost story whose readers may wonder whether they have a product of Churchill's fancy in fictional mode or the history of a supernatural encounter that he believed had really taken place.

For the sake of clarity while discussing "The Dream," I shall refer to the painter and narrator within the tale as Winston, the apparition as Lord Randolph, and the author of the story, to distinguish him from the character of the same name within it, as Churchill. The scene is set in Churchill's Chartwell studio "one foggy afternoon in November, 1947" while Winston copies an old 1886 portrait of his father, Lord Randolph Churchill:

> My easel was under a strong daylight lamp, which is necessary for indoor painting in the British winter. On the right of it stood the portrait I was copying, and behind me was a large looking glass, so that one could frequently study the painting in reverse. I must have painted for an hour and half, and was deeply concentrated on my subject. I was drawing my father's face, gazing at the portrait, and frequently turning round right-handed to check progress in the mirror. Thus I was intensely absorbed, and my mind was freed from

all other thoughts except the impressions of that loved and honoured
face now on the canvas, now on the picture, now in the mirror.[10]

Although Churchill offers no theory to account for the ensuing apparition,
his description of the occasion and setting of its manifestation suggests two
mutually exclusive explanations, one natural and one supernatural, without allowing either to be altogether dismissed. Entire attention focused for
a long interval on nothing but a triple representation of Lord Randolph's
face in different phases—complete in the old painting, in reverse of that
when seen in the mirror, and taking shape on Winston's canvas—might
well stimulate the painter's already activated imagination to the point of
making up a conversation while seeing in his mind's eye a kind of animated full-length picture of his father. Or just possibly—if one may
believe in such things—a son's intense and welcoming concentration on
"that loved and honoured face" could have summoned Lord Randolph's
shade from wherever it resides in the afterlife. Readers may accept either
implied line of explanation. Or else, as is always possible when dealing
with the fantastic in literature, they may simply suspend disbelief, take the
story as it comes, and push ahead without worrying about its dubious
probability.

This latter tack is most strongly encouraged by what follows because,
apart from materializing in the first place, the apparition does nothing
alarming or out of the ordinary. Unlike, say, the ghost of Hamlet's father,
Lord Randolph says nothing shattering, lays no task upon Winston, nor
provides any hair-raising hints about the nature of existence in the afterlife. The bulk of the tale consists of a calm dialogue between a ghost who
says he doesn't "remember anything after [eighteen] ninety-four" (the year
Lord Randolph declined into his terminal illness) and a living man satisfying the ghost's curiosity by answering questions about what happened
between that time and 1947. The exchange, unaccompanied by emotional
display or gestures on either side, might have taken place in some quiet
corner of a London club without attracting particular notice from others
present. Lord Randolph falls into conversation without any apparent sense
of the oddness of his own situation: "His eyes twinkled and shone. He
was evidently in the best of tempers. He was engaged in filling his amber
cigarette-holder with a little pad of cotton-wool before putting in the
cigarette." Winston, though remarking that he "suddenly felt an odd sensation" just before noticing the apparition, takes it well in stride: "I felt

no alarm, but I thought I would stand where I was and go no nearer."[11] This response not only displays an engaging mixture of sangfroid and prudence. It also nicely allows Churchill to maintain the tale's ambiguity as to the status of the ghost: real or imagined? Although apparent to sight and hearing, its presence is not put to a further test of the sense of touch.

Nor does Winston try to see if the ghost is tangible at a later moment toward the end of the conversation when its uncanny aspect at last strikes home as Winston notices the paradox that he and Lord Randolph are wearing the *same* watch chain, evidently one that Winston has inherited from his father:"He now took his matchbox from his watch-chain, which was the same as I was wearing. For the first time I felt a sense of awe. I rubbed my brush in the paint on the palette to make sure that everything was real. All the same I shivered."[12] This, however, offers no assurance that *everything*, including the ghost, was real. It only tests what the story never puts in doubt, namely, that the painting equipment was really there because it is reassuringly solid to the touch.

Equally ambiguous is another moment of confirmation, this time by the test of memory as Winston first sees the apparition: "I turned round with my palette in my hand, and there, sitting in my red leather upright armchair, was my father. He looked just as I had seen him in his prime, and as I had read about him in his brief year of triumph. He was small and slim, with the big moustache I was just painting, and all his bright, captivating, jaunty air."[13] This too could go either way. If the possibility of a ghost is granted as an allowable hypothesis for interpreting mysterious events in life or literature, the apparition may be accepted as really Lord Randolph because it conforms so perfectly to Winston's memories of his father. It passes the test of eyewitness identification in which what is seen is compared with what is remembered. Moreover the apparition's moustache, to which Winston is just attending on his canvas, is exactly like that in the 1886 portrait, presumably taken from life. Starting from a more skeptical view of the spirit world, however, it is equally possible to regard this apparition's resemblance to memories and pictures as the very hallmarks of an hallucination induced by concentrating on the portraits because such an hallucination at such a moment would be most likely to conform closely to memories of the actual man—memories stimulated, reinforced, and perhaps even to some degree reshaped by the old picture.

Winston's memories as described, moreover, are from three quite different sources. Some are long-term (and thus probably fading) memories of actual glimpses of his father "in his prime" well over fifty years before when Winston was young. Some are memories of reading about his father at his best during "his brief year of triumph." Some are short-term memories of the 1886 painting, its reversed reflection in the mirror, and the copy on Winston's canvas: memories that could merge into what amounts to an after-image as he looks up from his task and gazes at the red leather chair. Here also Churchill creates opposing possibilities. Winston's actual memories of his father's appearance may be taken as validated by historical sources in two forms: the 1886 portrait, and unspecified written accounts describing him in his heyday. Or else those memories may be taken as a kind of second-order memory, or, more accurately, as a mental image masquerading as a real memory but strongly shaped if not altogether created by the old picture and by other people's words that in turn may or may not have been accurate verbal portraits. In this case what Winston sees or imagines in the red leather chair is partly a literary construct derived from works that (like Churchill's own biography of Lord Randolph in certain respects) may have presented an idealized image. If the figure apparently seated in the chair is simply a projection of Winston's imagination, unusually focused on Lord Randolph at that moment in the studio, then the episode must be taken as only a wish-fulfilment fantasy of a father-son conversation with both meeting on equal terms as adults in a way denied to Churchill in reality by his father's early death and his reluctance while alive to confide in a boy who seemed so unpromising.

Most readers will take it as such a fantasy, if only to avoid the awkward complications of accepting the incident as an encounter with the supernatural. Either way the episode's outset arouses an expectation that the tale will end on a happy note as Lord Randolph at last has a chance, if only during his afterlife, to appreciate Winston's remarkable accomplishments while the son, for his part, gets an opportunity that he never had in reality to bask in a glow of paternal approval and applause for a life well lived. Churchill skillfully plays off against that expectation the tale's surprising turn away from such a sentimental—and trivial—happy ending.

Instead of saying anything about a political career that eventually led twice to the prime minister's office that eluded his father, who surely regarded it as the most praiseworthy of all possible achievements, or even mentioning that he wrote an admiring biography of his father, Winston merely reassures Lord Randolph that he is a professional writer not just an amateur painter:

His eye wandered round the studio, which is entirely panelled with scores of my pictures. I followed his travelling eye as it rested now on this one and on that. After a while: "Do you live in this cottage?"

"No," I said, "I have a house up on the hill, but you cannot see it for the fog."

"How do you get a living?" he asked. "Not, surely, by these?" indicating the pictures.

"No, indeed, Papa. I write books and articles for the Press."

"Ah, a reporter. There is nothing discreditable in that. I myself wrote articles for the *Daily Graphic* when I went to South Africa. And well I was paid for them. A hundred pounds an article!"[14]

Lord Randolph's approval—"Nothing discreditable in that"—is uncomfortably close to damning with faint praise, although at least more gratifying than his firm conclusion after a hasty survey that the paintings are not good enough to secure Winston his livelihood as an artist. Readers may at first take Winston's reticence about his political career and about his comfortable house on the hill above the studio as a sign of uncharacteristic modesty, or perhaps a considerate attempt to spare Lord Randolph's feelings by not revealing that his son, judged to be so unpromising, has in fact far outshone the father, proving him wrong. Neither explanation will quite do, however, because Churchill makes the tale a vehicle for issues that transcend concern with merely personal relationships and satisfactions. The main interest of "The Dream," arises neither from its effects as a ghost story nor from its psychological drama of a reunion between father and son, but from its witty juxtaposition of twentieth-century realities and the expectations of an aristocrat who lived and died during Queen Victoria's reign.

Via this interchange Churchill invites twentieth-century readers to regard their own era as it might appear to a time traveler from the late nineteenth century and *also* as it does appear to Winston, an inhabitant of mid-twentieth-century England who is himself a product of the Victorian fin de siècle and therefore views the ensuing years from the double perspective of a person who adapted to their shattering social, economic, and scientific changes but who started out steeped in the same Victorian certainties which Lord Randolph never had to abandon. A defamiliarized view of the twentieth century is thus created for readers because so much that they are inclined to take for granted seems strange to Lord Randolph and can only be explained to him with difficulty—or not at all—by Winston. He in turn remembers enough of the Victorian era's outlook to be acutely aware that from its perspective and according to its values the twentieth century must be judged to have turned out very oddly and on the whole very badly. The conclusion which emerges from Winston's dialogue with Lord Randolph is one of Churchill's characteristic reminders that Victorian ideas and hopes of progress have not been borne out by events. Churchill was never inclined to view the twentieth century as moving inexorably forward to some attainable utopia but rather as sliding back toward the prospect of what he calls in his "Finest Hour" speech "the abyss of a new Dark Age."[15]

Churchill's wide-ranging assessment of the twentieth century and comparison of it with the previous century makes "The Dream" stand out from its literary predecessors. From Lucian's "Dialogues of the Dead" through similar works with the same title by Fontenelle, Fénelon, Matthew Prior, and George Lyttleton to Walter Savage Landor's more widely known series of "Imaginary Conversations" and their avatars, focus is most often on dramatizing or inventing attitudes of the deceased in order to consider philosophical or literary issues, to satirize current but usually also perennial foibles, or simply as a means of envisioning a famous person such as Shakespeare or Henry VIII somewhat in the manner of an historical novel. By making readers look afresh at the history of their own century to notice its unique oddities and shortcoming as they might be viewed by a person from the past, "The Dream" is more akin to the newer genre of time-travel stories.

As a tale of time travel "The Dream" follows most closely the device of stories like Washington Irving's "Rip Van Winkle." Although Lord Randolph leaps ahead from 1895 to 1947 by supernatural means instead of sleeping as Rip does or remaining in some kind of hypnotic trance over the intervening years as do protagonists in stories such as Edward Bellamy's *Looking Backward*, Lord Randolph plays the conventional role in such tales of a man who wakes to find himself in what is to him a bewildering future time whose customs and history require explanation. "The Dream" is more remotely affiliated to stories of travel to the future presented as only dreams from which the time traveler finally awakes back in his own era, and to stories of travel to the future or past in a time machine. As I remarked in chapter 4, however, Churchill was much taken by the story in which H. G. Wells inaugurated what has become the most popular framework for such tales, the use of a machine with a vaguely explained but scientific rather than supernatural method of moving through time. Recall Churchill's enthusiastic description of a memorable first encounter: "when I came upon *The Time Machine*, that marvellous philosophical romance, not unworthy to follow at some distance, but nevertheless in the train of, *Gulliver's Travels*, I shouted with joy."[16] *The Time Machine* was published in 1895, the year of Lord Randolph's death. Perhaps it was read by Churchill then or at least associated by him with that fraught year whose events, good and bad, must have struck unusually resonant chords. In any case, for Churchill the appeal of Wells's "marvellous philosophical romance" endured.

Especially relevant to "The Dream" is the fact that *The Time Machine* was very much in Churchill's thoughts not long after he first mentioned the tale of that "foggy afternoon in November, 1947" when Winston is said to have talked with Lord Randolph. In a diary entry for December 7, 1947, Lord Moran records (as you'll also recall from chapter 4) that while Churchill "sat basking in the sun" musing on various topics he remarked that *The Time Machine* is "a wonderful book" and among those "I would like to take with me to Purgatory."[17] As evidence of where Churchill found inspiration or a partial literary model for "The Dream" it would be wrong to weigh heavily the curious associational link in this remark between a tale of time travel and a notion of the afterlife in Purgatory whimsically imagined as affording an opportunity to bring along and reread a few favorite books as one might to alleviate a tedious journey or rainy summer vacation. Nevertheless it is worth noting the approximate coincidence of this amiable remark and the genesis of "The Dream," in which Lord Randolph both travels through time and finds in a conversation with his son some diversion from whatever circumstances prevail for him in the afterlife. It is a telling sign of Churchill's originality that although this coincidence offers a clue to the story's literary lineage, similarities to Wells's masterpiece are more suggestive than exact.

The most notable parallel between "The Dream" and *The Time Machine*, apart from the presence in both of a man somehow displaced forward into what for him is future time, is that Lord Randolph and Wells's Time Traveler at his first destination both initially mistake the era in which they have arrived for a utopia, referred to in both works as a "Golden Age," whereupon they come to understand the disillusioning facts that mark their destinations as the very opposite of utopian in everything that matters most. The Time Traveler thinks himself in a utopia when he first sees the pretty and friendly though dim-witted Eloi apparently enjoying a life of ease and beauty in a land that seems like a new-model Garden of Eden: "The whole earth had become a garden." He muses upon the apparent discrepancy between those like him from the late nineteenth century and the inhabitants of England in 802,701 AD: "How wide the interval between myself and these of the Golden Age!"[18] Then he must revise his opinion when he is horrified to discover the hideous Morlocks living underground except for nightly raids to carry off Eloi and possibly himself to serve up at dinnertime in the caverns. Lord Randolph remarks early in his conversation with Winston, "You must be living in a very happy age. A Golden Age, it seems."[19] He arrives at this premature conclusion after initial questions have elicited assurance that despite several Socialist governments and introduction of the universal franchise ("Even the women have votes. . . . It did not turn out as badly as I thought") England's monarchy is still strong, the Carlton Club, the Turf Club, and horse racing continue as in his day, the Primrose League "has never had more members," Church of England bishops still sit in the House of Lords ("and make a lot of speeches"), and things are looking up in Ireland where Ulster at least remains loyal and where—here Winston is at his most sanguine—within a framework of Home Rule "They have built up a cultured Roman Catholic system in the South. . . . They are getting more happy and prosperous. The bitter past is fading. . . . And the Catholic Church has now become a great champion of individual liberty."[20] When the conversation proceeds from these rather overoptimistic observations to the darker side of the twentieth century, surveying its wars and massacres, Lord Randolph, like the Time Traveler after discovering the Morlocks, is horrified: "Winston, you have told me a terrible tale. I would never have believed that such things could happen. I am glad I did not live to see them."[21]

Except for their similar structure of ironic reversal from delight to horror within a tale of time travel, it is the differences between "The Dream" and *The Time Machine* that are most striking. If Churchill's favorite time-travel story served in some recess of his mind as an inspiration for "The Dream" he did not simply take it as a pattern any more than he exactly imitated the conventional dialogue of the dead or imaginary conversation. Wells's Time Traveler (he has no other name) must painfully and after much trial and error figure out for himself what is going on and what has led to the society in which he finds himself, whereas Winston is at hand to answer Lord Randolph's questions. The Time Traveler narrates his own adventure in the future, which is described as he sees and understands it, whereas Lord Randolph's excursion into the future is described, as is that future, by Winston. Thus Churchill shifts the narrative point of view from the traveler to the guide.

Winston becomes the character into whose mind readers are admitted—though not very far—and with whom they can most easily identify because he, more than Lord Randolph, is of their own era. "The Dream" is far less introspective and speculative, and thus far less what Churchill rightly termed a "philosophical romance," than *The Time Machine*. In portraying Winston's inner life Churchill's mode is understatement. There are only hints. We learn of Winston's "awe," of his doubts about the apparition's reality, and that after it vanishes he "felt too tired to go on" painting.[22] That's all. Otherwise, as is entirely the case for Lord Randolph, readers must infer what is thought from what is said. In this respect "The Dream" is closest to the archetypal dialogue of the dead, and to one of Churchill's favorite genres, the play, whether on stage or screen, with its confinement to dialogue, soliloquy, and scene. In "The Dream" there is no soliloquy from either character, whereas *The Time Machine*, though presenting its account of the trip forward to the future as a dialogue between the Time Traveler and his friends after he returns, reads more like an extended soliloquy or monologue in which he meditates upon the meaning of his experience and his various states of mind during it.

Unlike *The Time Machine* and most of its precursors and successors in the genres of fictional voyages through time or space to strange places, moreover, "The Dream" puts its readers in a position to judge—and indeed compels them to judge—the accuracy of what is said about the traveler's destination. For Churchill's audience in 1966 and for many years thereafter, that destination, Lord Randolph's future, is their present: the twentieth century. Every reader will have notions about its distinguishing features and opinions about its good and bad qualities. Accordingly every reader will be in a position to assess and perhaps debate the view of it offered by Winston as an explanation to Lord Randolph. Even for subsequent readers in the twenty-first century (and after), Lord Randolph's destination, 1947, will be a matter of historical record, unlike Wells's description of the Time Traveler's adventures in the year 802,701 AD and even further into our future. The significance of this imaginary far future for the reader's understanding of present reality may be considered, as for all fictional places that invite comparison of what is with what might be, but not its accuracy, or even its likelihood as a prediction. By setting his scenes so far forward in time, Wells relegates such questions to the notoriously irrelevant realm of debates about the number of Lady Macbeth's children. His division of humanity into hapless Eloi descended from the ruling classes and predatory Morlocks descended from workers must be taken as a fable allegorically inviting attention to potentially ruinous consequences of the widening gap between haves and have-nots in the reader's time. To this extent *The Time Machine* is a call to action that might remedy such dangerous disparities. "The Dream" is primarily a call to reflect on what cannot be changed: "the wars of nations, caused by demagogues and tyrants" that have already taken place bringing unprecedented slaughter and, not incidentally, undermining the British Empire and reducing Britain to the status of a much lesser power than the United States and Russia.[23]

"The Dream" is also an invitation for readers to compare their view of twentieth century upheavals with Churchill's as inferred from what Winston says. But his remarks offer only a few glimpses of Churchill's attitudes, not anything remotely approaching an account of all the twentieth century has meant to him and, in his view, to world history. For that one would have to read or reread (at a minimum) *The World Crisis, My Early Life, Thoughts and Adventures, Great Contemporaries, The Second World War*, and several volumes of collected speeches. Thanks to widespread familiarity with Churchill's long career as writer and speaker, however, it is easy for any likely reader of "The Dream" to recall or guess many of his opinions that remain unspoken in Winston's dialogue with Lord Randolph. So too, readers can easily appreciate typically devastating Churchillian irony in "The Dream," as when, after Lord Randolph is told that it is 1947 and dryly asks "Of the Christian era, I presume?" Winston replies: "Yes, that all goes on. At least, they still count that way."[24] Given Churchill's fame as a staunch defender of democracy in its most embattled hours, it is harder to accept the disturbing implications of Winston's report to Lord Randolph that "we have had nothing else but wars since democracy took charge."[25] This seems to allocate blame in a way uncharacteristic of Churchill even when analyzing elsewhere what he finds most problematic about democracy. Within the dialogue, however, Churchill quickly meliorates his critique of democracy by also remarking: "I have always been a strong supporter of the House of Commons, Papa. I am still very much in favour of it."[26] This is a more familiar Churchillian stance that could hardly be in doubt for readers.

But it evokes from Lord Randolph a stern admonition to be always a supporter of parliamentary democracy. For the seventy-three-year-old Winston this advice is superfluous indeed, although Lord Randolph, unlike readers of "The Dream," cannot be sure of this because he knows only how unpromising Winston seemed as a boy:

> "You had better be, Winston, because the will of the people must prevail. Give me a fair arrangement of the constituencies, a wide franchise, and free elections—say what you like, and one part of Britain will correct and balance the other."
>
> "Yes, you brought me up to that."
>
> "I never brought you up to anything. I was not going to talk politics with a boy like you ever. Bottom of the school! Never passed any examination, except into the Cavalry! Wrote me stilted letters. I could not see how you would make your living on the little I could leave you and Jack, and that only after your mother. I once thought of the Bar for you but you were not clever enough. . . . You were very fond of playing soldiers, so I settled for the Army. I hope you had a successful military career."
>
> "I was a Major in the Yeomanry."
>
> He did not seem impressed.[27]

This exchange elicits no comment from the adult Winston as narrator, despite Lord Randolph's unremittingly low opinion of Winston as a boy and now as apparently nothing more distinguished than a retired Territorial Army major. Churchill leaves his readers free to imagine if they can Winston's emotions on this rehearsal of the most painful aspect of his childhood, Lord Randolph's aloof lack of confidence in his son.

Without either providing any mitigating facts about his political career or any indication of how distressed he may still be at such early and now posthumously continued disapproval from his father, Winston simply mentions his forty years of marriage resulting in four children and five grandchildren, and then complies with Lord Randolph's request to be told "more about these other wars" that followed the Boer War.[28] Winston sums up these along with the empire's loss of India and Burma in a few

paragraphs. The horrific nature of both World Wars is sketched in a few
sentences:

> "Papa," I said, "in each of them about thirty million men were
> killed in battle. In the last one seven million were murdered in cold
> blood, mainly by the Germans. They made human slaughter-pens
> like the Chicago stockyards. Europe is a ruin. Many of her cities
> have been blown to pieces by bombs. Ten capitals in Eastern Europe
> are in Russian hands. They are Communists now, you know—Karl
> Marx and all that. It may well be that an even worse war is draw-
> ing near. A war of the East against the West. A war of liberal civi-
> lization against the Mongol hordes. Far gone are the days of Queen
> Victoria and a settled world order. But, having gone through so
> much, we do not despair."[29]

It is after hearing this bleak summary that Lord Randolph says he is glad
not to have lived to see such "terrible" events. His last remark before rather
incongruously giving Winston "a benignant smile" and vanishing is yet
another unwarranted rebuke for what he mistakenly takes to have been a
wasted life not lived to its full potential: "As I listened to you unfolding
these fearful facts you seemed to know a great deal about them. I never
expected that you would develop so far and so fully. Of course you are
too old now to think about such things, but when I hear you talk I really
wonder you didn't go into politics. You might have done a lot to help.
You might even have made a name for yourself." After this parting shot
from beyond the grave, "He vanished. The chair was empty. The illusion
had passed."[30] The episode is over. Winston has no further opportunity
to respond and perhaps get well-deserved approval at last by telling how
very helpful his political life had been and what a name he had made for
himself. Nor does he express regret at not doing so before Lord Randolph
vanished. It is on this point that Churchill keeps his fantasy in touch with
reality by in effect acknowledging a sad truth of the human condition: that
we cannot make the dead alter whatever opinions of us they had while
alive. The past is irrevocable.

It is otherwise for living readers of "The Dream." It closes by inviting them to remember, which is to imagine, Churchill's life, works, and
times in all their fullness. The few sentences in "The Dream" outlining
World War I, World War II, and the subsequent East-West confrontation

are an invitation to recollect—or better, revisit and reread—Churchill's six-volume *World Crisis* and six-volume *Second World War*, perhaps along with his Iron Curtain speech and his great wartime orations. Lord Randolph's speculation about what Churchill might have done had he gone into politics is an invitation for readers to remember and applaud what Churchill actually did. "The Dream" thus closes with an implied counterfactual history: Lord Randolph's mistaken imagination of retired Major of Yeomanry Churchill's life as a reporter supporting himself by writing "books and articles for the press." By fleetingly imagining that inconsequential alternative Churchillian life, and while doing so inevitably recognizing that it is only an alternative life that never happened as Lord Randolph supposes, readers of "The Dream" are also compelled to imagine in greater or lesser detail Churchill's actual life. These invitations are open-ended. "The Dream" is short. Churchill's life was long. His era was all too crowded with important events. His inclination as a writer was to chronicle such matters at length in expansive modes of history, biography, and memoir. In these works the Nobel laureate's own imagination could range at large in presenting his accounts. For his final literary legacy, however, Churchill chose to work in miniature by presenting readers with the posthumous gift of a narrative that is above all an invitation to exercise their own imaginations by recollecting for themselves Churchill's life as they think about all that Winston might have said about it to Lord Randolph but does not even hint at. As a last farewell to the story's—and the twentieth century's—Winston, the events of his remarkable and influential life are evoked but not spelled out. It is as though Churchill's own shade comes to us via the medium of "The Dream" proposing with engaging and irresistible charm that we do what the plaque devoted to him in Westminster Abbey more imperiously urges: "Remember Winston Churchill."

PREFACE

1. *Nobel Prize Library: Albert Camus, Winston Churchill* (New York: Alexis Gregory; Del Mar, CA: CRM Publishing, n.d.), 175. See also Burton Feldman, *The Nobel Prize: A History of Genius, Controversy, and Prestige* (New York: Arcade Publishing, 2000).

2. Manfred Weidhorn, *Sword and Pen: A Survey of the Writings of Sir Winston Churchill* (Albuquerque: University of New Mexico Press, 1974).

3. Isaiah Berlin, *Mr Churchill in 1940* (London: John Murray, n.d. [1949]).

4. David Reynolds, *In Command of History: Churchill Fighting and Writing the Second World War* (London: Allen Lane, 2004).

5. I list these in roughly chronological order to show the evolution of attention to Churchill's writing: Herbert Leslie Stewart, *Sir Winston Churchill as Writer and Speaker* (London: Sidgwick & Jackson, 1954); Maurice Ashley, *Churchill as Historian* (London: Secker & Warburg, 1968); J. H. Plumb, "The Historian," in A. J .P. Taylor, Robert Rhodes James, J. H. Plumb, Basil Liddell Hart, and Anthony Storr, *Churchill Revised: A Critical Assessment* (New York: Dial Press, 1969), 133–69; Plumb's essay in *Churchill Revised* is reprinted as "Churchill: The Historian," in J. H. Plumb, *The Making of an Historian: The Collected Essays of J. H. Plumb* (Athens, GA: University of Georgia Press, 1988), 225–52; James W. Muller, "'A Kind of Dignity and Even Nobility': Winston Churchill's *Thoughts and Adventures*," *Political Science Reviewer* 16 (Fall 1986): 281–315; James W. Muller, "Churchill the Writer," *Wilson Quarterly*, 18, no. 1 (Winter 1994): 38–48, and reprinted in a supplement entitled *Essays in Biography: The Best of the WQ* (1995): 23–33; Keith Alldritt, *Churchill the Writer: His Life as a Man of Letters* (London: Hutchinson, 1992); Patrick J. C. Powers, "*Savrola* and the Nobility of Politics: Winston Churchill's Premier Literary Work," *Finest Hour* 74 (First Quarter 1992): 6–13; Manfred Weidhorn, *A Harmony of Interests: Explorations in the Mind of Sir Winston Churchill* (Rutherford, NJ: Fairleigh Dickinson University Press, 1992); Frederick Woods, *Artillery of Words: The Writings of Sir Winston Churchill* (London: Leo Cooper, 1992); David Cannadine, "Winston Churchill as an Aristocratic Adventurer," in *Aspects of Aristocracy: Grandeur and Decline in Modern Britain* (New Haven: Yale University Press, 1994), 130–62; Victor Feske, "Winston Churchill, The Last Public Historian," in *From Belloc to Churchill: Private Scholars, Public Culture, and the Crisis of British Liberalism, 1900–1939* (Chapel Hill: University of North Carolina Press, 1996), 186–227; Stephen Bungay, "The Reason Why," in *The Most Dangerous Enemy: A History of the Battle of Britain* (London: Aurum Press, 2000), 7–26; David Cannadine, "Language: Churchill as the Voice of Destiny," in *In Churchill's Shadow: Confronting the Past in Modern Britain* (London: Allen Lane, 2002), 85–113; Algis Valiunas, *Churchill's Military Histories: A Rhetorical Study* (Lanham, MD: Rowman & Littlefield, 2002); John Ramsden, *Man of the Century: Winston Churchill and His Legend Since 1945* (London: HarperCollins, 2002).

6. For those who wish to visit or revisit Churchill's life, two especially valuable biographical studies are: Geoffrey Best, *Churchill: A Study in Greatness* (London: Hambledon

& London, 2001); Martin Gilbert, *In Search of Churchill: A Historian's Journey* (London: HarperCollins, 1994).

7. Winston S. Churchill, "Speech in the House of Commons May 13, 1940," in *Blood, Sweat, and Tears* (New York: G. P. Putnam's Sons, 1941), 276.

8. Winston S. Churchill, *My Early Life: A Roving Commission* (London: Thornton Butterworth, 1930), 31.

9. D. J. Wenden, "Churchill, Radio, and Cinema," in *Churchill*, ed. Robert Blake and W. Roger Louis (New York: W. W. Norton, 1993), 226–27.

10. Winston S. Churchill, "Fifty Years Hence," in *Thoughts and Adventures* (London: Thornton Butterworth Limited, 1932), 277.

11. Winston S. Churchill, *Marlborough: His Life and Times*, 2 vols. (London: George G. Harrap, 1947), 1:19.

CHAPTER ONE. IMAGINING LAWRENCE

1. Winston S. Churchill, "'These Are Great Days': A Speech to the Boys of Harrow School, October 29, 1941," in *The Unrelenting Struggle: War Speeches by the Right Hon. Winston S. Churchill, C.H., M.P.*, comp. Charles Eade (Boston: Little, Brown, 1942), 286–87.

2. Ibid., 287.

3. Among the myriad relevant works, good places to enter the labyrinth are Aaron S. Klieman, *Foundations of British Policy in the Arab World: The Cairo Conference of 1921* (Baltimore: Johns Hopkins Press, 1970), and David Fromkin, *A Peace to End All Peace: Creating the Modern Middle East* (New York: Henry Holt, 1989).

4. T. E. Lawrence, *The Mint* (1935; repr., New York: W. W. Norton, 1963), 218.

5. Jeremy Wilson, *Lawrence of Arabia: The Authorized Biography of T. E. Lawrence* (New York: Atheneum, 1990), 921–22.

6. Lawrence to Lionel Curtis, Bovington Camp, March 19, 1923, in *The Letters of T. E. Lawrence*, ed. David Garnett (New York: Doubleday, Doran, 1939), 411.

7. T. E. Lawrence, *Seven Pillars of Wisdom: A Triumph* (privately printed 1926; published 1935 by Jonathan Cape; repr., Harmondsworth, England: Penguin, 1962), 582.

8. Ibid., 30.

9. Ibid., 565.

10. Jeffrey Meyers, *The Wounded Spirit: T. E. Lawrence's "Seven Pillars of Wisdom,"* 2nd ed. (Houndmills: Macmillan, 1989), 64, 104.

11. Lawrence to Bernard Shaw, Karachi, May 7, 1928, in *Letters*, 603.

12. Lawrence, *The Mint*, 135.

13. Lawrence, *Seven Pillars*, 21.

14. Ibid., 469.

15. Lawrence, *The Mint*, 248.

16. Ibid.

17. Ibid., 249.

18. Ibid., 250.

19. Robert Graves, *Lawrence and the Arabs* (1927; repr., New York: Paragon House, 1991), 397.

20. Ibid., 396.

21. Wilson, *Lawrence of Arabia*, 651.

22. Ibid., 1118n29.

23. Lawrence, *Seven Pillars*, 582.

24. T. E. Lawrence to Winston S. Churchill, November 18, 1922, in Martin Gilbert, *Winston S. Churchill, Volume 4 Companion, Part 3: Documents April 1921–November 1922* (London: Heinemann, 1977), 2125.

25. T. E. Lawrence, "Draft Preface," November 18, 1922, in *Letters*, 345.

26. T. E. Lawrence to R. D. Blumenfeld, November 11, 1922, in Gilbert, *Churchill, Volume 4 Companion, Part 3*, 2122.

27. Lawrence, *Seven Pillars*, 283.

28. Winston S. Churchill, "Lawrence of Arabia," in *Great Contemporaries* (London: Thornton Butterworth, 1937), 160.

29. Ronald Storrs, *Orientations* (London: Ivor Nicholson & Watson, 1937), 525.

30. Winston Churchill, untitled essay on Lawrence in *T. E. Lawrence by His Friends*, ed. A. W. Lawrence (London: Jonathan Cape, 1937), 200.

31. Churchill, *Great Contemporaries*, 165.

32. Winston S. Churchill, *The World Crisis 1916–1918* (1927; repr., Norwalk, CT: Easton Press, 1991), 336–37.

33. T. E. Lawrence to Edward Marsh, Karachi, June 10, 1927, in *Letters*, 521.

34. Churchill, *Great Contemporaries*, 166.

35. Ibid., 155.

36. Frederick Woods, *A Bibliography of the Works of Sir Winston Churchill*, 2nd ed. (Toronto: University of Toronto Press, 1969), 167.

37. "Introduction to the Letters of T. E. Lawrence," in *The Home Letters of T. E. Lawrence and His Brothers*, ed. M. R. Lawrence (New York: Macmillan, 1954), xii.

38. A. W. Lawrence, ed., *T. E. Lawrence by His Friends*, 202.

39. Churchill, *Great Contemporaries*, 164.

40. Ibid., 166–67.

41. Winston S. Churchill, *The Second World War, Volume One: The Gathering Storm* (London: Educational Book Company, 1955), 115.

42. John Keble, *The Christian Year: Lyra Innocentium and Other Poems* (London: Oxford University Press, 1914), 4.

43. A. W. Lawrence, ed., *T. E. Lawrence by His Friends*, 201.

44. Churchill, *Great Contemporaries*, 166.

45. A. W. Lawrence, ed., *T. E. Lawrence by His Friends*, 201.

46. Churchill, *Great Contemporaries*, 164. Italics added.

47. Lowell Thomas, *With Lawrence in Arabia* (New York: Century, 1924), 349.

48. Churchill, *Gathering Storm*, 41.

49. Churchill, *Great Contemporaries*, 165.

50. Ibid., 167.

51. Ibid.

52. Adam Lindsay Gordon, "The Last Leap," in *Poems of the Late Adam Lindsay Gordon* (London, Samuel Mullen; Melbourne, Australia, A. H. Massina, n.d. [1900]), 91–92.

53. Ibid.

54. Winston S. Churchill, *My Early Life: A Roving Commission* (London: Thornton Butterworth, 1930), 205–6.

55. Ibid., 208.

56. Ibid., 210.

57. Winston S. Churchill, "Anglo-American Unity: A Speech on Receiving an Honorary Degree at Harvard University September 6, 1943," in *Onwards to Victory: War Speeches by the Right Hon. Winston S. Churchill, 1943*, comp. Charles Eade, 2nd ed. (London: Cassell, 1945), 182, 185.

58. Gordon, *Poems*, 125.

59. Ibid., 128.

60. Ibid., 92.

61. Adam Lindsay Gordon, *Selected Poems, with Brief Biographical Notes*, comp. Eustace A. Stedman (Tisbury: privately printed, 1933); Edith M. Humphris, *The Life of Adam Lindsay Gordon* (London: Eric Partridge, 1933); Douglas Sladen, *Adam Lindsay Gordon: the Life and Best Poems of the Poet of Australia, the Westminster Abbey Memorial Volume* (London: Hutchinson, n.d. [1934]).

62. Geoffrey Hutton, *Adam Lindsay Gordon: The Man and the Myth* (1978; repr., Melbourne: Melbourne University Press, 1996), 202.

63. [Cosmo Gordon Lang], *His Grace the Archbishop of Canterbury on Adam Lindsay Gordon: Delivered on the occasion of the Unveiling of The Adam Lindsay Gordon Memorial in Westminster Abbey on 11th May, 1934.* Reprinted by permission from Douglas Sladen's Westminster Abbey Memorial Volume (n.d. [1934]), n.p. [3].

64. Winston S. Churchill, *Thoughts and Adventures* (London: Thornton Butterworth, 1932), 34.

65. Ibid., 34–35.

66. Mary Soames, *Clementine Churchill: The Biography of a Marriage* (Boston: Houghton Mifflin, 1979), 299.

67. Oliver Garnett, *Chartwell, Kent* (1992; repr., London: National Trust, 1995), 58–59.

68. Mary Soames, ed., *Speaking for Themselves: The Personal Letters of Winston and Clementine Churchill* (London: Doubleday, 1998), 129.

69. Ibid., 132.

70. John Ramsden, *Man of the Century: Winston Churchill and His Legend Since 1945* (London: HarperCollins, 2002), 372.

71. Wilson, *Lawrence of Arabia*, 963.

72. Ibid.

73. Churchill, *Great Contemporaries*, 155.

74. Ibid., 157.

75. Ibid.

76. Charles Grosvenor, *An Iconography: The Portraits of T. E. Lawrence* (Pasadena, CA: Otterden Press, 1988), 22. Grosvenor discusses and includes reproductions of all the major portraits (excluding photographs) of Lawrence taken from life.

77. Churchill, *Thoughts and Adventures*, 318.

78. Ibid., 309–10.

79. Ibid., 310.

80. Lawrence [no specified recipient], London, February 15, 1922, in *Home Letters*, 355.

81. Lawrence, *Seven Pillars*, 385.

82. Mary Soames, *Winston Churchill: His Life as a Painter* (London: Collins, 1990), 64–65; David Coombs, *Churchill: His Paintings* (London: Hamish Hamilton, 1967), 11.

83. Churchill, *Thoughts and Adventures*, 317.

84. Ibid., 309–12. For Churchill's knowledge of cryptography and other aspects of intelligence see David Stafford, *Churchill and Secret Service* (Toronto: Stoddart, 1997; London, John Murray, 1997).

85. Churchill, *Thoughts and Adventures*, 317.

86. Ibid., 309, 314.

87. Ibid., 315.

88. Lawrence to D. G. Hogarth, October 29, 1922, in *Letters*, 373.

89. Churchill, *Great Contemporaries*, 157, 166.

90. Winston S. Churchill, "Lawrence's Great Book," in *The Collected Essays of Sir Winston Churchill*, Centenary Edition, vol. 3, *Churchill and People*, ed. Michael Wolff (London: Library of Imperial History, n.d. [1975]), 242.

91. Ibid.

92. C. S. Lewis, "On Stories," in *Of Other Worlds: Essays and Stories by C. S. Lewis*, ed. Walter Hooper (London: Geoffrey Bles, 1966), 17.

93. Winston S. Churchill to T. E. Lawrence, May 16, 1927, in *Letters to T. E. Lawrence*, ed. A. W. Lawrence (London: Jonathan Cape, 1962), 24.

94. Charles Grosvenor, "The Subscribers' *Seven Pillars of Wisdom*: The Visual Aspect," in *The T. E. Lawrence Puzzle*, ed. Stephen E. Tabachnick (Athens: University of Georgia Press, 1984), 177.

95. Churchill, *Great Contemporaries*, 162–64.

96. Churchill, *Collected Essays*, 3:242.

97. E. M. Forster to T. E. Lawrence, mid-February 1924, in *Letters to T. E. Lawrence*, 58, 61.

98. Lawrence, *Seven Pillars*, 622.

99. Churchill, *Collected Essays*, 3:241–42.

100. Ibid., 242.

101. Churchill, *Great Contemporaries*, 162.

102. Lawrence, *Seven Pillars*, 23.

103. Ibid., 568.

104. Churchill, *My Early Life*, 127.

CHAPTER TWO. IMAGINING SCENARIOS

1. Norman Rose, *Churchill: An Unruly Life* (London: Simon & Schuster, 1994), 201.

2. Michael Korda, *Charmed Lives: A Family Romance* (New York: Random House, 1979), 154.

3. Karol Kulik, *Alexander Korda: The Man Who Could Work Miracles* (New Rochelle, NY: Arlington House Publishers, 1975), 251.

4. Ibid., 257.

5. Charles Drazin, *Korda: Britain's Only Movie Mogul* (London: Sidgwick & Jackson, 2002), 242.

6. Andrew Kelly, James Pepper, and Jeffrey Richards, eds., *Filming T. E. Lawrence: Korda's Lost Epics* (London: I.B. Tauris, 1997), 3.

7. Ibid., 1–21.

8. Ibid., 22.

9. Ibid., 24.

10. Winston S. Churchill, "draft press announcement" September 12, 1934, in Martin Gilbert, *Winston S. Churchill, Volume 5 Companion Part 2: Documents, The Wilderness Years 1929–1935* (London: Heinemann, 1981), 869.

11. Ibid., 876.

12. Winston Churchill to David B. Cunynghame, October 22, 1937, Churchill Archives: Char 8/557.

13. David B. Cunynghame to Winston Churchill, October 22, 1937, Churchill Archives: Char 8/557.

14. Winston Churchill to David B. Cunynghame, November 3, 1937, Churchill Archives: Char 8/557. Subsequent references to this letter will be cited in my text by the page numbers on the letter. It is printed in Martin Gilbert, *Winston S. Churchill, Volume 5 Companion Part 3: Documents, The Coming of War 1936–1939* (London: Heinemann, 1982), 823–26.

15. T. E. Lawrence, *Seven Pillars of Wisdom: A Triumph* (privately printed 1926; published 1935 by Jonathan Cape; repr., Harmondsworth, England: Penguin, 1962), 601.

16. Lord Edward Turnour Winterton to Winston Churchill, October 27, 1937, Churchill Archives: Char 8/557.

17. Kelly, Pepper, and Richards, *Filming T.E. Lawrence*, 29–129.

18. Michael Edwardes, "'Oh to meet an Army Man': Kipling and the Soldiers," in *The Age of Kipling*, ed. John Gross (New York: Simon and Schuster, 1972), 44.

19. Winston S. Churchill, *My Early Life: A Roving Commission* (London: Thornton Butterworth, 1930), 57, 125, 127.

20. *Nobel Prize Library: Albert Camus, Winston Churchill* (New York: Alexis Gregory; Del Mar, CA: CRM Publishing, n.d.), 175.

21. Churchill, *My Early Life*, 57–58.

22. Ibid., 186.

23. Winston Spencer Churchill, *The River War: An Historical Account of the Reconquest of the Soudan* 2 vols. (London: Longmans, Green, 1899), 1:3–4.

24. Ibid., 1:235.

25. Winston Churchill, untitled memo on "Air scenario" to London Film Productions, June 10, 1935, Churchill Archives: Char 8/514.

26. Ibid.

27. Ibid.

28. Winston Churchill, untitled memo on "second revised non-technical script of the Reign of King George V" to London Film Productions, January 14, 1935, Churchill Archives: Char 8/514.

29. Winston S. Churchill to Alexander Korda, September 24, 1934, in Gilbert, *Volume 5 Companion Part 2*, 877.

30. Churchill, untitled memo on "Air scenario" to London Film Productions, June 10, 1935, Churchill Archives: Char 8/514.

31. Winston Churchill, "Air Defense Research," in *Arms and the Covenant: Speeches by the Right Hon. Winston S. Churchill*, comp. by Randolph S. Churchill (London: George G. Harrap, 1938), 245.

32. Churchill, untitled memo on "Air scenario," Churchill Archives: Char 8/514.

33. Ibid.

34. Ibid.

35. Ibid.

36. Quotations in this paragraph are from Winston S. Churchill, "The Effect of Air Transport on Civilization," in *The Collected Essays of Sir Winston Churchill*, Centenary Edition, ed. Michael Wolff (London: Library of Imperial History, n.d. [1975]), vol. 4, *Churchill At Large*, 427–34. This essay was first published in *News of the World*, May 8, 1938.

37. Churchill, *Collected Essays*, 4:428.

38. Churchill, untitled memo on "Air scenario," Churchill Archives: Char 8/514.

39. *The Encyclopedia of Science Fiction*, ed. John Clute and Peter Nicholls (New York: St. Martin's Press, 1993), 220; Drazin, *Korda*, 142.

40. Winston S. Churchill, *The Second World War, Volume One: The Gathering Storm* (London: Educational Book Company, 1955), 113.

41. David C. Smith, *H. G. Wells: Desperately Mortal* (New Haven: Yale University Press, 1986), 325.

42. Churchill, untitled memo on "Air scenario," Churchill Archives: Char 8/514.

43. Winston Spencer Churchill, "Author's Preface" dated "Cavalry barracks, Bangalore, 24 May 1898," in a typescript of *Savrola*, Churchill Archives: Char 8/7.

44. Winston Churchill to "Mr. Wimperis (London Films)," December 14, 1934, Churchill Archives: Char 8/495.

45. To Winston Churchill from London Film Productions, memo titled "King George V: Meeting on January 4th, 1935," Churchill Archives: Char 8/514.

46. Winston Churchill to Alexander Korda, October 3, 1934, "General Notes on the Film," Churchill Archives: Char 8/495.

47. Noel Coward, *Cavalcade* (London: William Heinemann, 1932).

48. Jeffrey Richards, *The Age of the Dream Palace: Cinema and Society in Britain 1930–1939* (London: Routledge & Kegan Paul, 1984), 324.

49. Ibid., 269–70.

50. Ibid., 271.

51. Churchill to Korda, October 3, 1934, "General Notes on the Film," Churchill Archives: Char 8/495.

52. Ibid.

53. Ibid.

54. Winston Churchill, "Scenario of the Reign of King George V" dated "mid-January 1935" (Churchill Archives: Char 8/526) printed in Gilbert, *Volume 5 Companion Part 2*, 994, 1023–24, 1031.

55. Ibid., 990.

56. Ibid.

57. Winston Churchill, undated "Preliminary Outline of Jubilee Film, Part 2, p. 10," Churchill Archives: Char 8/525.

58. Churchill, "Scenario of the Reign of King George V," in Gilbert, *Volume 5 Companion Part 2*, 1031.

59. Churchill's attendance at Royal Tournaments was confirmed to me by Sir Martin Gilbert and Celia Sandys in conversations during the International Churchill Conference in Leesburg, Virginia, September 19–22, 2002.

60. Churchill, "Scenario of the Reign of King George V," in Gilbert, *Volume 5 Companion Part 2*, 1000; Churchill Archives: London Film Productions memo titled "King George V (Meeting at Chartwell, December 28th, 1934)," Churchill Archives: Char 8/495; London Film Studio memo titled "Summary of Characters and Episodes Decided Upon at the Conference on December 21st," Churchill Archives: Char 8/525.

61. Churchill, "Scenario of the Reign of King George V," in Gilbert, *Volume 5 Companion Part 2*, 999.

62. Churchill to Alexander Korda October 3, 1934, "General Notes on the Film," Churchill Archives: Char 8/495.

63. Ibid.

64. Ibid.

65. London Film Productions memo titled "King George V (Meeting at Chartwell, December 28th, 1934)," Churchill Archives: Char 8/495.

66. Churchill, "Scenario of the Reign of King George V," in Gilbert, *Volume 5 Companion Part 2*, 1017.

67. London Film Production memo titled "Jubilee Film Story Conference," January 15, 1935, Churchill Archives: 8/824.

68. Churchill, "George V Scenario: Drafts and Correspondence," Churchill Archives: Char 8/824.

69. Churchill, "Scenario of the Reign of King George V," in Gilbert, *Volume 5 Companion Part 2*, 1012.

70. Churchill, "George V Scenario: Drafts and Correspondence," Churchill Archives: Char 8/824.

71. See Mary Soames, *Winston Churchill: His Life as a Painter* (London: Collins, 1990), 27.

72. Winston S. Churchill, introduction to A. P. Herbert, *The Secret Battle: With an introduction by the Right Hon. Winston S. Churchill*, 3rd ed. (London: Methuen, 1928), v.

73. Winston Churchill to R. C. Sherriff, February 1, 1929, in R. C. Sherriff, *No Leading Lady: An Autobiography* (London: Victor Gollancz, 1968), 113.

74. Ibid., 114.

75. See Algis Valiunas, *Churchill's Military Histories: A Rhetorical Study* (Lanham, MD: Rowman & Littlefield, 2002).

76. Churchill, "Scenario of the Reign of King George V," in Gilbert, *Volume 5 Companion Part 2*, 1015.

77. Ibid., 994.

78. London Film Productions memo titled "King George V (Meeting at Chartwell, December 28th, 1934)," Churchill Archives: Char 8/495.

79. Churchill, "Scenario of the Reign of King George V," in Gilbert, *Volume 5 Companion Part 2*, 1023.

80. Ibid., 1023–24.

81. Winston S. Churchill to Clementine Churchill, December 15, 1915, in Mary Soames, ed., *Speaking for Themselves: The Personal Letters of Winston and Clementine Churchill* (London: Doubleday, 1998), 133.

82. Gilbert, *Volume 5 Companion Part 2*, 1020n1.

83. Churchill, "Scenario of the Reign of King George V," in Gilbert, *Volume 5 Companion Part 2*, 1017–18.

84. Churchill, *Gathering Storm*, 459.

85. Churchill, "Scenario of the Reign of King George V," in Gilbert, *Volume 5 Companion Part 2*, 1019.

86. Ibid., 1020.

87. Gilbert, *Volume 5 Companion Part 2*, 1020n1.

88. Winston S. Churchill, "Everybody's Language," in *The Collected Essays of Sir Winston Churchill*, Centenary Edition, ed. Michael Wolff (London: Library of Imperial History, n.d. [1975]), vol. 3, *Churchill and People*, 246. This essay was first published in *Collier's*, October 26, 1935 and reprinted with the title "He Has Made the Whole World Laugh" in the *Sunday Chronicle*, February 9, 1936.

89. Churchill, *Collected Essays*, 3:246–47.

90. Churchill, *My Early Life*, 362.

91. Churchill, *Collected Essays*, 3:247.

92. Ibid., 247–50.

93. Ibid., 250.

94. Ibid., 250–51.

95. Ibid., 251.

96. "Anglo-American Unity: A Speech on Receiving an Honorary Degree at Harvard University September 6, 1943," in *Onwards to Victory: War Speeches the by Right Hon. Winston S. Churchill C.H., M.P., 1943*, comp. Charles Eade (London: Cassell and Company, 1944; repr., 1945), 185.

97. Churchill, *Collected Essays*, 3:251.

98. Churchill, *Onwards to Victory*, 185.

99. Churchill, "Author's Preface," *My Early Life*, n.p.

100. Churchill, *Collected Essays*, 3:252.

101. Ibid.

CHAPTER THREE. IMAGINING SCENES

1. David Coombs with Minnie Churchill, foreword by Mary Soames, *Sir Winston Churchill's Life through His Paintings* (London: Chaucer Press, 2003), 250–56.

2. See *Sir Winston Churchill 1874–1974: An Exhibition to commemorate the Centenary of the birth of Sir Winston Churchill, KG, OM, CH, MP, 10 May–30 September 1974, Somerset House Strand London WC2, David Jones Limited (Sydney) Australia May 5–17, 1975* (Sydney, Australia: David Jones, 1975). The David Jones Art Gallery in Sydney also issued an accompanying brochure listing the twenty-seven oil paintings by Churchill selected from the Somerset House centenary exhibition for display in the Australian exhibition.

3. Mary Soames, *Winston Churchill: His Life as a Painter* (London: Collins, 1990).

4. Richard M. Langworth, *A Connoisseur's Guide to the Books of Sir Winston Churchill*, rev. ed. (London: Brassey's, 2000), 288.

5. Ibid., 287–93 and 154–63.

6. Winston S. Churchill, "Painting as a Pastime," in *Thoughts and Adventures* (London: Thornton Butterworth Limited, 1932), 313.

7. Ibid., 305.

8. Ibid., 307–8.

9. Winston Spencer Churchill, *The River War: An Historical Account of the Reconquest of the Soudan*, 2 vols. (London: Longmans, Green, 1899), 2:111–12.

10. Winston S. Churchill, *My Early Life: A Roving Commission* (London: Thornton Butterworth, 1930), 199–200.

11. Ibid., 201.

12. Ibid., 186.

13. Celia Sandys, *From Winston With Love and Kisses: The Young Churchill* (London: Sinclair-Stevenson, 1994), 71.

14. Winston Churchill to Lady Randolph Churchill, January 1890, in Randolph S. Churchill, *Winston S. Churchill, Volume 1 Companion Part 1: 1874–1896* (London: Heinemann, 1967), 197.

15. Churchill, *My Early Life*, 55.

16. Winston Churchill to Lady Randolph Churchill, March 12, 1890, in Randolph S. Churchill, *Volume 1 Companion Part 1*, 201.

17. Winston Churchill to Lady Randolph Churchill, February 2, 1898, in Randolph S. Churchill, *Winston S. Churchill, Volume 1 Companion Part 2: 1896–1900* (London: Heinemann, 1967), 874.

18. Winston Churchill to Lord Randolph Churchill, [June 8, 1890] in Randolph S. Churchill, *Volume 1 Companion Part 1*, 203.

19. Winston Churchill to Lady Randolph Churchill, [November 1890], in Randolph S. Churchill, *Winston Churchill, Volume 1: Youth 1874–1900* (London: Heinemann, 1966), 134.

20. Winston Churchill to Lady Randolph Churchill, [postmark December 10, 1890], ibid., 135.

21. Winston S. Churchill, "Cartoons and Cartoonists," in *Thoughts and Adventures* (London: Thornton Butterworth, 1932), 23.

22. Ibid., 25–26.

23. Ibid., 35.

24. Lewis Carroll, *Alice's Adventures in Wonderland and Through the Looking-Glass* (New York: J. J. Little & Ives, n.d.), 11.

25. Winston Churchill to Lady Randolph Churchill, November 17, 1897, Randolph S. Churchill, *Volume 1 Companion Part 2*, 827.

26. Winston Churchill to Lady Randolph Churchill, November 24, 1897, ibid., 829.

27. Winston Churchill to Lady Randolph Churchill, January 1, 1897, ibid., 719–20.

28. Winston Churchill to Lady Randolph Churchill, January 5, 1898, ibid., 853. See also 812.

29. Winston Churchill to Lady Randolph Churchill, November 24, 1897, ibid., 829.

30. Winston Churchill to Lady Randolph Churchill, December 2, 1897, ibid., 834.

31. Randolph S. Churchill, *Winston S. Churchill, Volume 1: Youth*, 362.

32. Lady Randolph Churchill to Winston Churchill, December 16, 1897, in Randolph S. Churchill, *Volume 1 Companion Part 2*, 851.

33. Winston Churchill to Lady Randolph Churchill, January 5, 1898, ibid., 852.

34. Winston Churchill to Lady Randolph Churchill, January 19, 1898, ibid., 862.

35. Churchill, *River War*, 1:ix.

36. Winston Churchill to Lady Randolph Churchill, Savoy Hotel, Cairo, April 3, 1899, in Randolph S. Churchill, *Volume 1 Companion Part 2*, 1020.

37. Churchill, *River War*, 1:x.

38. Winston Spencer Churchill, "'Man Overboard!' An Episode of the Red Sea," *Harmsworth Monthly Pictorial Magazine* 1 (1898–99): 662–64.

39. Winston Churchill, "Fifty Years Hence," *Strand Magazine* 82 (July to December 1931): 549–58.

40. Winston Spencer Churchill, "My African Journey," *Strand Magazine* 35 (January to June 1908): 299–306, 385–94, 490–96, 680–88; *Strand Magazine* 36 (July to December 1908): 50–56, 137–45, 251–58, 374–81, 491–98.

41. Winston Spencer Churchill, *My African Journey* (London: Hodder and Stoughton, 1908), title page.

42. See, for example, the six illustrations in Winston Churchill, "Alphonso the Unlucky," *Strand Magazine* 82 (July to December 1931): 15–23, and the single illustration of "Alfonso XIII," a slightly expanded version of the essay, commenting also on the Spanish civil war, in Churchill's *Great Contemporaries* (London: Thorton Butterworth, 1937), 209–20.

43. Winston S. Churchill, *The Second World War Volume One: The Gathering Storm* (London: Educational Book Company, n.d. [1955]), xi.

44. Winston Churchill to Lady Randolph Churchill, January 19, 1898, in Randolph S. Churchill, *Volume 1 Companion Part 2*, 862.

45. Viscount [Alexander Edward] Fincastle and P. C. Eliott-Lockhart, *A Frontier Campaign: A Narrative of the Operations of the Malakand and Buner Field Forces, 1897–1898*, 2nd ed. (London: Methuen, 1898).

46. Winston Churchill to Lady Randolph Churchill, February 25, 1898, in Randolph S. Churchill, *Volume 1 Companion Part 2*, 883.

47. Fincastle and Eliott-Lockhart, *Frontier Campaign*, opposite 55.

48. E[dmund] A[rthur] P[onsonby] Hobday, *Sketches on Service during the Indian Frontier Campaigns of 1897* (London: James Bowden, 1898).

49. Fincastle and Eliott-Lockhart, *Frontier Campaign*, preface, n.p. [5].

50. Ibid., 11.

51. Winston Spencer Churchill, *The Story of the Malakand Field Force: An Episode of Frontier War*, 2nd ed. (London: Longmans, Green, 1899), 41.

52. Fincastle and Eliott-Lockhart, *Frontier Campaign*, 102.

53. Winston Churchill to Lady Randolph Churchill, January 26, 1898, in Randolph S. Churchill, *Volume 1 Companion Part 2*, 863.

54. Winston Churchill to Lady Randolph Churchill, June 1, 1898, ibid., 942.

55. Winston Churchill to Lady Randolph Churchill, June 2, 1898, ibid., 943.

56. Winston Churchill to Lady Randolph Churchill, February 23, 1899, ibid., 1010–11.

57. Robert Jay, "Alphonse de Neuville's *The Spy* and the Legacy of the Franco-Prussian War," *Metropolitan Museum Journal*, 19/20 (1984–85): 151–62, 153, 159. See also Christopher Forbes and Margaret Kelly, *War A La Mode: Military Pictures by Meissonier, Detaille, de Neuville and Berne-Bellecour from the FORBES Magazine Collection* (Exhibition Catalogue, Amherst College, Mead Art Museum, c. 1975).

58. Jay, "Legacy," 154.

59. Ibid., 152–53. The village name is wrongly given as Balan in Forbes and Kelly, *War A La Mode*, 21.

60. Jay, "Legacy," 153.

61. Philippe Chabert, *Alphonse de Neuville: l'épopée de la défaite* (Paris: Editions Copernic, 1979). See also François Robichon, *L'armée française vue par les peintres 1870–1914* (Paris: Hersher/Ministère de la Défense, 2000), 24–25.

62. Churchill, *Malakand Field Force*, 205.

63. Ibid., 201.

64. Ibid., 205.

65. Ibid., 200–201.

66. Ibid., 206.

67. William Shakespeare, *The Tempest*, ed. Anne Righter (Anne Barton) (London: Penguin Books, 1968), 120 (act 4, scene 1).

68. Churchill, *Malakand Field Force*, 223.

69. Ibid., 141.

70. Ibid.

71. William Shakespeare, *As You Like It*, act 2, scene 7.

72. Churchill, *Malakand Field Force*, 300.

73. Ibid., 301.

74. Ibid., 127–28.

75. Ibid.

76. Ibid., 128.

77. Ibid., 217.

78. Ibid., 127n1.

79. Ibid., vii.

80. Ibid., 268.

81. Ibid., 142.

82. Ibid., 136.

83. Ibid., 138.

84. Ibid., 139.

85. Thomas Babington Macaulay, "Von Ranke," in *Critical and Historical Essays Contributed to the Edinburgh Review*, 3 vols. (London: Longman, Brown, Green, & Longmans, 1843), 2:208–9.

86. Churchill, *Malakand Field Force*, 139.

87. Rudyard Kipling, "Recessional," in *The Book of Living Verse*, ed. Louis Untermeyer (New York: Harcourt, Brace, 1945), 492

88. Churchill, *Malakand Field Force*, 139.

89. Winston S. Churchill, "Their Finest Hour," in *Blood, Sweat, and Tears* (New York: G. P. Putnam's Sons, 1941), 314.

90. Paula Rea Radisich, *Hubert Robert: Painted Spaces of the Enlightenment* (Cambridge: Cambridge University Press, 1998), 129–33.

91. I. F. Clarke, introduction to Jean-Baptiste François Xavier Cousin de Grainville, *The Last Man*, trans. I. F. and M. Clarke, with an intr. and Critical Material by I. F. Clarke (Middletown, CT: Wesleyan University Press, 2002), xxviii.

92. For reproductions of the pictures by Gandy, Doré, and Saunier, see Clarke, introduction, xxviii, xxxvii, and facing preface, n.p.

93. Churchill, *Malakand Field Force*, 157–58.

94. Ibid., 161.

95. Ibid., 162.

96. Ibid., 11.

97. Ibid., 17.

98. Ibid.

99. Ibid., 159.

100. Ibid., 11–12.

101. Ibid., 286.

102. Ibid., 198.

103. Ibid., 154–56.

104. Ibid., 174.

105. Ibid., 154.

106. E. H. Gombrich, *Art and Illusion: A Study in the Psychology of Pictorial Representation*, 2nd ed. (Princeton, NJ: Princeton University Press, 1961), 38–39.

107. Churchill, *Malakand Field Force*, 304.

108. Ibid.

109. Ibid., 128.

110. Winston S. Churchill, *Marlborough: His Life and Times*, 2 vols. (London: George G. Harrap, 1947), 1:749.

111. Winston S. Churchill, *The World Crisis 1911–1918: Abridged and Revised with additional chapter on the Battle of the Marne* (London: Thornton Butterworth, 1931), 168, 176.

112. Ibid., *World Crisis*, 180, 178.

113. Churchill, *River War*, 1:364.

114. Ibid., 2:142–43.

115. Churchill, *My Early Life*, 204.

116. Ibid., 205.

117. Winston Spencer Churchill, *Savrola: A Tale of the Revolution in Laurania* (November 1899; repr., New York: Longmans, Green, January 1900), 277–78.

118. Ibid., 25.

119. Coombs, Catalogue numbers C 199 and C 279 (illustrated in figures 269 and 190).

120. See Coombs, Catalogue numbers C 280 and C 281 (illustrated in figures 188 and 191).

121. See Coombs, Catalogue numbers C 298, C 299, C 300, C 301, C 307, C 309, C 417 (illustrated in figures 278, 277, 301, 279, 327, 58, 451).

122. Churchill, *Savrola*, 1.

123. Ibid., 2.

124. Ibid., 289.

125. Ibid., 25.

126. Ibid., 18–19.

127. Ibid., 185–86.

128. Ibid., 185.

129. Coombs, Catalogue numbers C 189, C 10, C 22, C 157 (illustrated in figures 52, 139, 140, 100).

130. Churchill, *Savrola*, 39.

131. Ibid., 39–40.

132. Ibid., 45.

133. Ibid., 40.

134. Ibid., 41.

135. Ibid.

136. Winston Churchill to Lady Randolph Churchill, February 25, 1898, in Randolph S. Churchill, *Volume 1 Companion Part 2*, 884.

137. Churchill, *Savrola*, 45.

138. Ibid., 45–46.

139. Ibid., 47.

140. Ibid., 46.

141. Winston Churchill to Mrs. John Leslie, May 3, 1898, in Randolph S. Churchill, *Volume 1 Companion Part 2*, 925.

142. Churchill, *Savrola*, 117–19.

143. Winston Churchill to Lady Randolph Churchill, August 24, 1897, in Randolph S. Churchill, *Volume 1 Companion Part 2*, 779.

144. Winston Churchill to Mrs. John Leslie, May 3, 1898, ibid., 924.

145. Churchill, *Savrola*, 39, 3.

146. Ibid., 344.

147. Ibid., 344–45.

148. Ibid., 343.

149. Soames, figures 3 & 4; Coombs, Catalogue numbers C 1, C 2, C 3, C 4 (illustrated in figures 7, 6, 8, 5).

150. Churchill, *Savrola*, 77.

151. Ibid., 72.

152. Ibid., 70–71.

CHAPTER FOUR. IMAGINING SCIENCE

1. Winston S. Churchill, *The World Crisis 1911–1914* (New York: Charles Scribner's Sons, 1924), 125–48.

2. Winston S. Churchill, *The Second World War*, "Chartwell" Edition, Volume Two: *Their Finest Hour* (London: Educational Book Company, n.d. [1955]), 292–304.

3. See R. F. Harrod, *The Prof: A Personal Memoir of Lord Cherwell* (London: MacMillan, 1959); Frederick, second Earl of Birkenhead, *The Professor and the Prime Minister: The Official Life of Professor F. A. Lindemann, Viscount Cherwell* (Boston: Houghton Mifflin, 1962); Thomas Wilson, *Churchill and the Prof* (London: Cassell, 1995); Adrian Fort, *Prof: the Life of Frederick Lindemann* (London: Jonathan Cape, 2003). On Churchill's speech at Churchill College see Martin Gilbert, *Winston S. Churchill: Vol. 8 'Never Despair' 1945–1965* (Boston: Houghton Mifflin, 1988), 1302–3. For the text of that speech, see Winston S. Churchill, *The Unwritten Alliance: Speeches 1953 to 1959*, ed. Randolph S. Churchill (London: Cassell, 1961), 328–30.

4. Winston S. Churchill, *My Early Life: A Roving Commission* (London: Thornton Butterworth, 1930), 57.

5. Winston S. Churchill, "Their Finest Hour: A Speech delivered first to the House of Commons and then broadcast, June 18, 1940," in *Blood, Sweat, and Tears* (New York: G. P. Putnam's Sons, 1941), 314.

6. Winston S. Churchill, *Shall We Commit Suicide?* (1924; repr., International

Churchill Societies, 1994), 3. The 1924 Eilert Printing Company pamphlet, of which the 1994 International Churchill Societies edition is a photographic facsimile, dropped the word "All" from the title, which in other printings of the entire essay during Churchill's lifetime appears as "Shall We All Commit Suicide?". He evidently preferred the slightly longer and much more arresting title.

7. Ibid.

8. Ibid., 4.

9. Winston S. Churchill, *The World Crisis 1916–1918*, 2 vols. (New York: Charles Scribner's Sons, 1927), 2:193–217.

10. Churchill, *Shall We Commit Suicide?*, 8–9.

11. Ibid., 11.

12. Winston S. Churchill, "If Lee Had Not Won the Battle of Gettysburg," *Scribner's* 88 (December 1930): 587–97. Reprinted in *If It Had Happened Otherwise: Lapses into Imaginary History*, ed. J. C. Squire (London: Longmans, Green, 1931), 173–96; and in *If, or History Rewritten*, ed. J. C. Squire (New York: Viking Press, 1931), 259–87.

13. See Paul Alkon, "Alternate History and Postmodern Temporality," in *Time, Literature and the Arts: Essays in Honor of Samuel L. Macey*, ed. Thomas R. Cleary, English Literary Studies Monograph Series, no. 61 (Victoria, B.C.: University of Victoria, 1994), 65–85. See also Barton C. Hacker and Gordon B. Chamberlain, "Pasts That Might Have Been, II: A Revised Bibliography of Alternative History," in *Alternative Histories: Eleven Stories of the World as It Might Have Been*, ed. Charles G. Waugh and Martin H. Greenberg (New York: Garland, 1986), 301–63.

14. See I. S. Bloch, *The Future of War in Its Technical Economic and Political Relations*, trans. R. C. Long (Boston: Ginn, 1899).Churchill perhaps incorrectly recalled the date of this English translation of Jan Bloch's six-volume work of the same name, or of the 1902 reprint of Long's translation.

15. Churchill, *Blood, Sweat, and Tears*, 314.

16. Winston S. Churchill, *The World Crisis—1918–1928: The Aftermath* (New York: Charles Scribner's Sons, 1929), 221–22. Hereafter cited as *Aftermath*.

17. Ibid., 390, 466. In a private communication to me, Edward L. Saslow implies that Churchill's phrasemaking may owe more to his struggles with Latin than he is usually given credit for. Commenting on Churchill's choice of *The Hinge of Fate* as a title for volume 4 of *The Second World War*, Saslow writes: "'The Hinge of Fate' has the force of 'pivot' of fate, as the Roman door hinge was a pole and socket arrangement. The figurative use of 'cardo' (hinge) as 'that on which matters depend' dates only from the Augustan period. The specific place in Vergil from which I think Churchill took his title is *Aeneid*, l. 672, which has hinge of events ('rerum,' which is a word of wide application)."

18. Churchill, *World Crisis 1916–1918*, 2:217.

19. Churchill, *Aftermath*, 7.

20. Ibid., 11–12.

21. Ibid., 12.

22. Winston S. Churchill, "Dunkirk: A Speech in the House of Commons, June 4, 1940," in *Blood, Sweat, and Tears*, 293.

23. James W. Muller, "'A Kind of Dignity and Even Nobility': Winston Churchill's *Thoughts and Adventures*," *Political Science Reviewer*, 16 (Fall 1986): 297.

24. Winston S. Churchill, *Thoughts and Adventures* (London: Thornton Butterworth, 1932), 270.

25. Ibid., 273.

26. For the backgrounds of future history as a form of imaginative literature, see Paul K. Alkon, *Origins of Futuristic Fiction* (Athens: University of Georgia Press, 1987).

27. Churchill, *Thoughts and Adventures*, 276.

28. Ibid., 277.

29. Ibid., 280.

30. Ibid., 274.

31. Fort, *Prof*, 308–10.

32. Warren F. Kimball, *Forged in War: Roosevelt, Churchill, and the Second World War* (New York: William Morrow, 1997), 220–21; David Reynolds, *In Command of History: Churchill Fighting and Writing the Second World War* (London: Allen Lane, 2004), 399–401.

33. Winston S. Churchill, "Defense: A Speech to the House of Commons 1 March 1955," in *The Unwritten Alliance: Speeches 1953 to 1959*, ed. Randolph S. Churchill (London: Cassell, 1961), 226.

34. Ibid., 230.

35. Ibid., 234.

36. Ibid., 229.

37. Winston S. Churchill, "The Hydrogen Bomb: A Speech to the House of Commons 5 April 1954," in *The Unwritten Alliance*, 130.

38. Churchill, *Thoughts and Adventures*, 279.

39. Ibid.

40. On Churchill's efforts to avert or end wars, see James W. Muller, ed., *Churchill as Peacemaker* (Cambridge: Woodrow Wilson Center Press and Cambridge University Press, 1997).

41. Churchill, *Thoughts and Adventures*, 278.

42. Winston S. Churchill, *Savrola: A Tale of the Revolution in Laurania* (November 1899; repr., New York: Longmans, Green, January 1900), 46–47.

43. For an excellent survey of relationships between Wells and Churchill that does not, however, dwell on the Wellsian affinities in Churchill's own writing, see Manfred Weidhorn, *A Harmony of Interests: Explorations in the Mind of Sir Winston Churchill* (Rutherford, NJ: Fairleigh Dickinson University Press, 1992), 25–30, 40–44. I am indebted to this map of the bumpy road along which Wells and Churchill traveled together.

44. David C. Smith, *H. G. Wells: Desperately Mortal* (New Haven, CT: Yale University Press, 1986), 398.

45. Randolph S. Churchill, *Winston S. Churchill: Volume 2, Young Statesman 1901–1914* (London: Heinemann, 1967), 255.

46. H. G. Wells, *Experiment in Autobiography: Discoveries and Conclusions of a Very Ordinary Brain (Since 1866)*, (New York: Macmillan, 1934), 583–84.

47. Winston S. Churchill, *The World Crisis, 1915* (New York: Charles Scribner's Sons, 1923), 69–70.

48. Smith, *H. G. Wells*, 280, 565n23.

49. H. G. Wells, *Star Begotten: A Biological Fantasia* (London: Chatto & Windus, 1937), dedication page (unnumbered).

50. Smith, *H. G. Wells*, 328, 580n.30.

51. Michael Foot, *H. G.: The History of Mr Wells* (1995; repr., London: Black Swan, 1996), 275.

52. Smith, *H. G. Wells*, 272.

53. Winston S. Churchill, "H. G. Wells," in *The Collected Essays of Sir Winston Churchill*, Centenary Edition, ed. Michael Wolff (London: Library of Imperial History, n.d. [1975]), vol. 3, *Churchill and People*, 51. This essay was first published in the *Sunday Pictorial*, August 23, 1931.

54. H. G. Wells, *Men Like Gods: A Novel* (New York: Macmillan, 1923), 245.

55. Ibid., 21.

56. Ibid., 21–22.

57. Ibid., 100.

58. Ibid., 173.

59. Ibid., 219–20.

60. Ibid., 229.

61. Ibid., 125.

62. Smith, *H. G. Wells*, 284.

63. H. G. Wells, *Meanwhile (The Picture of a Lady)* (New York: George H. Doran, 1927), 199–200.

64. Ibid., 202–3.

65. George Orwell, "Wells, Hitler and the World State," in *Dickens, Dali and Others* (1946; repr., San Diego: Harcourt Brace, Jovanovich, 1973), 123.

66. Churchill, *Blood, Sweat, and Tears*, 314.

67. Orwell, *Dickens, Dali and Others*, 123.

68. Churchill, *Collected Essays*, 3:52–53.

69. Lord Moran [Charles Wilson], *Churchill: Taken from the Diaries of Lord Moran* (Boston: Houghton Mifflin, 1956), 352.

70. Churchill, *Collected Essays*, 3:53.

CHAPTER FIVE. TIME AND IMAGINATION

1. Isaiah Berlin, *Mr Churchill in 1940* (London: John Murray, n.d. [1949]), 12.

2. "Their Finest Hour: A Speech delivered first to the House of Commons and then Broadcast, June 18, 1940," in Winston S. Churchill, *Blood, Sweat, and Tears* (New York: G. P. Putnam's Sons, 1941), 314.

3. For one of the most influential attacks on counterfactual history, see David Hackett Fischer, *Historian's Fallacies: Toward a Logic of Historical Thought* (New York: Harper & Row, 1970), 15–21. Counterfactuals are also referred to, especially by literary critics, as "alternate history" or "alternative history." See my chapter 4, note 13. For a survey of the controversy, a defense of counterfactuals as a method of serious historical enquiry, and a collection of essays using the method of counterfactuals, see Niall Ferguson, ed., *Virtual History: Alternatives and Counterfactuals* (London: Picador, 1997). See also the article "Alternate History" in Samuel L. Macey, ed., *Encyclopedia of Time* (New York: Garland, 1994).

4. Hugh Trevor-Roper, "History and Imagination," in *History and Imagination: Essays in Honor of H. R. Trevor-Roper*, ed. Hugh Lloyd-Jones, Valerie Pearl, and Blair Worden (New York: Holmes & Meier, 1982), 356, 364.

5. Winston S. Churchill, "A Second Choice," in *Thoughts and Adventures* (London: Thornton Butterwoth, 1932), 11, 14.

6. Winston S. Churchill, *The Second World War*, "Chartwell" Edition, 6 vols. (London: Educational Book Company, n.d. [1955]), vol. 1, *The Gathering Storm*, 14.

7. Churchill, *The Second World War*, vol. 2, *Their Finest Hour*, 170–72.

8. Winston S. Churchill, "If Lee Had Not Won the Battle of Gettysburg," *Scribner's Magazine* 88 (December 1930): 587–97; reprinted in *If, or History Rewritten*, ed. J. C. Squire (New York: Viking Press, 1931), 259–87.

9. Winston S. Churchill, *Marlborough: His Life and Times*, 2 vols. (London: George G. Harrap, 1947), 1:16.

10. Ibid.

11. For the text of *The Battle of Dorking* along with related tales, see I. F. Clarke, ed., *The Tale of the Next Great War, 1871–1914: Fictions of Future Warfare and of Battles Still-to-come* (Syracuse, NY: Syracuse University Press, 1995). For a history of the genre, see I. F. Clarke, *Voices Prophesying War: Future Wars 1763–3749*, 2nd ed. (Oxford: Oxford University Press, 1992).

12. For the text of "The Time-Table of a Nightmare" see Randolph S. Churchill, *Winston S. Churchill, Vol. 2: Young Statesman 1901–1914* (London: Heinemann, 1967), 613–25.

13. Winston S. Churchill, *The World Crisis 1911–1914* (1923; repr., Norwalk, CT: Easton Press, 1991), 153–54.

14. Churchill, *Marlborough*, 1:285–86.

15. Churchill, for example, refers to the death of Charles II of Spain as "one of the great turning-points in the history of France" (*Marlborough*, 1:457). For other uses of "turning-point," see Winston S. Churchill, *The World Crisis: The Aftermath 1918–1928* (New York: Charles Scribner's Sons, 1929), 390, 466. Volume IV of Churchill's *The Second World War* is titled *The Hinge of Fate*. See also my chapter 4, note 17.

16. J. R. Jones, *Marlborough* (Cambridge: Cambridge University Press, 1993), 4.

17. Manfred Weidhorn, *Sword and Pen: A Survey of the Writings of Sir Winston Churchill* (Albuquerque: University of New Mexico Press, 1974), 128.

18. Churchill, *Marlborough*, 1:105.

19. Ibid., 1:331.

20. Ibid., 1:400–401.

21. Ibid., 1:333.

22. Ibid., 1:978–79.

23. Ibid., 2:401.

24. Ibid.

25. Ibid., 2:550–51.

26. Ibid., 2:1040.

27. Ibid., 1:19.

28. Robert Eden, "Churchill's *Marlborough*: An Introduction to his Collaboration with Roosevelt," paper presented at the Churchill Centre's Third Winston Churchill Symposium, Blenheim Palace, May 15–16, 1998.

29. Churchill, *Marlborough*, 1:16.

30. Victor Feske, *From Belloc to Churchill: Private Scholars, Public Culture, and the Crisis of British Liberalism, 1900–1939* (Chapel Hill: University of North Carolina Press, 1996), 226.

31. Feske's chapter "Winston Churchill: The Last Public Historian" (*From Belloc to*

Churchill, 186–227) is an excellent account of Churchill's political impact as Whig historian. For an argument from a professional historian's viewpoint that Whig history, especially in *Marlborough*, interferes with accuracy, see J. H. Plumb, "The Historian" in A. J. P. Taylor, Robert Rhodes James, J. H. Plumb, Basil Liddell Hart, and Anthony Storr, eds., *Churchill Revised: A Critical Assessment* (New York: Dial Press, 1969), 133–69. This essay is reprinted with additional comments in J. H. Plumb, *The Making of an Historian: The Collected Essays of J. H. Plumb* (Athens: University of Georgia Press, 1988), 225–52. For his summing up of Churchill's cultural and especially political value as an historian, espousal of Whig history and all, see J. H. Plumb, "The Dominion of History," in *Winston Churchill: Resolution, Defiance, Magnanimity, Good Will*, ed. R. Crosby Kemper III (Columbia: University of Missouri Press, 1996), 63–78.

32. Churchill, *Marlborough*, 2:22.

33. Ibid., 1:427–28.

34. For the classic definition and condemnation of Whig history, see Herbert Butterfield, *The Whig Interpretation of History* (London: G. Bell, 1931).

35. Churchill, *Marlbrough*, 1:40.

36. Ibid., 1:41.

37. Ibid., 1:823.

38. Ibid., 1:42.

39. Ibid., 1:428–29.

40. Ibid., 1:556.

41. Ibid.

42. Ibid., 1:18.

43. Ibid.

44. Ibid., 1:296.

45. Ibid., 1:297.

46. Ibid., 1:19.

47. Ibid.

48. Ibid.

49. Ibid., 1:487.

50. Ibid., 1:488.

51. Ibid.

52. Samuel Richardson, *Clarissa. Or, the History of a Young Lady: Comprehending the most Important Concerns of Private Life*, 8 vols., 3rd ed. (London: S. Richardson, 1751), 1:viii.

53. Churchill, *Marlborough*, 1:79.

54. Ibid., 1:434.

55. Ibid., 1:77.

56. James Boswell, *Life of Johnson*, ed. R. W. Chapman, new edition corrected by J. D. Fleeman (London: Oxford University Press, 1970), 21.

57. Ibid., 22.

58. Churchill, *Marlborough*, 2:20.

59. Ibid., 2:22.

60. Ibid., 2:492.

61. Ibid., 1:83, 489.

62. Ibid., 1:516.

63. Ibid., 1:358–61.

64. Ibid., 1:116–17.

65. Ibid., 1:372.

66. Ibid., 1:214.

67. Ibid., 1:112.

68. Ibid., 2:22.

69. Ibid., 1:568.

70. Ibid., 1:489.

71. Ibid., 2:1036.

CHAPTER SIX. ENVOI

1. Winston S. Churchill, *The Second World War,* "*Chartwell*" *Edition,* 6 vols., (London: Educational Book Company, n.d. [1955]), vol. 1, *The Gathering Storm,* 522–23.

2. Ibid., 325.

3. Ibid., 199.

4. Lord Moran [Charles Wilson], *Churchill: Taken from the Diaries of Lord Moran* (Boston: Houghton Mifflin, 1956), 653.

5. Ibid., 395, 420, 429, 496, 501, 723.

6. Churchill, *The Second World War,* vol. 3, *The Grand Alliance,* 484.

7. Churchill, *The Gathering Storm,* 199.

8. Winston S. Churchill, *The World Crisis—1918–1928: The Aftermath* (New York: Charles Scribner's Sons, 1929), 7–12.

9. Randolph Churchill, "How He Came to Write It," *Sunday Telegraph,* January 30, 1966, 4.

10. Winston Churchill, "The Dream," *Sunday Telegraph,* January 30, 1966, 4–5; repr. in Martin Gilbert, *Winston S. Churchill, Volume 8: Never Despair, 1945–1965* (Boston: Houghton Mifflin, 1988), 364–72, 365 quoted. My citations to "The Dream" are to its pagination in Gilbert's volume. "The Dream" is also in Winston S. Churchill, *The Collected Essays of Sir Winston Churchill,* Centenary Edition, ed. Michael Wolff (London: Library of Imperial History, n.d. [1975]), vol. 4, *Churchill at Large,* 504–11. Limited single-volume editions of "The Dream" were published by the International Churchill Societies in 1987 and (with introduction by Richard M. Langworth and illustration by Sal Asaro) in 1994. In 2005 Levenger Press published a handsome edition with a new introduction by Richard M. Langworth.

11. Churchill, "The Dream," 365.

12. Ibid., 371.

13. Ibid., 365.

14. Ibid., 368–69.

15. Winston S. Churchill, "Their Finest Hour: A Speech delivered first to the House of Commons and then broadcast, June 18, 1940," in *Blood, Sweat, and Tears* (New York: G. P. Putnam's Sons, 1941), 314.

16. Winston S. Churchill, "H. G. Wells," in *Collected Essays,* vol. 3, *Churchill and People,* 53.

17. Moran, 352.

18. H. G. Wells, *The Time Machine: An Invention,* ed. Nicholas Ruddick (Peterborough, Ontario, Canada: Broadview Press, 2001), 90, 101.

19. Churchill, "The Dream," 368.
20. Ibid., 366–68.
21. Ibid., 372.
22. Ibid.
23. Ibid., 370.
24. Ibid., 365.
25. Ibid., 369.
26. Ibid., 370.
27. Ibid.
28. Ibid.
29. Ibid., 371.
30. Ibid., 372.

Works Cited
PRIMARY SOURCES: WORKS BY WINSTON SPENCER CHURCHILL

Citations in my notes to CHAR with various reference numbers refer to documents, often untitled, in the Churchill Archives at Churchill College, Cambridge University. I cite the following published works by Churchill, and list them here alphabetically for ease of reference. For their order of first publication, see my Chronology, pp. xxi–xxiii above.

"Alphonso the Unlucky." *Strand Magazine* 82 (July to December 1931): 15–23.

Arms and the Covenant: Speeches by the Right Hon. Winston S. Churchill. Compiled by Randolph S. Churchill. London: George G. Harrap, 1938.

Blood, Sweat, and Tears. New York: G. P. Putnam's Sons, 1941.

The Collected Essays of Sir Winston Churchill. Centenary Edition. 4 vols. Edited by Michael Wolff. London: Library of Imperial History, n.d. [1975].

"The Dream." *Sunday Telegraph*, January 30, 1966, 4. Reprinted in Martin Gilbert, *Winston S. Churchill, Volume 8: Never Despair, 1945–1965*, 364–72. Boston: Houghton Mifflin, 1988.

"Fifty Years Hence." *Strand Magazine* 82 (July to December 1931): 549–58.

Great Contemporaries. London: Thornton Butterworth, 1937.

"If Lee Had Not Won the Battle of Gettysburg." *Scribner's* 88 (December 1930): 587–97. Reprinted in *If It Had Happened Otherwise: Lapses into Imaginary History*, edited by J. C. Squire, 173–96. London: Longmans, Green, 1931. Also reprinted in *If, or History Rewritten*, edited by J. C. Squire, 259–87. New York: Viking Press, 1931.

Introduction to A. P. Herbert, *The Secret Battle: With an Introduction by the Right Hon. Winston S. Churchill.* 3rd ed.. London: Methuen, 1928.

"Man Overboard! An Episode of the Red Sea." *Harmsworth Monthly Pictorial Magazine* 1 (1898–99): 662–64.

Marlborough: His Life and Times. 2 vols. London: George G. Harrap, 1947.

"My African Journey." *Strand Magazine* 35 (January to June 1908): 299–306, 385–94, 490–96, 680–88; *Strand Magazine* 36 (July to December 1908): 50–56, 137–45, 251–58, 374–81, 491–98.

My African Journey. London: Hodder and Stoughton, 1908.

My Early Life: A Roving Commission. London: Thornton Butterworth, 1930.

Onwards to Victory: War Speeches by the Right Hon. Winston S. Churchill, 1943. 2nd ed. Compiled by Charles Eade. London: Cassell, 1945.

The River War: An Historical Account of the Reconquest of the Soudan. 2 vols. London: Longmans, Green, 1899.

Savrola: A Tale of the Revolution in Laurania. New York: Longmans, Green, January 1900.

The Second World War, "Chartwell" Edition. 6 vols. London: Educational Book Company, 1955.

Shall We Commit Suicide? New York: Eilert, 1924; facsimile reprint, USA, Canada, UK, Australia, New Zealand: International Churchill Societies, 1994.

The Story of the Malakand Field Force: An Episode of Frontier War. 2nd ed. London: Long-
  mans, Green, 1899.
Thoughts and Adventures. London: Thornton Butterworth, 1932.
The Unrelenting Struggle: War Speeches by the Right Hon. Winston S. Churchill, C.H., M.P.
  Compiled by Charles Eade. Boston: Little, Brown, 1942.
The Unwritten Alliance: Speeches 1953 to 1959. Edited by Randolph S. Churchill. London:
  Cassell, 1961.
The World Crisis 1911–1914. New York: Charles Scribner's Sons, 1923.
The World Crisis 1915. New York: Charles Scribner's Sons, 1923.
The World Crisis 1916–1918. 2 vols. New York: Charles Scribner's Sons, 1927.
The World Crisis–1918–1928: The Aftermath. New York: Charles Scribner's Sons, 1929.
*The World Crisis 1911–1918: Abridged and Revised with additional chapter on the Battle of the
  Marne.* London: Thornton Butterworth, 1931.
The World Crisis 1911–1914. Norwalk, CT: Easton Press, 1991.
The World Crisis 1916–1918. Norwalk, CT: Easton Press, 1991.

SECONDARY SOURCES

Alkon, Paul. "Alternate History and Postmodern Temporality." In *Time, Literature and the
  Arts: Essays in Honor of Samuel L. Macey,* edited by Thomas R. Cleary, 65–85. Vic-
  toria: University of Victoria, 1994.
———. *Origins of Futuristic Fiction.* Athens: University of Georgia Press, 1987.
Alldritt, Keith. *Churchill the Writer: His Life as a Man of Letters.* London: Hutchinson,
  1992.
Ashley, Maurice. *Churchill as Historian.* London: Secker & Warburg, 1968.
Berlin, Isaiah. *Mr Churchill in 1940.* London: John Murray, n.d. [1949].
Best, Geoffrey. *Churchill: A Study in Greatness.* London: Hambledon & London: 2001.
Birkenhead, Frederick, second Earl of Birkenhead. *The Professor and the Prime Minister:
  The Official Life of Professor F. A. Lindemann, Viscount Cherwell.* Boston: Houghton
  Mifflin, 1962.
Bloch, I. S. [Jan]. *The Future of War in Its Technical Economic and Political Relations.* Trans-
  lated by R. C. Long. Boston: Ginn, 1899.
Boswell, James. *Life of Johnson.* Edited by R. W. Chapman. New edition corrected by
  J. D. Fleeman. London: Oxford University Press, 1970.
Bungay, Stephen. "The Reason Why." In *The Most Dangerous Enemy: A History of the Bat-
  tle of Britain,* 7–26. London: Aurum Press, 2000.
Butterfield, Herbert. *The Whig Interpretation of History.* London: G. Bell, 1931.
Cannadine, David. "Language: Churchill as the Voice of Destiny." In *In Churchill's
  Shadow: Confronting the Past in Modern Britain,* 85–113. London: Allen Lane, 2002.
———. "Winston Churchill as an Aristocratic Adventurer." In *Aspects of Aristocracy:
  Grandeur and Decline in Modern Britain,* 130–62. New Haven, CT: Yale University
  Press, 1994.
Carroll, Lewis. *Alice's Adventures in Wonderland and Through the Looking-Glass.* New York:
  J. J. Little & Ives, n.d.
Chabert, Philippe. *Alphonse de Neuville: l'épopée de la défaite.* Paris: Editions Copernic,
  1979.

Churchill, Randolph S. "How He Came to Write It." *Sunday Telegraph*, January 30, 1966, 4.

———. *Winston Churchill, Volume 1: Youth 1874–1900*. London: Heinemann, 1966.

———. *Winston S. Churchill, Volume 1 Companion Part 1: 1874–1896*. London: Heinemann, 1967.

———. *Winston S. Churchill, Volume 1 Companion Part 2: 1896–1900*. London: Heinemann, 1967.

———. *Winston S. Churchill, Volume 2: Young Statesman 1901–1914*. London: Heinemann, 1967.

Clarke, I. F. "Introduction." In Jean-Baptiste François Xavier Cousin de Grainville, *The Last Man*, translated by I. F. and M. Clarke. Middletown, CT: Wesleyan University Press, 2002.

———, ed. *The Tale of the Next Great War, 1871–1914: Fictions of Future Warfare and of Battles Still-to-come*. Syracuse: Syracuse University Press, 1995.

———. *Voices Prophesying War: Future Wars 1763–3749*. 2nd ed. Oxford: Oxford University Press, 1992.

Clute, John, and Peter Nicholls, eds. *The Encyclopedia of Science Fiction*. New York: St. Martin's Press, 1993.

Coombs, David. *Churchill: His Paintings*. London: Hamish Hamilton, 1967.

———. With Minnie Churchill, foreword by Mary Soames. *Sir Winston Churchill's Life through His Paintings*. London: Chaucer Press, 2003.

Coward, Noel. *Cavalcade*. London: William Heinemann, 1932.

Drazin, Charles. *Korda: Britain's Only Movie Mogul*. London: Sidgwick & Jackson, 2002.

Edwardes, Michael. "'Oh to meet an Army Man': Kipling and the Soldiers." In *The Age of Kipling*, edited by John Gross, 37–44 New York: Simon & Schuster, 1972.

Feldman, Burton. *The Nobel Prize: A History of Genius, Controversy, and Prestige*. New York: Arcade Publishing, 2000.

Ferguson, Niall, ed. *Virtual History: Alternatives and Counterfactuals*. London: Picador, 1997.

Feske, Victor. "Winston Churchill, The Last Public Historian." In *From Belloc to Churchill: Private Scholars, Public Culture, and the Crisis of British Liberalism, 1909–1939*, 186–227. Chapel Hill: University of North Carolina Press, 1996.

Fincastle, Viscount Alexander Edward, and P. C. Eliott-Lockhart. *A Frontier Campaign: A Narrative of the Operations of the Malakand and Buner Field Forces, 1897–1898*. 2nd ed. London: Methuen, 1898.

Fischer, David Hackett. *Historian's Fallacies: Toward a Logic of Historical Thought*. New York: Harper & Row, 1970.

Foot, Michael. *H. G: The History of Mr Wells*. London: Black Swan, 1996.

Forbes, Christopher, and Margaret Kelly, *War A La Mode: Military Pictures by Meissonier, Detaille, de Neuville and Berne-Bellecour from the Forbes Magazine Collection*. Exhibition Catalogue, Amherst College, Mead Art Museum, c. 1975.

Fort, Adrian. *Prof: The Life of Frederick Lindemann*. London: Jonathan Cape, 2003.

Fromkin, David. *A Peace to End All Peace: Creating the Modern Middle East*. New York: Henry Holt, 1989.

Garnett, Oliver. *Chartwell, Kent*. 1992. Repr., London: National Trust, 1995.

Gilbert, Martin. *In Search of Churchill: A Historian's Journey*. London: HarperCollins, 1994.

————. *Winston S. Churchill: Vol. 8 "Never Despair" 1945–1965*. Boston: Houghton Mifflin, 1988.

————, ed. *Winston S. Churchill, Volume 4 Companion, Part 3: Documents April 1921–November 1922*. London: Heinemann, 1977.

————, ed. *Winston S. Churchill, Volume 5 Companion Part 2: Documents, The Wilderness Years 1929–1935*. London: Heinemann, 1981.

————, ed. *Winston S. Churchill, Volume 5 Companion Part 3: Documents, The Coming of War 1936–1939*. London: Heinemann, 1982.

Gombrich, E. H. *Art and Illusion: A Study in the Psychology of Pictorial Representation*. 2nd ed. Princeton, NJ: Princeton University Press, 1961.

Gordon, Adam Lindsay. *Poems of the Late Adam Lindsay Gordon*. London: Samuel Mullen; Melbourne: A. H. Massina, n.d. [1900].

————. *Selected Poems, with Brief Biographical Notes*. Compiled by Eustace A. Stedman. Tisbury: privately printed, 1933.

Graves, Robert. *Lawrence and the Arabs*. 1927. Repr., New York: Paragon House, 1991.

Grosvenor, Charles. *An Iconography: The Portraits of T. E. Lawrence*. Pasadena: Otterden Press, 1988.

————. "The Subscribers' *Seven Pillars of Wisdom*: The Visual Aspect." In *The T. E. Lawrence Puzzle*, edited by Stephen E. Tabachnick, 159–84. Athens: University of Georgia Press, 1984.

Hacker, Barton C., and Gordon B. Chamberlain. "Pasts That Might Have Been, 2: A Revised Bibliography of Alternative History." In *Alternative Histories: Eleven Stories of the World as It Might Have Been*, edited by Charles G. Waugh and Martin H. Greenberg, 301–63. New York: Garland, 1986.

Harrod, R. F. *The Prof: A Personal Memoir of Lord Cherwell*. London: MacMillan, 1959.

Herbert, A. P. *The Secret Battle: With an Introduction by the Right Hon. Winston S. Churchill*. 3rd ed. London: Methuen, 1928.

Hobday, Edmund Arthur Ponsonby. *Sketches on Service during the Indian Frontier Campaigns of 1897*. London: James Bowden, 1898.

Humphris, Edith M. *The Life of Adam Lindsay Gordon*. London: Eric Partridge, 1933.

Hutton, Geoffrey. *Adam Lindsay Gordon: the Man and the Myth*. 1978. Repr., Melbourne, Australia: Melbourne University Press, 1996.

Jay, Robert. "Alphonse de Neuville's *The Spy* and the Legacy of the Franco-Prussian War." *Metropolitan Museum Journal* 19/20 (1984–85): 151–62.

Jones, J. R. *Marlborough*. Cambridge: Cambridge University Press, 1993.

Keble, John. *The Christian Year: Lyra Innocentium and Other Poems*. London: Oxford University Press, 1914.

Kelly, Andrew, James Pepper and Jeffrey Richards, eds. *Filming T. E. Lawrence: Korda's Lost Epics*. London: I. B. Tauris, 1997.

Kimball, Warren F. *Forged in War: Roosevelt, Churchill, and the Second World War*. New York: William Morrow, 1997.

Kipling, Rudyard. "Recessional." In *The Book of Living Verse*, edited by Louis Untermeyer, 492. New York: Harcourt, Brace, 1945.

Klieman, Aaron S. *Foundations of British Policy in the Arab World: The Cairo Conference of 1921*. Baltimore: Johns Hopkins Press, 1970.

Korda, Michael. *Charmed Lives: A Family Romance.* New York: Random House, 1979.

Kulik, Karol. *Alexander Korda: The Man Who Could Work Miracles.* New Rochelle, NY: Arlington House Publishers, 1975.

Lang, Cosmo Gordon. *His Grace the Archbishop of Canterbury on Adam Lindsay Gordon: Delivered on the Occasion of the Unveiling of the Adam Lindsay Gordon Memorial in Westminster Abbey on 11th May, 1934.* N.p. N.d. [1934].

Langworth, Richard M. *A Connoisseur's Guide to the Books of Sir Winston Churchill.* Rev. ed. London: Brassey's 2000.

Lawrence, A. W., ed. *Letters to T. E. Lawrence.* London: Jonathan Cape, 1962.

———, ed. *T. E. Lawrence by His Friends.* London: Jonathan Cape, 1937.

Lawrence, M. R., ed. *The Home Letters of T. E. Lawrence and His Brothers.* New York: Macmillan, 1954.

Lawrence, T. E. *The Letters of T. E. Lawrence.* Edited by David Garnett. New York: Doubleday, Doran, 1939.

———. *The Mint.* New York: W. W. Norton, 1963.

———. *Seven Pillars of Wisdom: A Triumph.* Harmondsworth, England: Penguin, 1962.

Lewis, C. S. *Of Other Worlds: Essays and Stories by C. S. Lewis.* Edited by Walter Hooper. London: Geoffrey Bles, 1966.

Macaulay, Thomas Babington. "Von Ranke." In *Critical and Historical Essays Contributed to the Edinburgh Review,* 2:207–54. 3 vols. London: Longman, Brown, Green, and Longmans, 1843.

Macey, Samuel L., ed. *Encyclopedia of Time.* New York: Garland, 1994.

Meyers, Jeffrey. *The Wounded Spirit: T. E. Lawrence's "Seven Pillars of Wisdom."* 2nd ed. Houndmills: Macmillan, 1989.

Moran, Lord [Charles Wilson]. *Churchill: Taken from the Diaries of Lord Moran.* Boston: Houghton Mifflin, 1956.

Muller, James W., ed. *Churchill as Peacemaker.* Cambridge: Woodrow Wilson Center Press and Cambridge University Press, 1997.

———. "Churchill the Writer." *Wilson Quarterly* 18, no. 1 (Winter 1994): 38–48. Repr. in *Essays in Biography: The Best of the WQ* (1995): 23–33.

——— "'A Kind of Dignity and Even Nobility': Winston Churchill's *Thoughts and Adventures.*" *Political Science Reviewer* 16 (Fall 1986): 281–315.

Nobel Prize Library: Albert Camus, Winston Churchill. New York: Alexis Gregory; Del Mar, CA: CRM Publishing, n.d.

Orwell, George. "Wells, Hitler and the World State." In *Dickens, Dali and Others.* San Diego, New York, London: Harcourt Brace, Jovanovich, 1973.

Plumb, J. H. "The Dominion of History." In *Winston Churchill: Resolution, Defiance, Magnanimity, Good Will.* Edited by R. Crosby Kemper III. Columbia: University of Missouri Press, 1996.

———. "The Historian." In *Churchill Revised: A Critical Assessment,* edited by A. J. P. Taylor, Robert Rhodes James, J. H. Plumb, Basil Liddell Hart, and Anthony Storr, 133–69. New York: Dial Press, 1969.

———. *The Making of an Historian: The Collected Essays of J. H. Plumb.* Athens: University of Georgia Press, 1988.

Powers, Patrick J. C. "*Savrola* and the Nobility of Politics: Winston Churchill's Premier Literary Work." *Finest Hour* 74 (First Quarter 1992): 6–13.

Radisich, Paula Rea. *Hubert Robert: Painted Spaces of the Enlightenment.* Cambridge: Cambridge University Press, 1998.

Ramsden, John. *Man of the Century: Winston Churchill and His Legend Since 1945.* London: HarperCollins, 2002.

Reynolds, David. *In Command of History: Churchill Fighting and Writing the Second World War.* London: Allen Lane, 2004.

Richards, Jeffrey. *The Age of the Dream Palace: Cinema and Society in Britain 1930–1939.* London: Routledge & Kegan Paul, 1984.

Richardson, Samuel. *Clarissa. Or, the History of a Young Lady: Comprehending the most Important Concerns of Private Life.* 3rd ed. 8 vols. London: S. Richardson, 1751.

Robichon, François. *L'armée française vue par les peintres 1870–1914.* Paris: Hercher/Ministère de la Défense, 2000.

Rose, Norman. *Churchill: An Unruly Life.* London: Simon & Schuster, 1994.

Sandys, Celia. *From Winston With Love and Kisses: The Young Churchill.* London: Sinclair-Stevenson, 1994.

Sherriff, R. C. *No Leading Lady: An Autobiography.* London: Victor Gollancz, 1968.

Sladen, Douglas. *Adam Lindsay Gordon: The Life and Best Poems of the Poet of Australia, The Westminster Abbey Memorial Volume.* London: Hutchinson, n.d. [1934].

Smith, David C. *H. G. Wells: Desperately Mortal.* New Haven, CT: Yale University Press, 1986.

Soames, Mary. *Clementine Churchill: The Biography of a Marriage.* Boston: Houghton Mifflin, 1979.

———, ed. *Speaking for Themselves: The Personal Letters of Winston and Clementine Churchill.* London: Doubleday, 1998.

———. *Winston Churchill: His Life as a Painter.* London: Collins, 1990.

Stafford, David. *Churchill and Secret Service.* Toronto: Stoddart, 1997; London, John Murray, 1997.

Steward, Herbert Leslie. *Sir Winston Churchill as Writer and Speaker.* London: Sidgwick & Jackson, 1954.

Storrs, Ronald. *Orientations.* London: Ivor Nicholson & Watson, 1937.

Thomas, Lowell. *With Lawrence in Arabia.* New York and London: Century, 1924.

Trevor-Roper, Hugh. "History and Imagination." In *History and Imaginatioin: Essays in Honor of H. R. Trevor-Roper,* edited by Hugh Lloyd-Jones, Valerie Pearl, and Blair Worden, 356–69. New York: Holmes & Meier, 1982.

Valiunas, Algis. *Churchill's Military Histories: A Rhetorical Study.* Lanham, MD: Roman & Littlefield, 2002.

Weidhorn, Manfred. *A Harmony of Interests: Explorations in the Mind of Sir Winston Churchill.* Rutherford, NJ: Fairleigh Dickinson University Press, 1992.

———. *Sword and Pen: A Survey of the Writings of Sir Winston Churchill.* Albuquerque: University of New Mexico Press, 1974.

Wells, H. G. *Experiment in Autobiography: Discoveries and Conclusions of a Very Ordinary Brain (Since 1866).* New York: Macmillan, 1934.

———. *Meanwhile (The Picture of a Lady).* New York: George H. Doran, 1927.

———. *Men Like Gods: A Novel.* New York: Macmillan, 1923.

———. *Star Begotten: A Biological Fantasia.* London: Chatto & Windus, 1937.

———. *The Time Machine: An Invention.* Edited by Nicholas Ruddick. Peterborough, Ontario, Canada: Broadview Press, 2001.

Wenden, D. J. "Churchill, Radio, and Cinema." In *Churchill*, edited by Robert Blake and W. Roger Louis, 215–39. New York and London: W. W. Norton, 1993.

Wilson, Jeremy. *Lawrence of Arabia: The Authorized Biography of T. E. Lawrence.* New York: Atheneum, 1990.

Wilson, Thomas. *Churchill and the Prof.* London: Cassell, 1995.

Woods, Frederick. *Artillery of Words: The Writings of Sir Winston Churchill.* London: Leo Cooper, 1992.

———. *A Bibliography of the Works of Sir Winston Churchill.* 2nd ed. Toronto: University of Toronto Press, 1969.

Index

Page numbers in italics refer to illustrations. *Plate* or *plates* indicates the color photographs grouped together within the volume as well as the discussion in the captions.

Abyssinia, 11
aestheticism, 65
Afghanistan, 135, 136
Africa, 108, 180
Air Defense Research Committee, 57
Alcock, John, 58
Alexander the Great, 134
Alkon, Paul K., 243n.13, 244n.26
Alldritt, Keith, 229n.5
Allenby, Edmund, 1st Viscount, 8–9, 46, 53
American Revolution, 184
anarchism, 172
Anne, Queen, 185, 186–87, 188, 189, 192
Antwerp, xiii
Arab Bureau, 45–46, 47
Arab Revolt, 3, 4, 5, 8, 9, 45–46, 47, 50, 53
Aristotle: *Poetics*, 140
Armistice, 66, 156, 160, 161, 215
Ashley, Maurice, 229n.5
astronomy, 150–51
atheism, 151
atomic age/bomb, xvi, 155, 160, 164–65
Attlee, Clement, 164
Auda Abu Tayi, 48
Augustine, Saint: *Confessions*, 98
Augustus Caesar, 90
Austin, Henry, 108
autogiro, 59–60, 61–62, 64
Australia, 18, 22–23, 60, 97, 237n.2
aviation: Churchill's views of and interest in, xiii, 12–14, 20, 33, 34, 54–55, 57–65, 155, 160, 173; and Lawrence, 2–3, 12–14. *See also* autogiro

bacteriological warfare, 157
Baldwin, Stanley, 12, 24, 56, 57, 195
Balfour Declaration, 2
Balzac, Honoré de, 120
Bangalore, 102, 115
Barrie, James, 22; *The Admirable Crichton*, 85

Bayeux tapestry, 99–100
Bazeilles, *plate*
Beerbohm, Max, 103
Bellamy, Edward: *Looking Backward*, 221
Belgium, 77, 198, *plate*
Bentley, Thomas: *Royal Cavalcade*, 67–68
Berlin, Isaiah, xii, 177
Best, Geoffrey, 229–30n.6
Bible, 16–17, 121, 149
Biddulph, Major, 110
biological engineering, xvi
Birkenhead, Frederick, 2nd Earl of, 242n.3
Bismarck, Otto von, 39, 103
Blackhead, Stephen, 207
Blake, William, 32
Blenheim, Battle of, 142, 208
Blenheim Palace, 101, 146
Blériot, Louis, 58
Blitz, 1, 50, 63
Bloch, Jan: *The Future of War*, 158, 243n.14
Blood, Sir Bindon, 104, 105, 110, 113, *114*, 115, 128
Blumenfeld, R. D., 7
Board of Film Censors, 42
Boccaccio, Giovanni: *Decameron*, 149
Boer War, 23, 36, 66, 67, 71–72, 89, 108–9, 179, 184
Bonaparte, Napoleon, 7, 9, 10, 34, 41, 53, 180, 181, 190, 192–93, 196
Boswell, James, 203; *Life of Johnson*, 205–6
Bracken, Brendan, 168
Bridgeman, William Clive, 34
Brighton, 101, 103
Bristol University, 25
Britain, Battle of, 1, 156, 158
British Broadcasting Corporation, 93
British Gazette, 171
Brown, Arthur Whitten, 58
Buner Field Force, 112
Bungay, Stephen, 229n.5

Bunyan, John: *Pilgrim's Progress*, 33, 38
Burke, Edmund: *Speech at Bristol on Declining the Poll*, 121, 123
Burma, 226
Butterfield, Herbert, 196, 247n.34
Buxton, Robert V., 45

Cairo, 36, 106
Cairo settlement of 1921, 2, 7, 34
Cambridge University, 49, 155
Cannadine, David, 229n.5
Čapek, Karel, xiii, xvi, 175; *Rossum's Universal Robots*, 162–63, 164
capitalism, 167
Carlton Club, 223
Carroll, Lewis: *Alice in Wonderland*, 104
cartography, 49, 102, 105–6, 107, 108, 109–10, 115, 156, 191, 209. *See also* topography
cartoons, political, 24, 103–2, 108
Catholicism, 223
cavalry, 9, 18, 19–20, 24, 49, 51–52, 72, 93, 105, 106, 117, 144, 156, 226
Cézanne, Paul, 32
Chakdara, 112
Chamberlain, Gordon B., 243n.13
Chamberlain, Neville, 12, 24, 195, 214
Chaplin, Charlie, xv, 87–95
Charles II, King (Spain), 246n.15
Chesney, George T.: *The Battle of Dorking*, 181, 182, 183
Chartwell, 25, 75, 79, 97, 106, 153, 215, 216
Childers, Erskine: *The Riddle of the Sands*, 181
chemical warfare, 155, 157
China, 60
Christianity, 112
Churchill, Arabella, 197
Churchill, Clementine, 25, 81, 82, 83, 84
Churchill, John Strange, 226
Churchill, Lady Randolph, 226; Churchill's correspondence with, 104, 105, 106, 113, 115, 116, 150; Sargent's sketch of, 108
Churchill, Lord Randolph (father of Winston), xvii–xviii, 24, 89, 101, 102, 215–28
Churchill, Randolph (son of Winston), 44, 216
Churchill, Sarah (daughter of Winston), 216
Churchill, Sir Winston (father of Marlborough), 207
Churchill, Winston: attention to grim reality of war by, 19–20, 75–79, 81–84, 119–24,

156, 165–66, 199, 209, 244n.40; as colonial secretary, xiv, 2, 6; as Conservative MP, 23; critical attention to writings of, xi–xii, 229n.5; "Dark Age" motif of, 83, 156, 158–59, 172, 177–78, 180–81, 221; as defense minister, 84, 184, 193; dismissal after World War II of, 153; education of, xiv, 24, 49–50, 101–2, 156, 171, 226; as First Lord of the Admiralty, xiii, 71, 93, 155, 181; folklore regarding, 41; generic literary range of, xi, 23, 56, 66, 141, 215, 228; as home secretary, 172; and Independent Liberal candidate, 167; as journalist/war correspondent, 23, 56, 58, 66, 105, 127, 215, 220, 228; legendary dullness of, xv; and love of debate, 55, 93; moments of depression of, 21–22; moral imagination of, 65, 120–21, 123, 131, 163, 164, 165–66, 177, 199, 201, 214; as munitions minister, 160; as Nobel laureate, xi, xii, xvi, 24, 49–50, 93, 139, 175, 228; and political goals in writing, xi, xii, 11–14, 17, 23, 34, 39, 70–71, 78–79, 103–4, 123, 193; as prime minister, 1, 24, 41, 84, 146, 155, 164, 166, 181, 184, 193, 213, 219; revisionist biographers of, 34–35; as rhetorician, xi, xii, 14, 23, 30, 78, 93, 131, 135, 137, 139, 158, 169; self-promotion and ambitiousness of, 23, 115–16, 153, 195; theatricality and dress of, 24–26, 104, 109; use of assistants in writing by, xii; "wilderness years" in the 1930s of, xiii, 12, 14, 39, 42, 70. *See also* cinema; painting; science; World War I; World War II
—Works:
—Addresses: "Anglo-American Unity," 20, 92–93; "Defense," 164–65; "Dunkirk," 161; "The Hydrogen Bomb," 165; "The Sinews of Peace," 228; "A Speech at a Tree-Planting at Churchill College," 155, 242n.3; "Their Finest Hour," 130–31, 158–59, 172, 177–78, 181, 221; "'These Are Great Days,'" 1–2
—Fiction: "The Dream," xvii–xviii, 216–28, 248n.10; "Man Overboard!" 108; *Savrola*, xv–xvi, 23, 65, 73, 105, 107, 115–24, 142, 144–54, 166–67, 207, *plates*
—Nonfiction: *The Aftermath*, 156, 159, 160, 215, 246n.15; "Alphonso the Unlucky,"

239n.42; "A Bolt from the Grey," 182; "Cartoons and Cartoonists," 24–25, 102–3, 108; "The Effect of Air Transport on Civilization," 57, 60–61, 64; "Everybody's Language," xv, 87–95; "Fifty Years Hence," 108, 161–63, 165–66; *The Gathering Storm*, 15, 84, 156; *Great Contemporaries*, 11–17, 21–22, 27, 28, 29, 33, 38, 109, 225, 239n.42; "H. G. Wells," 173–74; *A History of the English-Speaking Peoples*, 141; "Hobbies," 97; *Ian Hamilton's March*, 23, 36, 209; "If Lee Had Not Won the Battle of Gettysburg," xvi, 157–58, 180, 215; "The King's Twenty-Five Years," 44; "Lawrence of Arabia's Name Will Live!" 10–19, 21–23, 26, 27, 28, 29, 30, 33, 34, 36, 38, 39; "Lawrence's Great Book," 33–34, 36–37, 39; *London to Ladysmith via Pretoria*, 23, 36, 209; *Lord Randolph Churchill*, 23, 108, 141, 219; *Marlborough*, xvi–xvii, 36, 44, 49, 55, 109, 141, 142, 143, 178, 180–211, 246–47n.31; *My African Journey*, 23, 36, 108; *My Early Life*, xiv, xv, 19–20, 23, 36, 39, 51, 89, 99–100, 108, 144, 209, 225; "Painting as a Pastime," 30–32, 97–99, 154; *Painting as a Pastime*, xv, 97, 139; "Preliminary Outline of Jubilee Film," 70–71; *The River War*, 23, 24, 35, 51–52, 54, 99, 106–7, 116, 141, 143–44, 153, 209; "The Scaffolding of Rhetoric," 131; "Scenario of the Reign of King George V," 69, 75; "A Second Choice," 179; *The Second World War*, xii, 109, 141, 155, 156, 179–80, 204, 225, 228, 243n.17; "Shall We All Commit Suicide?" 156–57, 161, 165–66, 242–43n.6; *The Story of the Malakand Field Force*, xv–xvi, 23, 35, 104, 109–10, 112–13, 114, 115, 118–41, 153, 209, plate; *Thoughts and Adventures*, 23, 97, 108, 156, 161, 225; "The Time-Table of a Nightmare," 181; *The World Crisis*, 8, 9, 23, 36, 109, 141, 142–43, 155, 157, 159–60, 168, 182, 204, 225, 228, 246n.15

—Paintings: *The Banqueting Hall, Knebworth House 1920s*, 149; *Coast Scene on the Riviera*, 145, plate; *The Dining-room at Chartwell with Miss Diana Churchill 1933*, 149; *The Dining-room at Knebworth c. 1928*, 149; *The Dining-room of Sir Philip*

Sassoon's House, Lympne c. 1930, 149; *Lawrence Farm*, 33, 152–53; "*Plugstreet*" *under Shell-fire*, 33, 77, 152; *Study of Boats*, plate; *A View of Marrakech with the Tower of the Katoubia Mosque*, 36; *View of Monte Carlo*, plate; *View of Monte Carlo and Monaco*, 145

Churchill College, Cambridge, 155, 242n.3
Church of England, 223
cinema, xv, 41–95, 104, 138, 142–44; and animation, 68, 73–74; and Churchill's concern for verisimilitude and historical accuracy, 45–48, 50, 58, 59, 68, 69, 74; and Churchill's fondness for movies, xv, 41, 42; Churchill's work as scriptwriter and consultant in, xv, 42–87, 94–95, 215; and newsreels, 56, 67–68, 74; and political uses of film, 56–57, 92–94; and silent vs. "talkie" movies, xv, 42, 68, 72–73, 88, 90–94, 144; technological impact on Churchill's narratives of, 142–44. *See also* Korda, Alexander
Civil War, American, 103, 158–59
Clark, Cosmo, 35
Clarke, I. F., 240n.92, 246n.11
class system, 66–67, 85–86, 90
Clemenceau, Georges, 160, 215
Clements, John, 43
Cleveland, Duchess of (Barbara Villiers), 196, 197
Clio, 70, 71, 73
Clive, Robert (Baron Clive of Plassey), 34
Cold War, 164
Colonel Blimp, 156
Columbia Pictures, 42
comedy, 24, 86, 89–91, 93, 188–89, 204, 205, 207, 210
Communism, 168, 169, 227
Constantinople, 7, 8
counterfactual history. *See* history, alternative
Coward, Noel: *Cavalcade*, 66–67
Cromwell, Oliver, 25–26, 187
Crosland, Alan: *The Jazz Singer*, 144
Cruikshank, George, 132
Crusades, 48, 99–100
cryptography, 31–32, 233n.84
Cuba, 23
cubism, 30
Cunynghame, David B., 44–45
Curtis, Lionel, 3

Dahoum (Salim Ahmed), 38
Damascus, 48–49, 51
Dardanelles, xiii, 8
Darwin, Charles: *Origin of Species*, 149
David Jones Art Gallery, 237n.2
Defoe, Daniel: *Robinson Crusoe*, 33, 34, 38
Degas, Edgar, 31
democracy, xiii, 93, 195, 199, 225–26
de Neuville, Alphonse Marie de, 115–20, 122,
    plates; *La défense de Reorke's Drift*, 117;
    Les dernières cartouches, 117–18, *plate*
Deraa, 37–38, 39
Dervish army/war, 19, 99–100, 106
dialogues of the dead, 221, 223, 224
Dibdin, Thomas John, 70
Dickens, Charles, 89
Disraeli, Benjamin, 24
Donat, Robert, 43
Doré, Gustave, 240n.92; *The New Zealander*, 131
Dostoevksy, Fyodor, 4, 38
Doyle, Sir Arthur Conan: *The Adventures of*
    Sherlock Holmes, 171; *A Study in Scarlet*,
    171
drama, 122–25, 142, 144–45, 162–63, 164, 224
dreams, xvii–xviii, 213–16
dream vision, 160–61, 215
Drew, George, 26
Dunkirk, 183

Eden, Anthony, 214
Eden, Robert, 194
Edwardes, Michael, 47
Eliot, T. S., 175
Eliott-Lockhart, P. C.: *A Frontier Campaign*
    (second author to Fincastle), 104–5, 109–
    10, *111*, 112–13, *114*
empire, xvii, 7, 12, 20, 22–23, 66, 70, 69, 79, 83,
    84, 92–93, 123–24, 129–31, 167–71,
    177–78, 200, 205, 225, 226
Enlightenment, 91–92, 156
Evans, Clifford, 43
Everest, Elizabeth Anne, 149
evolution, 151
expressionism, 32

fairy tales. *See* Grimm's fairy tales
Fascism, xiii, 10, 173
Feisal I, Emir, 28, 30, 49
Fénelon, François de Salignac de La Mothe-:
    Dialogues of the Dead, 221

Ferdinand, Archduke, 72
Ferguson, Niall, 245n.3
Feske, Victor, 195, 229n.5, 246–47n.31
Few, the, 58, 161
film. *See* cinema
Fincastle, Alexander Edward, Viscount:
    A Frontier Campaign, 104–5, 109–10, *111*,
    112–13, *114*
Fischer, David Hackett, 245n.3
Flaubert, Gustave, 120
Fontenelle M. de (Bernard le Bovier):
    Dialogues des morts, 221
Forbes, Christopher, 239nn.57 and 59
Foreign Office, 42
Forster, E. M., 36–37
4th Queen's Own Hussars, 25, 102
France, xiii, 9, 180, 181, 182, 183–84, 189–93,
    198, 205, 246n.15
France, Battle of, 213
Franco-Prussian War, 117–18, *plate*
French Revolution, 192
Freud, Sigmund, 209
Fromkin, David, 230n.3

Gallipoli, 8, 9, 159, 179
Galsworthy, John, 22
Gandy, Joseph, 240n.92; *Architectural Ruins:*
    A Vision, 131
gardens, 146, 148–49, 154
Garnett, Edward, 7
Gaza, 9
General Strike (1926), 171–72
Genghis Khan, 174
geography, 48–49. *See also* cartography;
    topography
George V, King, 44, 56, 65–67, 67, 69, 79, 83
George VI, King, 22
Germany, xiii, 1, 10, 11, 34, 72, 137, 142–43,
    158, 159, 168, 180, 181, 183, 198, 227. *See*
    also Nazis
Gettysburg, Battle of, 157
Ghosam, 128
Gibbon, Edward, 112; *Decline and Fall of the*
    Roman Empire, 129, 130, 149
Gilbert, Martin, 229–30n.6, 235n.59, 242n.3
Gladstone, William Ewart, 24
Glorious Revolution, 201. *See also* James
    Francis Edward Stuart; William III, King
Godolphin, Sidney, 1st Earl of, 192, 206, 207
Goes, Count, 207

Gombrich, E. H.: *Art and Illusion*, 139
Gordon, Adam Lindsay: as hero of
    Australia/the empire, 22–23; suicide of,
    21. Works: *Bush Ballads and Galloping
    Rhymes*, 21; "The Last Leap," 18–19, 21–
    22; "The Roll of the Kettledrum; or, the
    Lay of the Last Charger," 20–21; *Sea
    Spray and Smoke Drift*, 18
Goya, Francisco, 77
Grand Alliance, 184, 191, 192, 196
Grant, Cary, 43
Graves, Robert, 2, 6
Grimm's fairy tales, 132–34, 136
Grosvenor, Charles, 35, 232n.76
Guthrie, Duncan, 46

Hacker, Barton C., 243n.13
Haifa, 9
Hamilton, Emma, Lady, xv, 41
Harrod, R. F., 242n.3
Harrow, xiv, 1–2, 101, 102, 171
Harvard University, 20, 92, 93
Hawkins, Sir John, 206
Hegel, Georg Wilhelm Friedrich, 149
Hentsch, Richard, 142–43
Herbert, A. P.: *The Secret Battle*, 78
Hewett, Captain, 110, 112
Hill, Abigail, 205
Hiroshima, 164
history, alternative, xvii–xvii, 7, 8, 17, 91,
    156–61, 178–88, 190–94, 207, 215, 228,
    245n.3, 246n.11
Hitler, Adolf, xiii, 3, 10, 15, 57, 63, 70–71, 158,
    168, 172, 178, 180, 196
Hobbes, Thomas, 156
Hobday, Edmund Arthur Ponsonby, 104;
    "Cavalry Reconnaissance from Mala-
    kand," 110, *111*, 113; *Sketches on Service
    during the Indian Frontier Campaigns of
    1897*, 110, *114*
Holland, 189–91, 205
Home Guard, 183
Homer: *Odyssey*, 64
Home Rule, 223
horses, 18–21, 72, 223. *See also* cavalry; polo
House of Commons. *See* Parliament
House of Lords. *See* Parliament
Howard, Leslie, 42, 43
Hudd, Walter, 42
Huguenots, 198

Hughes-Stanton, Blair, 35
Hurst, Brian Desmond, 46
Huxley, Aldous, xiii; *Brave New World*, xvi, 163

illustration, book, xvi, 3–4, 5, 31, 32–33, 35,
    101, 102, 104–18, 132, 133, 153, 191, 209,
    239n.42, *plate*
imperialism. *See* empire
impressionism, 30, 32, 101, 215
India, 23, 24, 49, 105, 113, 124, 129–37, 205,
    226. *See also* Bangalore; Malakand Field
    Force/expedition; Sarai Valley
Invasion Committee of the Committee of
    Imperial Defense, 181
Iraq, 2
Ireland, 223
irony, 197, 199
irony, dramatic, 204–5
Irving, Washington: "Rip Van Winkle," 221
Isandhlwana, Battle of, 117
Islam, 100, 112, 135–37
Italy, 10, 11

Jacobites, 185–86, 188
James, Henry, 175
James II, King, 182, 186, 197, 207
James Francis Edward Stuart ("James III," the
    Pretender), 185–89, 201
Japan, 60, 214
Jazz Singer, The. See Crosland, Alan: *The Jazz
    Singer*
Jerusalem, 8, 36
John, Augustus Edwin, 27, 28, 33
Johnson, Samuel, 200, 205–6; *Rasselas*, 149
Jones, J. R., 184
Joyce, James, 175
Julius Caesar, 174

Kant, Immanuel, 149
Karachi, 4
Keble, John: "Morning," 13
Kellogg Pact, 173
Kelly, Margaret, 239nn.57 and 59
Kennington, Eric, 5, 32, 35
Kipling, Rudyard, 22, 47, 92, 170; "Recessional,"
    130
Kitchener, Horatio, 1st Earl, 24, 47, 51
Klieman, Aaron S., 230n.3
Korda, Alexander, xv, 41–87, 94–95, 215; as
    British agent, 41–42; and film project on

Lawrence, xv, 42–54; knighthood of, 42; proposed topical films of, 43–44, 54–87. Works: *Lady Hamilton* (*That Hamilton Woman*), xv, 41; *Things to Come*, 63–64

Lamb, Henry, 35; *Irish Troops in the Judean Hills Surprised by a Turkish Bombardment*, 32–33
Landor, Walter Savage: "Imaginary Conversations," 221
Langley, Samuel Pierpont, 58
Latham, Hubert, 58
Lavery, Mrs. John, 98–99
Lawrence, T. E., xiv, xv, 2–26, 27, 28, 29, 30–39, 232n.76; as advisor to Churchill, xiv, 2, 6–7; and Arab Revolt or nationalism, 2, 3, 4, 5, 8, 9, 10, 15, 26, 28, 38, 45–46, 47, 50, 53; Churchill's elegiac essay on, xiv, 10–19, 21–23, 26, 27, 28, 29, 30, 33, 34, 36, 38, 39; and costume, 5, 24, 25, 26, 27, 28, 29; death of, 10, 19, 23, 42; education and training of, 24; ego of, xiv, 7; Korda's proposed film on, xv, 42–54; literary and imaginative concerns of, 2, 3–5, 24, 30–31, 32–33, 35–37; mythologizing of, xiv, 5, 8, 11, 14–15, 17, 22, 34, 38, 39, 50, 52–53; nihilism of, 3, 5, 21. Works: *The Mint*, 2, 3, 5, 13; *Revolt in the Desert*, 42; *Seven Pillars of Wisdom: A Triumph*, xiv, 3–4, 6–7, 9, 31–39, 44–45, 50, 51–52; "To S. A.," 38
League of Nations, 157, 180, 196
Lean, David: *Lawrence of Arabia*, 53, 54
Lecky, William Edward Hartpole: *History of European Morals*, 149
Leigh, Vivien, 41
Leslie, Sir John, 107
Leslie, Lady Leonie, 151
Lewis, C. S., 34
Lindbergh, Charles, 58
Lindemann, Frederick, 155, 164
Lloyd, Frank: *Cavalcade*, 66–67
Lloyd George, David, 160, 215
London, 62–63, 64, 71, 85, 88, 89, 129, 131, 172
London Film Productions, xv, 42–44, 52, 55, 56, 66, 83, 86, 94, 95, 215
Long, R. C., 243n.14
Louis XIV, 180, 181, 182, 184, 187, 188, 196
Lucian: "Dialogues of the Dead," 221

Luftwaffe, 12, 57
Lyttleton, George: *Dialogues of the Dead*, 221

Macaulay, Thomas Babington, 55, 149, 189, 195, 206; "Von Ranke," 129, 130
Malakand Field Force/expedition, 104–5, 109–10, 112–13, 118–21, 124, 126–28, 131–32, 134
Malleson, Miles, 42, 46
Malplaquet, Battle of, 189
Manet, Edouard, 32
Manhattan Project, 164
maps. *See* cartography
Marius, Gaius, 173–74
Marlborough, Duchess of (Sarah Churchill), 197, 204–5, 206, 207, 208
Marlborough, 1st Duke of (John Churchill), xvi–xvii, 109, 141, 178, 180–81, 182–211; Churchill's alternative history sketches featuring, xvi–xvii, 180–81, 182–88, 190–94, 207; Churchill's defense of, 188–89, 194–97, 201, 206; and impact on Churchill's efforts in 1930s and World War II, 183, 184, 196
Marne, Battle of the, 142
Marrakech, 36
Marsh, Edward, 9, 169
Marx, Karl, 227
Massey, Raymond, 63
Matisse, Henri, 32
Matthew, Book of, 16–17
McNeill, Angus John, 106, 115, 116
Medina, 49, 50, 51
Mediterranean Sea, 145–46, *plate*
Melville, Herman, 38
metaphor, 22, 122–24, 125, 140–41, 202
Meyers, Jeffrey, 230n.10
Middle East, 2, 6, 7
MI5, 41
Military Co-ordination Committee, 84
Ministry of Information, 42
Miracle of the Air (film), 55
modernism, 175
Moloch, 75, 169
Monet, Claude, 32
Moran, Lord (Charles Wilson), 213–14, 222
Morris, William, 4, 33
mosaics, 147
Moses, 169
Muller, James W., 161, 229n.5, 244n.40

music, 66–70, 72, 80, 88, 94, 101
Mussolini, Benito, 10

Nagasaki, 164
Nash, Paul, 35
Nazis, xiii, 10, 14, 92, 158, 164, 183, 184
Nelson, Horatio, xv, 41
Nero, 90–91
New World Films, 42
New Zealand, 97
Nicholson, William, 35
Nietzsche, Friedrich Wilhelm, 4
9th East Surreys, 78
Norway, xiii
novel, 120, 122, 149, 203–5, 209
nuclear energy. *See* atomic age/bomb

Office of Strategic Services (OSS), 41
Oldham, 23
Olivier, Laurence, 41, 43
Omdurman, Battle of, 19, 51, 52, 99–100, 107,
    109, 143, 144, 156
Orwell, George, xvi, 161, 162; "Wells, Hitler
    and the World State," 172
Other Club, 167
Oxford High School for Boys, 10, 11
Oxford University, 24, 49, 179

painting: and Churchill's sense of narrative
    description, xvi, 35–36, 75, 77, 81–82, 100,
    118–28, 131–34, 138–42, 145–46, 149,
    153–54, 202; Churchill's understanding
    of, xv–xvi, 30–32, 35, 99–101, 139; de
    Neuville and the military genre of,
    117–19, 124, *plates*; as hobby/practice of
    Churchill, xv, xvii, 30, 31, 32–33, 35, 36,
    72, 87, 95, 97–101, 145–46, 153–54, 214–
    15, 216–20, 237n.2, *plates*; and interiors,
    30, 149, 214; and landscapes/ruins, 30,
    35–36, 101, 126, 128, 131–32, 133, 138–39,
    145–46, 149, 214, *plates*; and perspective,
    32–33, 145; and portraiture, xvii, 30, 109,
    216–19; realism in, 120, 122, 124, 126, 215
Palestine Expedition, 8–9
Paramount Pictures, 42
Paris, 34–35, 36
Parliament, xi, 23, 56, 57, 151, 164–65, 167, 223,
    226
Parnell, William, 82, 86
Passchendaele, 78

Pater, Walter, 37
Pearl Harbor, 41
photography, 31, 73–75, 104, 108, 109, 110, 113,
    114
Picasso, Pablo, 30
picturesque, 134–37, 141
Plato: *Republic*, 149
Ploegsteert, 77
Plumb, J. H., 229n.5, 246–47n.31
Poe, Edgar Allan, 37–38, 76, 77; "The Cask
    of Amontillado," 38; "The Pit and the
    Pendulum," 38
polo, 18, 19, 72
Powers, Patrick J. C., 229n.5
Primrose League, 223
Prince of Wales (ship), 214
Prior, Matthew: *Dialogues of the Dead*, 221
Privy Council, 25
Proust, Marcel, 52
Prussia, 181
Punch, 102

Quebec conference, 164
Quiller-Couch, Arthur, 22

race, 92–93, 123
Raemakers, Louis, 103
Ramsden, John, 229n.5
realism, 20, 119–20, 122, 124, 126, 133–34, 141,
    150, 215
religion, 112, 151
Repulse, 214
Restoration comedy, 188
Reynolds, David, xii
Richardson, Ralph, 63
Richardson, Samuel, 205; *Clarissa*, 203–4
rifles, 136–37
Riviera, French, 145–46
Robert, Hubert: *Vue Imaginaire de la Grande
    Galerie en Ruines*, 131
Roberts, William, 35
robots, xvi, 162
Roman Empire, 129
romanticism, 131, 132, 135, 150, 171, 197
Roosevelt, Franklin Delano, xii, 171, 164
Rorke's Drift, Battle of, 117, 118
Rothenstein, William, 35
Roundheads, 25–26
Royal Academy, 33, 97
Royal Air Force, 2, 4, 5, 12, 13, 34, 183

Royal Auxiliary Air Force, 25
Royal Navy, 9, 159, 183
Royal Navy Field Gun Competition, 71
Royal Scots Fusiliers, 47, 77, *plate*
Royal Tournaments, 71, 72, 235n.59
Rump Parliament, 187
Russia, 1, 168, 225, 227
Ryswick, Treaty of, 196

Saint-Simon, duc de (Louis de Rouvroy),
    149
Salonica, 8
Sandhurst, 24, 49, 50, 101, 102, 109, 115, 156
Sandys, Celia, 235n.59
Sarai Valley, 128–31
Sargent, John Singer, 108
Saslow, Edward L., 243n.17
Sassoon, Siegfried, 78
satire, 163, 188–89
Saunders, John Monk, 42
Saunier, Octave, 250n.92; *Paris en ruines*, 131
Sayers, Dorothy, 86
Schopenhauer, Arthur, 149
science: Churchill's engagement with, xvi, 64,
    155–57, 161–62, 164–65, 168, 174–75,
    199, 220. *See also* atomic age/bomb;
    aviation
science fiction, xiii, xvi, 62–63, 157, 160,
    161–75, 179, 183, 221–22. *See also* history,
    alternative
Scott, Lady, 22
sculpture, 146, 149–50
Seaforth Highlanders, 106
Sedan, Battle of, *plate*
Shakespeare, William: *Hamlet*, 11–12, 217;
    Macbeth, 153, 225; *The Tempest*, 123–24
Shaw, George Bernard, 4; *Too True to Be Good*,
    42
Sherriff, R. C.: *Journey's End*, 78, 83
Sickert, Walter R., 31
Sidney Street shootout, 172
16th Lancers, 112
skepticism, 151
Soames, Mary, Lady (née Churchill), 25, 97
socialism, 170, 171, 172, 223
Somerset House, 237n.2
Somme, Battle of the, 86
South Africa, 23
Soviet Union, 164, 167, 168, 169, 227
Spain, 11, 239n.42, 246n.15

Spurrier, Steven, 108
Stalin, Josef, xii
Stafford, 233n.84
Stapledon, Olaf, xiii, 175; *Last and First Men*,
    163–64
Stendhal (Marie-Henri Beyle), 209
Stewart, Herbert Leslie, 229n.5
Storrs, Ronald, 7, 46
Sudan, 23, 51–52, 106, 143
suffrage, 56, 69, 79–81, 197
surrealism, 32
Swat Valley, 112
Swift, Jonathan, 24, 199; *Gulliver's Travels*, 33,
    34, 38, 173, 174, 222
symbolism, 20, 75, 76, 77, 81, 88, 116, 150, 169
Syria, 9

Tafas, 32
Talal el Hareidhin, Sheikh of Tafas, 53
tanks, xiii, 155, 159, 167–68, 174
television, 104
Tenniel, Sir John, 103, 104
10th Bengal Lancers, 110
Thackeray, William Makepeace, 149
theater. *See* drama
Thomas, Lowell, 15, 23
Thomson, Kate and Charlotte: school of, 101,
    103
Thompson, James, 70
Thrale, Hester, 206
time, narrative, xvii, 177–78, 191, 194, 196,
    200–207, 210
time travel, 221–25
Todd, Ann, 63
Tolstoy, Leo, 209
topography, 49, 102, 109, 117, 139, 140, 156.
    See also cartography
Torbay, 185
totalitarianism, xvi, 17, 163–64, 166, 195, 215
Trafalgar, Battle of, 41
Transjordan, 2
travel literature, 134, 138
Trevor-Roper, Hugh, 179
Trinity House, 25, 109
Turf Club, 223
Turks, 8–9, 37, 42, 50, 52–53
Turner, J. M. W., 32
Twain, Mark, 89; *Huckleberry Finn*, 89
21st Lancers, 19–20, 52, 109, 143, 156
Tube Alloys, 164

Ulster, 223

Ulysses, 64

United States of America, 92, 97, 200; and the American Revolution, 184; and the atomic age, 164, 165; Civil War of, 103, 157–58; isolationism of, 41; and the film industry, 91; social fluidity of, 90; as a power, 225

Utman Khel area, 131–34, 136

utopias, xii, 86, 146–52, 156, 158–62, 165, 167, 169, 171, 172–73, 184, 192, 193, 194, 215, 222–23, plate

Utrecht, Treaty of, 196

Valiunas, Algis, 229n.5

Venus, 149–50

Versailles, Treaty of, 159, 160

"V" for victory sign, 25

Verne, Jules, xiii, 174; Twenty Thousand Leagues Under the Sea, 117, plate

Victoria, Queen, xvii, 47, 93, 130, 220, 227

Victorian era, xvii–xviii, 92–93, 141, 156, 174, 220–21

Victoria Station, 75

Virgil: Aeneid, 243n.17

Von Richthofen, Manfred, 58

Wadi Rumm, 31

Wadsworth, Edward, 35

War of the League of Augsburg, 198

warships, 155

Waterloo, Battle of, 189, 190, 196

Weidhorn, Manfred, xi, 184, 229n.5, 244n.43

Wejd, 48, 51

Wells, H. G., xiii, 63, 159, 160, 167–75, 244n.43; "The Land Ironclads," xiii, 168; Meanwhile, 171–72; Men Like Gods, 169–71; Mr. Britling Sees It Through, 168; Queer Side of Things, 173; Select Conversations with an Uncle, 173; The Shape of Things to Come, 63–64, 160; Star Begotten, 168; The Time Machine, 167, 173, 174, 222–25; The War in the Air, 160; The World Set Free, 160

Westminster Abbey, 22–23, 228

Whig history, 195, 196, 205, 246–47n.31, 247n.34

Whistler, James McNeill, 31

Wilde, Cornel: The Naked Prey, 94

Wilde, Oscar, 65

Wilhelm II, Kaiser, 103, 157, 180, 181

William III, King, 185, 186, 187, 189, 201, 207

Wilson, Gordon, 108

Wilson, Thomas, 242n.3

Wilson, Woodrow, 160, 215

Wimperis, Arthur, 66, 75

Winterton, 6th Earl (Edward Turnour), 45–47

Woods, Arthur B., 67

Woods, Frederick, 11, 229n.5

Woodville, R. Caton: The Charge of the 21st Lancers at Omdurman, 109

World War I, xiii, 78, 142, 158, 159–60, 168, 174, 199, 227; and Churchill's experience/memories of the front, 25, 33, 47, 76–77, 81–83, 152–53, plate; development of aviation and other technologies during, 58–59, 155, 156–57, 174; and filmic representation, 66, 67, 72–73, 75–77, 79, 82–83; and possibility of German invasion of England, 181–83. See also Armistice

World War II, xiii, 49, 153, 168, 172, 179–80, 183, 199, 213–14, 227; and Churchill's visions of victory, xiii, 25, 158; and Marlborough's impact on Churchill, xvii, 183, 184; and technological developments, 155–56. See also Blitz

Wratislaw, Count (John Wenzel), 207

Wright, Orville and Wilbur, 58

Young, Robert, 207

Zola, Emile: La Curée, 149

Zulu War, 11